THE CATECHIST'S
MAGIC KIT

80 Simple Tricks for Teaching Catholicism to Kids

So then, faith comes from hearing the message,
and the message comes through preaching Christ.
—Romans 10:17

by

ANGELO STAGNARO

Illustrated by
SEAN PRYOR

Iconic Images by
ADE BETHUNE

NIHIL OBSTAT: Reverend John Cush, S.T.L., Diocesan Censor
IMPRIMATUR: Most Reverend Nicholas DiMarzio, Ph.D., D.D., Bishop of Brooklyn
Brooklyn, New York
January 12, 2009

THE CROSSROAD PUBLISHING COMPANY
www.cpcbooks.com

All rights reserved. No part of this book may be reproduced, stored in a retrieval system, or transmitted, in any form or by any means, electronic, mechanical, photocopying, recording or otherwise, without the written permission of The Crossroad Publishing Company.
© 2009 by Angelo Stagnaro

In continuation of our 200-year tradition of independent publishing, The Crossroad Publishing Company proudly offers a variety of books with strong, original voices and diverse perspectives. The viewpoints expressed in our books are not necessarily those of The Crossroad Publishing Company, any of its imprints or of its employees. No claims are made or responsibility assumed for any health or other benefit.

Publisher: Gwendolin Herder
Technical Writer/Project Editor: Sylke Jackson
Illustrator: Sean Pryor
Iconographer: Ade Bethune
Book Designer: Eve Vaterlaus
Cover Designer: Stefan Killen
Proofreader: Elizabeth Mechem Carroll
Thanks to Salesians of Don Bosco for providing the photo of Saint Don Bosco on the Dedication page

Printed in Canada

Library of Congress Cataloging-in-Publication Data

Stagnaro, Angelo, 1962-

The catechist's magic kit : 80 simple tricks for teaching Catholicism to kids /
Angelo Stagnaro; illustrated by Sean Pryor; iconic images by Ade Bethune.
p. cm.

ISBN-13: 978-0-8245-2518-7 (alk. paper)

ISBN-10: 0-8245-2518-3 (alk. paper) 1. Catechetics—Catholic Church.
2. Christian education of children. 3. Spiritual formation—Catholic Church.
4. Initiation rites—Religious aspects—Catholic Church.
5. Children—Religious life. I. Pryor, Sean. II. Bethune, Ade, 1914-2002 III. Title.

BX1968.S775 2009
268'.432088282--dc22
2009000657

1 2 3 4 5 6 7 8 9 10   14 13 12 11 10 09

All scripture quotations in this publication are from the Good News Translation in Today's English Version–Second Edition © 1992 by American Bible Society. Used by Permission.

Sancte Ioannes Bosco, ora pro nobis.
Sancte Nicholaus Audoinus, ora pro nobis.
Sancte Laurenti, ora pro nobis.
Sancte Genesius, ora pro nobis.

DEDICATION
To my mother, Guisepina, whose love
has always been real magic

and to St. John Don Bosco, the Apostle of Joy,
the world's first Gospel Magician,
and to the work of his Salesians worldwide.

Da mihi animas, caetera tolle.
(Give me souls, leave the rest.)

The Catechist's Magic Kit is by far the most thorough treatise I have ever read concerning how to powerfully present the proper magic effects to illustrate, emphasize and make more memorable to the viewers, essential Catholic theological principles. Angelo Stagnaro's book explains, not only the construction and performance of each of the magic tricks and its presentation, but also has extensive Biblical and even some literary references to the religious lessons each effect represents. If spreading the word by entertainingly presenting the important concepts of Catholicism is your goal, (and I can't think of a better one), this well written volume should be at the top of your list. One more reason you should buy this book is, when you arrive at that big front gate, St. Peter may say, "I see you are a magician and have done some good work for us. Yes, you are certainly welcome here. But, wait till you see our Magic!!"
    —MARK WILSON, Stage Magician, Author

The Catechist's Magic Kit will be a great aid to many catechists who want the Good News to come alive and be remembered by the student long after the spoken word has been forgotten. This book is designed to engage the eye as well as the ear in its presentation of the message. It will demand some practice and preparation for the catechist, but the result will be very rewarding and entertaining.
    —His Excellency BISHOP PAUL ZIPFEL, Bismarck, North Dakota, Stage Magician

St. Francis Xavier used songs to teach people the truths of Catholicism. The Baltimore catechism used easy-to-understand images and questions. Archbishop Fulton Sheen used a television show. Now Angelo Stagnaro introduces the practice of simple magic tricks not only to delight and amaze children, but also to invite them to think about the mysteries of the faith in a charming way. St. Francis of Assisi said, "Preach the Gospel. Use words when necessary." Angelo Stagnaro says, "Preach the Gospel to children. Use magic tricks when you can!"
    —Fr. JAMES MARTIN, S.J., author of **My Life with the Saints**

For religion teachers looking for ways to engage children's attention and impart to them the truths of the Catholic faith – Presto! – here is your book.
    —BRIAN FINNERTY, National Communications Officer, Opus Dei

Catechism classes are full of magical moments: instants when children suddenly grasp the deep truths of faith. Now, thanks to Angelo Stagnaro, catechists can bring magic literally into the classroom. In **The Catechist's Magic Kit** a professional magician explains how to teach Catholic doctrine through easily mastered tricks. This book is ideal for first-time magicians and can be used in the family as well in parishes. It can even be employed to dazzle inquiring friends. Stagnaro offers a unique fusion of the wonder of magic and the splendour of Truth which will appeal to Christians of all traditions.
    —LUKE COPPEN, Editor of **The Catholic Herald** (London)

Angelo Stagnaro has done an outstanding job in this book. **The Catechist's Magic Kit** is excellently written and presented. His approach to teaching religious concepts through the use of magic is very creative as is his choice of magic tricks. It's sure to impress catechism classes. He's done a fantastic job. I am proud to have a copy of his book in my collection.
    —MARÍA IBÁÑEZ, MI, AIMC, President of the Society of American Magicians

This book represents a landmark in the history of magic in the Catholic Church, and as such should be on the shelf of every magician of faith. Stagnaro has written clear explanations using Biblical text and patter within well defined sections devoted to all aspects of the catechism. Tips, definitions and many easy to follow illustrations round out his manuscript. It is guaranteed to give many hours of joy to the reader, and ensure the retention of the catechism for audience members. This is a must-read book for Gospel Magicians.
    —JOAN CAESAR, President of the International Brotherhood of Magicians

The idea and objective behind Angelo Stagnaro's **The Catechist's Magic Kit** is very creative. He definitely researched the doctrines and coordinated magic tricks relative to each one. The tie-ins to the catechism lessons are very relevant, and an excellent teaching methodology. The use of magic as a medium of instruction stirs interest, and stretches the attention span of every child, regardless of age. I've used MAGIC to Motivate And Give Inspiration to Children. Angelo Stagnaro has taken it to the next level.
    —Sr. CAROL ANN NAWRACAJ, Gospel Magician

Angelo Stagnaro has pulled one out of the hat with this comprehensive, informative, and fun approach to catechesis for Catholic children. If providing sleight-of-hand to accompany the Catechism wasn't enough, religious educators will also find here a rich collection of scripture passages and wisdom from saints and sages to enlighten both themselves and those they teach. Bravo!
    —BRYAN CONES, Managing Editor, **U.S. Catholic Magazine**

Angelo Stagnaro has written perhaps the most monumental and complete resource for using Gospel magic as a teaching tool.
    —Rev. DAVID REED-BROWN, Baptist Church, Suffield, CT

This new book is a magical guide for teaching the Catechism to students of all ages. Stagnaro is especially skilled at explaining the difficult subjects of creed, sacraments, morality, and prayer with simple and easy-to-perform magic tricks. Learning the Catechism makes us wiser—with this new book, it makes us happier as well.
    —Fr. VINCENT JOHN PAZHUKKAKULAM, O. Carm., India's best-known Gospel Magician

Angelo has done a great job of taking many classical magic effects and breaking them down for the novice magician. Any catechetical instructor interested in using magic in their lessons simply must own this book.
    —ROB MURRAY, Stage Magician

[The Church] is called catholic, then, because it extends over the whole world, from end to end of the earth, and because it teaches universally and infallibly each and every doctrine which must come to the knowledge of men, concerning things visible and invisible, heavenly and earthly, and because it brings every race of men into subjection to godliness, governors and governed, learned and unlearned, and because it universally treats and heals every class of sins, those committed with the soul and those with the body, and it possesses within itself every conceivable form of virtue, in deeds and in words and in the spiritual gifts of every description.

— Catechetical Lectures 18:23

TABLE OF CONTENTS
Numbers in parentheses are sections from catechism.

- 11 **Forward**
- 14 **Preface**
- 16 **Introduction**
  Catholic Catechetical Gospel Magic
- 43 **Part One: THE PROFESSION OF FAITH**
- 44 **The Desire for God — (27-30)**
  Christ unites us with God.
- 46 **The Revelation of God — (51-73)**
  God has a plan for us.
- 48 **The Apostolic Tradition — (75-79)**
  The ancient tradition of the Church unites past, present and future.
- 50 **Sacred Scripture — (101-141)**
  The Bible is the source of our knowledge of God.
- 52 **I Believe — (144-165)**
  Belief in God means trusting Him.
- 54 **Only One Faith — (172-175)**
  God acts in our lives every day.
- 56 **I Believe in One God — (200-202)**
  The One, Eternal God is our Father and Creator.
- 58 **The Father — (232-267)**
  The Father, Son, and Holy Spirit are one.
- 60 **The Almighty — (268-274)**
  Out of nothing, God created the universe.
- 63 **The Creator — (279-324)**
  The creative force of love illuminates us.
- 66 **The Angels — (328-336)**
  Angels are signs of God's love.
- 68 **Where Sin Abounded, Grace Abounded All the More — (386-389)**
  Man sins, God's grace heals.
- 70 **The Son of God Became Man — (456-483)**
  The loving power of God shines in our lives.
- 72 **The Incarnation — (461-463)**
  We offer ourselves to God.
- 74 **Born of the Virgin Mary — (487-507)**
  In God, the impossible is possible.
- 76 **Jesus Christ Suffered Under Pontius Pilate, Was Crucified, Died and Was Buried — (571-630)**
  Jesus died for our sins.
- 78 **Jesus Christ Was Buried — (624-628)**
  The emptiness of Christ's tomb brings forth great blessings.
- 80 **He Descended into Hell. On the Third Day He Rose Again — (631-658)**
  Do not look here, He has risen.
- 82 **On the Third Day He Rose from the Dead — (638-658)**
  We share in Christ's resurrection.
- 84 **He Ascended into Heaven and Is Seated at the Right Hand of the Father — (659-667)**
  New life in Christ is our sure hope.

- **86** **From Thence Will He Come Again to Judge the Living and the Dead — (668-686)**
  God is our loving Judge.
- **88** **The Joint Mission of the Son and the Spirit — (689-690)**
  The actions of the Holy Spirit are apparent in our lives.
- **90** **The Mystery of the Church — (770-776)**
  The Word was made flesh and dwelt among us.
- **92** **The Church is the Temple of the Holy Spirit — (797-801)**
  The Church is directed by the Holy Spirit.
- **94** **The Church is One — (813-822)**
  We are all part of God's plan.
- **96** **The Hierarchical Constitution of the Church — (874-896)**
  The Church guides and teaches.
- **98** **Communion in Spiritual Goods — (949-953)**
  God shares His blessings with us constantly.
- **100** **Mary – Mother of Christ, Mother of the Church — (963-975)**
  Mary is the mother of us all.
- **102** **The Power of the Keys — (981-983)**
  The authority of the Church is a sign of God's love and grace.
- **104** **I Believe in the Resurrection of the Body — (988-1019)**
  We share in Christ's resurrection.
- **106** **The Final Purification, or Purgatory — (1030-1032)**
  We must be prepared before we can stand before God.
- **108** **The Last Judgment — (1038-1041)**
  We stand before God's throne.
- **110** **Part 2: THE CELEBRATION OF THE CHRISTIAN MYSTERY**
- **112** **The Liturgy – Work of the Holy Trinity — (1077-1112)**
  God Heals and Restores us.
- **114** **The Paschal Mystery in the Church's Sacraments — (1113-1134)**
  We are invited to experience God.
- **116** **Celebrating the Church's Liturgy — (1136-1199)**
  We come together in our love for God.
- **118** **Liturgical Diversity and the Unity of the Mystery — (1200-1209)**
  Many voices unite to worship God.
- **120** **The Sacrament of Baptism — (1213-1284)**
  We are reborn in Christ.
- **122** **The Sacrament of Confirmation — (1285-1321)**
  We are sealed with the Holy Spirit.
- **124** **The Sacrament of the Eucharist — (1322-1419)**
  We commune with Christ and with each other.
- **126** **The Sacrament of Penance and Reconciliation — (1422-1498)**
  We find healing in Christ's love and forgiveness.
- **128** **The Anointing of the Sick — (1499-1532)**
  We are truly healed in Christ.
- **130** **The Sacrament of Holy Orders — (1536-1600)**
  We are invited to serve the community of believers.

TABLE OF CONTENTS
Numbers in parentheses are sections from catechism.

132 The Sacrament of Matrimony — (1601-1666)
God's love is abundant and without limit.

134 Sacramentals — (1667-1679)
God invites us to experience His love in our lives.

136 Christian Funerals — (1680-1690)
Death is not the end.

138 Part 3: LIFE IN CHRIST

140 Man: The Image of God — (1701-1715)
We are reflections of God's love.

142 The Beatitudes — (1716-1717)
Christ explains how we must behave towards each other.

144 Man's Freedom — (1730-1748)
Sin binds and restricts us.

146 The Morality of Human Acts — (1749-1761)
God teaches us right and wrong in the silence of our hearts.

148 The Morality of the Passions — (1762-1775)
With God's grace comes maturity and proper control of our emotions.

150 Moral Conscience — (1776-1802)
The choice between good and evil is ever before us.

152 The Gifts and Fruits of the Holy Spirit — (1830-1832)
The Spirit bestows His gifts on us.

154 Sin — (1846-1876)
Christ sacrificed Himself for us.

156 The Person & Society — (1878-1896)
By showing compassion towards others, we show our love for God.

158 Participation in Social Life — (1897-1927)
Man is a social creature.

160 The Moral Law — (1950-1986)
By understanding good and evil, we come to make better choices in our lives.

162 Grace & Justification — (1987-2029)
God shines His magnificent grace upon us.

164 The Church: Mother and Teacher — (2030-2051)
The Church is an expression of God's love.

166 The Second Commandment — (2142-2167)
We show respect to God when we respect His name.

168 The Third Commandment — (2168-2195)
We demonstrate our love of God by keeping His day holy.

170 The Fourth Commandment — (2196-2257)
By loving and respecting our parents, we come to know and love God.

172 The Fifth Commandment — (2258-2330)
Jesus is Eternal Life.

174 The Sixth Commandment — (2331-2400)
We show respect by keeping our promises.

176 The Seventh Commandment — (2401-2463)h
What you do to the least of your brothers, that you do unto Me.

178	**The Eighth Commandment — (2464-2513)**	
	By understanding the nature of truth, we come to experience God.	
180	**To Bear Witness to the Truth — (2471-2474)**	
	As Christians, we are witnesses for Christ.	
182	**The Ninth Commandment — (2514-2533)**	
	Through God's love and grace we come to know the difference between good and evil.	
184	**The Tenth Commandment — (2534-2557)**	
	Where your riches are, so too is your heart.	
186	**Part 4: CHRISTIAN PRAYER**	
188	**In the Old Testament — (2568-2597)**	
	The ancient forms of prayer show us the way to God.	
190	**In the Fullness of Time — (2598-2622)**	
	God has a plan for the world.	
192	**In the Age of the Church — (2623-2649)**	
	Prayer is a lifeline to God.	
194	**At the Wellsprings of Prayer — (2652-2662)**	
	The power of prayer leads us to God.	
196	**The Way of Prayer — (2663-2682)**	
	God uses prayer to develop a relationship with us.	
198	**Guides for Prayer — (2683-2696)**	
	Those experienced in developing a relationship with God can teach us how to pray.	
200	**The Life of Prayer — (2697-2865)**	
	Prayer helps us grow as individuals and as part of God's family.	
202	**Persevering in Love — (2742-2745)**	
	Prayer changes us.	
204	**The Prayer of the Hour of Jesus — (2746-2758)**	
	Jesus is the aim and support of our prayer.	
206	**The Lord's Prayer — (2765-2766)**	
	The Bible teaches and inspires us to lead prayerful lives.	
208	**Our Father Who Art in Heaven — (2777-2802)**	
	Prayer restores us.	
210	**But Deliver Us From Evil — (2850-2854)**	
	We rest in God and He keeps us safe.	
212	**Final Doxology — (2855-2865)**	
	We show our thankfulness to God in prayer.	
214	**Bible Passages and Tricks That Apply**	
222	**Tricks Across Religions**	
224	**Glossary of Magic Terms**	
228	**Cutouts and Extra Materials**	
245	**About the Author**	
246	**About the Graphic Artist, Editor and Designer**	
247	**About Ade Bethune, the Iconographer**	
248	**About the Consultants**	

FOREWORD

The Bible assures us that Jesus used parables and examples from history to instruct His disciples to which they listened with pleasure. St. Don Bosco, the great patron of young people, would retell his divinely inspired dreams to his students to help them understand the importance of our Faith. And during medieval times, theatrical plays were used to relate doctrinal truths. Our predecessors understood that the shortest distance between a human person and the Truth was the use of a story, an historical account, a theatrical presentation or even a game of skill. All of these were used to gain the attention and stir the imagination of the Faithful. Further, Anthony de Mello once said: "Despise neither history nor games. A lost treasure of gold is found once again thanks to a candle that is worth mere pennies; similarly, a deep Truth can be found through the vehicle of a simple game properly introduced."

For years, since I was a child, I've tried to pay attention to homilists who spoke at great length and at too high and too monotonous a level as they endeavored to describe our faith's Eternal Truths. Of all of these lessons, I can honestly say I recall absolutely nothing unless they were told to me by means of interesting stories, especially those of St. Don Bosco. Don Bosco, as a child, observed that his fellow countrymen avoided church because they were attracted to games of skill set up by charlatans in the town square. He remarked, "If priests, in their homilies or their other sacramental functions, were as interesting as these charlatans and jugglers, certainly our religion and the knowledge of the Truth would be greatly profited." If this is the case, we should endeavor to take advantage of Don Bosco's admonishments and suggestions and those of our ancestors and introduce Catholic Truths in the guise of games, especially those of magic tricks.

From his many years of experience, Angelo Stagnaro's book seeks to overcome this great instructional void. He is a true professional, especially in the field of mentalism, and has kindly placed his knowledge and experience in magic at the service of the Catholic faith. This precious and indispensable textbook will benefit every Catholic catechetical instructor. Each magic trick described in this book will arouse curiosity and will ultimately and effectively present one evangelical Truth. With some minor preparations on the part of the reader, all of the tricks described in this book can be used to render both interesting and effective catechetical lessons.

The purpose of every catechist is to communicate the truth and to invite his or her listeners to grasp the greatest Truth that God loves us. Such a wonderful fact cannot be imposed upon our catechetical students. To present such an idea, a teacher must be both interesting and benevolent. The magic tricks presented in Angelo's book are designed to produce a winning and comprehensive, faith-filled message.

Cesario di Heisterbach tells that, in the 13th century, the Cistercian abbot Gerald, preached to several particularly sleepy monks who had seemed to be wandering in their thoughts. The abbot stopped in the middle of his homily and said, "Now I will show you a trick." Suddenly all of the monks become alert in expectation of the trick. At that, Gerald noted, "When I spoke about God you slept, and when I offered you a trick, you woke up." Angelo's book encompasses the very same scope; it can wake the sleeper to give the opportunity for the catechist to teach the Truth of our faith. In this, it succeeds perfectly.

Moreover this book is the first great work in the Catholic Gospel Magic tradition. In fact the overwhelming number of titles of previous writings on Gospel Magic were meant solely for professional magicians with the standard training and were little more than photocopied and self-published booklets. Further they were all meant for Protestant audiences and had a decidedly Calvinist bent which is thoroughly inappropriate for Catholic audiences.

Angelo Stagnaro's book is certainly a magic book, but more importantly, it is a true Catholic catechism; a magical catechism. It has earned the right to be in the libraries of all Catholic catechists, beginning with mine. I predict that it will not gather dust there like so many other books of high philosophy or theology, but, instead, will be a working text from which catechists will draw continually. It certainly is now my preferred textbook in my ministry of catechesis to the world.

My thanks to Mr. Stagnaro for producing this great treasure; it offers its readers the real possibility to reach the hearts of catechumens and above all, those of children, and to help them understand God's greatest gift of His Son. The joy of Christ, the approval of St. Don Bosco and the smiles of the children are with you.

Sincerely,

Fr. Don Silvio Mantelli, **SDB,** (a.k.a. "Mago Sales"), Salesian Gospel magician
Torino, Italy
Palm Sunday, 2008

FOREWORD

There can be an inherent difficulty in teaching children anything, considering their short attention span, lack of discipline and resistance to the material. This difficulty seems especially true for religious education. Adding magic tricks to a lesson plan may just do the trick, so to speak. Capturing the imagination of the students with magic tricks allows the student to enter into religious material with a sense of wonder and awe. When a magician combines magic with spiritual lessons or even performs to secular audiences, it is not to become a miracle worker but to entertain and bring new insights. Angelo Stagnaro does an excellent job at this. The magic tricks in this book are not self-referential, as to say, "Look at what I can do." But, like most signs and symbols, they point to something greater, the mystery of faith.

Blending magic and the Gospel message is difficult. Either the message is too strong for the effect or the effect is stronger then the message. But the tricks in this book are object lessons and thus are not designed to be woven into a whole show. Instead, they spark discussion in the classroom. If done well they should evoke the response of "How true!" or "Wow!" not "How did you do that?"

The systematic following of the outline of the catechism of the Catholic faith is utilized well to fit into a comprehensive catechism of any Christian Church or parish. One aspect of faith may flow into another; Trinity into Christology and then onto the Incarnation so that any particular routine can be used to illumine other aspects of faith. Angelo Stagnaro has provided a great tool for communicating the faith to others. While there are other books about Gospel magic, they may be limited strictly to the Gospel text. Our Christian faith, while rooted in part in the gospel, also grows out of the history and traditions from which the Gospels came. The tradition and history fill out the fullness of the faith.

I have been utilizing object lessons, combining magic with the message, to hundreds of large and small crowds, young and old alike, and people respond positively to consider the aspects of faith with newer and deeper understanding. Magic and faith go hand in hand since they both point to the greater mysteries of life. While you might not perform every trick in this book, you will find many that you will do and do well.

As with all magic books, take your time and prepare well. Your audience deserves that and they will be most disappointed if you don't, not only in the trick and lesson, but in you. The same could be said for your teaching the catechism; take your time and prepare well. Your audience deserves that much. Learn the mysteries, teach the mysteries, and live the mysteries.

Your friend in the True Mystery,

Fr. Daniel Rolland, O.P.

Quoniam apud te fons vitae in lumine tuo videbimus lumen. — PSALMS 36:9
(You are the source of all life, and because of Your light we see the light.)

PREFACE

This book is the result of many years of both performing magic and teaching Catholic catechism in a variety of situations. I began writing this book while on a pilgrimage to the major centers of Christendom in 2005. It was difficult working that way but it gave me a great opportunity to consult with many other Gospel Magicians, pastors and theologians throughout Europe.

Like most magicians, I started studying magic when I was a young boy; it's always been a part of my life. In the professional magic community, many magicians will try to combine the art with another interest inevitably to promote or teach some other idea. Magicians who are police officers will frequently use magic to teach children about bike safety and avoiding drugs. Magicians who are businessmen will use magic to highlight a business presentation. Magicians who are physicians or dentists will use magic to put children at ease while they are undergoing treatment. And so, there we have it; an art applied to perform positive social functions. It's little wonder that St. John Don Bosco specifically used magic to draw unchurched children to him so that he might minister to them. Magic is an attractive artistic medium; there are very few people who can honestly say they dislike magic performances. If magic can initially attract people's attention and help them remember an object lesson, then it should be used like any other pedagogic tool. After all, Ad Majorem Dei Gloriam.

The principle reason for writing this book is to share my experience as a Gospel Magician and because I saw the need for a book on basic magic for Catholic catechists. Creating a magic book based specifically on the Catholic catechism was a daunting task. There were many fevered phone calls to my publisher whining that this task might be beyond my ability to complete. I think we are still both in shock that this project is finished.

I hope this book serves you positively as the experience of writing it has served me. Gospel Magic has offered me many wonderful opportunities to combine three loves: magic, teaching and my Catholic faith. I hope all of your Gospel Magic experiences are full of faith, love, joy and wonder.

Angelo Stagnaro
Naples, Italy
The Feast of the Assumption
August 15, 2008

In the Catholic Church ... a few spiritual men attain [wisdom] in this life, in such a way that ... they know it without any doubting, while the rest of the multitude finds [its] greatest safety not in lively understanding but in the simplicity of believing....(T)here are many other things which most properly can keep me in her bosom. The unanimity of peoples and nations keeps me here. Her authority, inaugurated in miracles, nourished by hope, augmented by love, and confirmed by her age, keeps me here. The succession of priests, from the very see of the apostle Peter, to whom the Lord, after His resurrection, gave the charge of feeding His sheep (John 21:15–17), up to the present episcopate, keeps me here. And last, the very name Catholic, which, not without reason, belongs to this Church alone, in the face of so many heretics, so much so that, although all heretics want to be called 'Catholic,' when a stranger inquires where the Catholic Church meets, none of the heretics would dare to point out his own basilica or house.

— Against the Letter of Mani Called "The Foundation" 4:5

There are different kinds of spiritual gifts, but the same Spirit gives them. There are different ways of serving, but the same Lord is served. There are different abilities to perform service, but the same God gives ability to all for their particular service.

— 1 Corinthians 12:4-6

Gospel Magic *n. :* the use of stage magic to instruct, illuminate and edify the Faithful in Christian catechism — **Gospel Magician** *n.*

Preach the Gospel at all times and, when necessary, use words. — St. Francis of Assisi

CATHOLIC CATECHETICAL GOSPEL MAGIC

INTRODUCTION

This book represents the first Catholic Gospel Magic book in publishing history. There is a substantial amount of material on Gospel Magic, many titles of which can be found in the bibliography at the end of the book. Unfortunately, most of it is self-published photocopies and none of it is specifically based on orthodox Christian theology suitable for Catholic catechists and Gospel Magicians. The texts are of varying quality and difficult to obtain unless one attends Gospel Magic conventions where one can examine the contents of each volume. They are written for the experienced magician who has access to very expensive magic equipment. Though experienced Christian magicians who wish to explore Gospel Magic will find this book useful, I designed this book for catechists without any magical training. All of the props for the tricks described in this book can be made at home inexpensively.

This book is not meant to be a replacement for orthodox religious training. It is, instead, meant to offer the catechetical teacher an additional means by which to present the material at hand. A catechetical teaching session should not degrade into a magic show. But a single, well-practiced and well-executed magic trick used to introduce a specific topic will greatly enhance your class's learning experience.

WHAT IS MAGIC?

Magic is older than the word itself. The word 'magic' comes from the Greek word "magi," the word used to refer to the priestly caste of the Zoroastrian religion. Zoroaster, their founding prophet, was born in ancient Persia (Iran) c.628 BC - c.551 BC. The ancient magi (plural for 'magus') were seen as wise men and were said to have power over spirits and the elements. The three wise men of the New Testament are still referred to as "magi." The Spanish refer to them as "los Reyes Magos;" "the Magician Kings."

But certainly, magic existed long before the sixth century BC. I don't think it was very long after we came out of the trees and differentiated from the apes that the first cave child hid a pebble in his hand and asked his friend to guess which hand held the rock. I recall the performance "Magic: Witness the Impossible" which played at the Arena Players Turntable Theatre in New York in 1997 and a line I heard in it: "Magic is one of the oldest art forms known to man. In fact, you can be certain that as soon as two people began walking on the face of the earth, it was just a matter of time before one tried to fool the other. I suppose it's just a part of our human nature."

But even before that cave child fooled his first cave playmate, there were the apes. Primatologists have documented many instances of monkeys and apes (presumably the magician monkeys and apes) intentionally deceiving their fellow primates in the hope of securing some kind of benefit for themselves. One case I came across, explored by the anthropologist Sarah Hrdy, was an experiment that involved leaving food in such a position that only the alpha male of a particular troupe of African capuchin monkeys could see it; the rest of his troupe couldn't view the food left out by the scientists. Immediately upon spying the food, the alpha male let out an alarm and headed into the woods in the opposite direction. After getting the entire troupe to follow him, he circled around and immediately made his way to the food thereby assuring that he alone would get the larger share of the choicer fruits. One might wonder how good a card trick that monkey could do if given the training.

But what is it that ties together the experiences of our ancient ancestors and our modern audiences? I would say it is the sense of wonder. That gasp that someone lets out when your assistant floats off the stage or when you correctly divine someone's phone number or are able to reveal a previously selected card, is the thing at which we aim. After all, what is the purpose of our deceptions if not the effect they have on our audiences? Magicians refer to their tricks as "effects" for a reason.

It can be said that deception is a part of who we are as a species; evidence certainly exists for that interpretation. A single glance at the evening's newspaper will positively convince you of mankind's capacity to willfully deceive itself and each other. But I believe deception, as in the case of our art, is meant to bring us back to our ancestral past to a point where we were, as a species, still amazed by the stars, eclipses, childbirth, the change in seasons, thunderstorms, earthquakes and fire.

The Merriam-Webster Dictionary defines "magic" as being: 1: the use of means (as charms or spells) believed to have supernatural power over natural forces 2: an extraordinary power or influence seemingly from a supernatural force or creature 3: sleight-of-hand. Looking over this definition, I have to wonder what citizens of the 17th century would think when presented with a flashlight. Most probably this prosaic modern-day tool would be seen back then as witchcraft. Velcro would have really thrown them for a loop. Frankly, it surprises me at times. It is interesting to note that we have the technology now to do things we couldn't have dreamt of accomplishing even 25 years ago, let alone 100 years ago or 1,000 years ago. We can now fly, speak to people on the other side of the globe, withstand diseases that would previously have killed us, travel into outer space, prepare our toast without completely burning the bread, and flip through hundreds of television stations from the comfort of our easy chairs.

This discussion should serve as a lesson for magicians. To protect this sense of awe that we willingly offer our audience, we must be vigilant in keeping our secrets. There can be no awe when the audience knows what's coming. How else can we hope to transport our audience emotionally back to our caveman days if not by jealously protecting our secrets from them. At the same time, just as we are protectors of ancient mysteries, we should also be morally vigilant and our audiences' protectors against fraud. I specifically refer to magicians and mentalists who intentionally deceive their audiences in the hope of creating personality cults and accruing wealth by fraudulent means.

But this aside, I think it would behoove all of us to pay more attention to the gasps of surprise, the round-eyed stares and the silent, uncomprehending and breathless finger-pointing that our magic solicits; they are all signs of a good magician, an outstanding trick and an excellent performance. I'll never forget the first time I performed "Metamorphosis" on stage. It's the magic trick where a bound magician steps into a trunk which is subsequently locked and shackled. His assistant stands on top of the trunk with a large curtain and quickly envelops herself with it. In a flash, the magician is seen in her place. The assistant is found to be tied up in the trunk instead. The sound of the vast majority of 600 audience members gasping simultaneously is the most satisfying sound in the world. I highly recommend reveling in it next time you find yourself in a similar position. Remember that the same sound was expressed hundreds of thousands of years ago when our ancestors huddled in the dark around a campfire under a sky gravid with stars with the wind blowing past them as they watched their tribe's magician perform amazing tricks. There we were; surprised, awe-struck, amazed and full of wonder of the magic around us.

TYPES OF MAGIC PERFORMANCES

Magic is generally categorized by the distance the performer needs to keep between himself and his audience. Very intimate magic done with cards and coins, must be performed at a very close distance simply because no one will otherwise be able to see the performance. Some tricks are of such grand scale that they need to be performed on a large stage.

CLOSE-UP – Magic that involves cards, coins, thimbles, balls and other small objects. Because of the intimate nature of close-up magic, generally, it is performed within 5 feet of one's audience.

PARLOR/PLATFORM – This is fairly intimate magic in that it can be done between 5 and 15 feet away from one's audience. Platform tricks use larger props and, more often than not, are angle-sensitive. That is, they sometimes cannot be performed if the magician is completely surrounded.

STAGE ILLUSIONS – Large-scale stage tricks that involve humans or large animals. Because of the nature of these types of tricks, they must be performed no closer than 20 feet of one's audience. Stage tricks usually use enormous props and involve the use of assistants and/or animals. "Sawing a Lady in Half" or "Lady to Tiger" are two examples of such tricks neither of which are described in this book.

MENTALISM – An aspect of magic that specializes in "magic of the mind" (tricks that simulate such mythological ideas as ESP/clairvoyance, telepathy, telekinesis, precognition/prediction and mesmerism/hypnosis). As Marc Salem, one of American's top mentalists, once put it, "An illusionist tries to fool the eye. A ventriloquist tries to fool the ear. And a mentalist tries to fool the mind."

ESCAPOLOGY – Magic tricks that involve escaping from seemingly impossible situations or conditions.

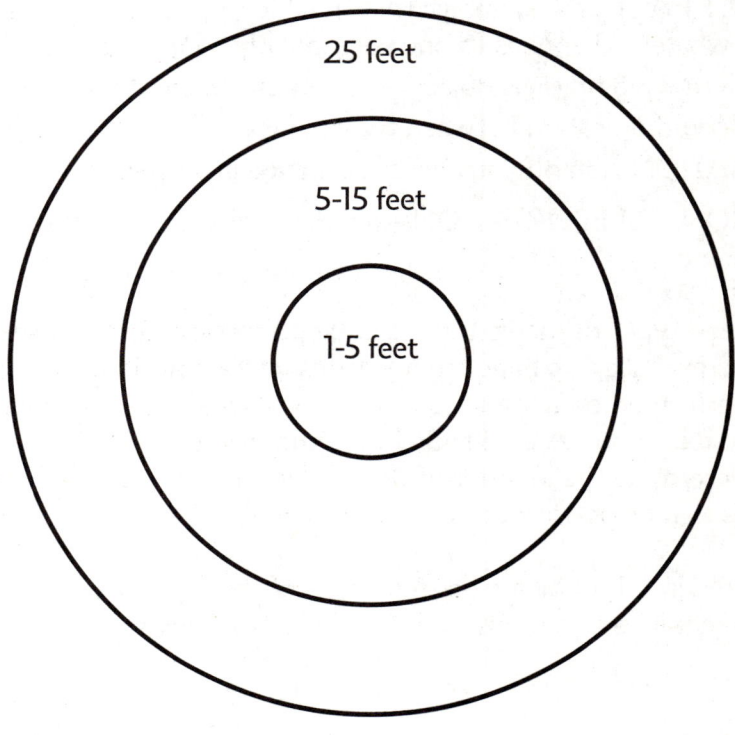

performance distances

TYPES OF MAGIC TRICKS

Even though there are several specialties in magic as described above, magic tricks are multifarious and can be of any of the types described below. There have been many categorizations of types of magic tricks throughout the centuries and none are truly definitive. Here are the categorizations that seem most effective in my experience:

1. ANTI-GRAVITY/LEVITATION – a magic trick in which an object rises into the air in apparent defiance of the law of gravity.
2. APPEARANCES AND VANISHES – an act or instance of an object seemingly coming into or out of sight.
3. ESCAPES – to break loose from confinement or containment.
4. ESP/CLAIRVOYANCE (includes psychometry) – the seeming ability to sense or otherwise experience objects, venues or situations at a distance.
5. MESMERISM/HYPNOSIS – tricks wherein the performer seemingly induces a state that resembles sleep and in which the subject responds to suggestions.
6. PENETRATIONS, RESTORATIONS AND INVULNERABILITY – the physical destruction and reconstitution of an object.
7. PRECOGNITION – a prediction as to a future outcome.
8. SPECTATOR SUCCESS/FAILURE – a comical magic trick wherein the performer always succeeds but the spectator loses.
9. SYMPATHETIC REACTION – a magic trick in which a pair of objects are somehow "linked" in that whatever happens to one will similarly happen to the other.
10. TELEKINESIS – moving physical objects without an apparent means.
11. TELEPATHY – communication between two minds.
12. TRANSFORMATION – an obvious physical change in an object.
13. TRANSPOSITION/TELEPORTATION – a switch, exchange or relocation of a physical positioning.

Each of these thirteen types of magic tricks can be performed either close-up or on stage. For example, a trick where a balled up handkerchief turns into a dove is an example of a transformation but must be performed on a stage as it requires a substantial distance from the audience or the secret will be found out. A card trick where the magician is able to "read the spectator's mind" in order to determine the identity of the card is an example of ESP or clairvoyance and, like most card tricks, can be performed very close to one's spectators.

The magic tricks listed in this book are permutations of the types of magic described above. I've selected tricks that require a minimum of practice and no expensive or specialized professional magic equipment.

> ### 1 CORINTHIANS 9:19-23
> I am a free man, nobody's slave; but I make myself everybody's slave in order to win as many people as possible. While working with the Jews, I live like a Jew in order to win them; and even though I myself am not subject to the Law of Moses, I live as though I were when working with those who are, in order to win them. In the same way, when working with Gentiles, I live like a Gentile, outside the Jewish Law, in order to win Gentiles. This does not mean that I don't obey God's law; I am really under Christ's law. Among the weak in faith I become weak like one of them, in order to win them. So I become all things to all people, that I may save some of them by whatever means are possible. All this I do for the gospel's sake, in order to share in its blessings.

THE ORIGINS OF GOSPEL MAGIC

Biblical references to "magic" are, without exception, the manipulation of supposed preternatural powers usually associated with conjuring spirits in order to foretell the future (1 Samuel 28:7) or dealing with astrology (Isaiah 47:13) Suffice it to say that, inevitably, the kind of "magic" that is referenced in the ßible is not stage magic.

To make an obvious point even more obvious, this book is a collection of instructions to create illusions only. If anything other than stage magic actually existed, this book would be unnecessary.

St. John Melchoir ßosco, an Italian priest born in ßecchi, Castelnuovo d'Asti, Piedmont, Italy, invented what later came to be called "Gospel Magic." As magic is a richly sensory experience, one can see the "spiritual applications" that magic can offer as a pedagogic tool. Typical magic tricks used by Gospel Magicians look very much like any other magic trick one has come across but the patter, or story weaved by the magician, is directed to demonstrate such theological principles as God's love and forgiveness, Christ's parables, the Immaculate Conception, the Sacraments. Even free will can be the subject of a Gospel Magic performance.

> ### COLOSSIANS 3:16
> Christ's message in all its richness must live in your hearts. Teach and instruct one another with all wisdom. Sing psalms, hymns, and sacred songs; sing to God with thanksgiving in your hearts.

THE PROPER USE OF GOSPEL MAGIC

Among Catholics, many forms of art, including the performing arts, have been used throughout history to convey an understanding of the Gospel. It's understandable that Christians would want to honor their Creator with their artistic expression. Music, writing, singing, dancing, painting, sculpture, architecture and poetry have all been used to glorify God throughout Christian history. Stage magic is simply yet another art by which we may honor God. And, after the example of St. John Don Bosco, who used magic tricks he learned from professional magicians who worked in traveling circuses, Catholic stage magicians hope to emulate their patron saint and do the same.

Though Gospel Magic is quite commonly practiced in the course of a prayer session in Protestant circles, I believe this is totally inappropriate for Catholics as the dignity and uniqueness of the liturgy must be preserved. It would be no more appropriate for a Gospel Magician to do a trick during the Mass than it would be for any congregant or presider to start telling jokes during the Consecration.

The proper use of Catholic Gospel Magic is during catechetical classes (missions, discussion groups, sacramental preparation for children, and RCIA classes) or any non-liturgical situation including school assemblies and parish fellowship. Similarly, it would be inappropriate to use Gospel Magic in a non-religious venue or at least one in which one's hosts had not been alerted.

Gospel Magic is a very sensitive and delicate art. When a magician performs his regular act on stage, he can allow people to think as they wish. It's the goal of a good performer to bring his audience to such a point that they can suspend disbelief and accept the performance but the goal of a Gospel magician is to use his art to bear witness to Christ our Savior and to bring others to a better understanding of His love and His sacrifice.

> Catechesis is an education of children, young people and adults in the faith, which includes especially the teaching of Christian doctrine imparted, generally speaking, in an organic and systematic way, with a view to initiating the hearers into the fullness of Christian life.
> — Pope John Paul II

CATHOLIC CATECHESIS

Catechesis comes from the Greek meaning "to resound" or "to echo." This echoing refers to the repeating or recounting of the teachings of the Church to those in need of instruction whether they are children preparing for instruction, young people preparing for the sacraments or adults who are converting to Catholicism or preparing to be married in the Church.

Catechetical instruction includes explaining the meaning of Scripture and tradition, salvific history, the teachings of Jesus Christ, and the teachings of the Church that are inspired and guided by the Holy Spirit so that all who receive instruction might come to a deeper and fuller understanding of God and His Church. (Sources for points in the Catholic Catechesis and Cathechism in the Early Christian Church sections are listed in parentheses. Vatican II, Decree on the Pastoral Office of Bishops in the Church #14; General Catechetical Directory #17.) **Jesus is the cause, the heart and the goal of all catechesis. Catechesis can never be simple communication of abstract ideas but the proclamation of Christ's living Gospel for the strengthening of faith among the Faithful** (General Catechetical Directory #16).

CATECHISM IN THE EARLY CHRISTIAN CHURCH

Instruction by dialogue has always been a part of Christianity. From the parables that Christ taught His disciples, to the gospels and epistles of the New Testament, when Jesus offered instruction in the Temple and in synagogues throughout Israel, He was catechizing. When His Apostles spread throughout the world in order to win souls for the kingdom of Heaven, they too catechized. This style of teaching was understandably used by the ancient Jews. Knowledge had to be transmitted and dialogue was the most efficient means of handing down knowledge intact and free of doctrinal error.

Many theologians and historical scholars believe that the Gospels were the product of such catechetical schools. The ancient Christian historian, Eusebius explains in his "Ecclesiastic History" that St. Mark the Evangelist started his school in Alexandria. According to Eusebius, St. Mark came to Egypt between AD 61 and 68, during the first or third year of the Roman Emperor Claudius's reign. Two famous catechists, Clement of Alexandria and Origen, taught at this school.

> MATTHEW 21:23
> Jesus came back to the Temple; and as He taught, the chief priests and the elders came to Him and asked, "What right do You have to do these things? Who gave You such right?"
>
> LUKE 21:37
> Jesus spent those days teaching in the Temple, and when evening came, He would go out and spend the night on the Mount of Olives.
>
> JOHN 7:28
> As Jesus taught in the Temple, He said in a loud voice, "Do you really know Me and know where I am from? I have not come on My own authority. He who sent Me, however, is truthful. You do not know Him."
>
> JOHN 18:20
> Jesus answered, "I have always spoken publicly to everyone; all My teaching was done in the synagogues and in the Temple, where all the people come together. I have never said anything in secret."
>
> ACTS 5:42
> And every day in the Temple and in people's homes they continued to teach and preach the Good News about Jesus the Messiah.
>
> MARK 6:34
> When Jesus got out of the boat, He saw this large crowd, and His heart was filled with pity for them, because they were like sheep without a shepherd. So He began to teach them many things.

Catechesis is an essential ministry of the Church and is an important part of the ministries of evangelization and of the Word. We are all catechists even in our daily lives in the same sense that we are all a priesthood of believers. (Lumen Gentium, 10; Evangelii Nuntiandi, 6, 14, 15, 59, 60; Catechesi Tradendae, 16; NCD 30, 93).

Catechesis is not merely an intellectual pursuit. It is more appropriately a spiritual development whose end is a greater acceptance of Christ's salvation and submission to His will. Though an academic understanding is essential to this development, the main goal of catechesis is growth in faith.

Successful catechesis considers the human cognitive and affective dimensions in order to maintain a holistic Christian spirituality. It is imperative to maintain continuity in tradition while incorporating the human experience in the process of developing a life of faith.

Gospel magicians are catechists also. Like all catechists, they: 1) proclaim God's Word in their performances so that others might learn; 2) lead others in prayer and worship to honor and give glory to their Creator; 3) develop a sense of community among those they instruct so that they are unified in their love of God and 4) foster service to God and the world in order to realize social justice in our communities and throughout the world.

The Gospel Magician must be a Catholic of strong faith; one who receives the sacraments regularly and is trained in pedagogy (Vatican II, Decree on the Pastoral Office of Bishops in the Church #14). Gospel Magicians should be thoroughly acquainted with Christian theology, interested in the principles of magic and the cultivation thereof, and have the desire, enthusiasm, ability and sensitivity required to teach and serve in the capacity of teacher. He or she must be familiar with the stages of children's growth and development (Sharing the Light of Faith #177–189) and more specifically the intimate relationship of faith to human development (Sharing #173–175) The Gospel Magician must be a faithful and prayerful Christian, one who receives the sacraments regularly and is trained in pedagogy (Vatican II, Decree on the Pastoral Office of Bishops in the Church #14). Gospel Magicians should be thoroughly acquainted with Christian theology, interested in the principles of stage magic and the cultivation thereof, has the desire, enthusiasm, ability and sensitivity required to teach and wishes to serve in the capacity of teacher. He or she must be familiar with the stages of children's growth and development (Sharing #177–189) and more specifically the intimate relationship of faith to human development (Sharing #173–175).

A catechist must consider the level of comprehension and personal maturity of the individuals in the classes. Furthermore, catechetical materials and activities should be adapted to the stages of intellectual, academic, spiritual, and emotional development of the class (On Evangelization in the Modern World #44). In the book, Sharing the Light of Faith, catechists are reminded that communication fosters human development and is capable of contributing to the growth of religious understanding and faith experience (Sharing #252). Catechists are encouraged to look for the most suitable ways and means of catechizing through use of social communications (On Catechesis in Our Time #46). Modern methods of teaching catechism have included retreats, prayer, group discussion, liturgical celebrations, guided reflection, community service projects, group study, games, role playing, resolution development, dramatic presentation and creative writing or art. Keeping this in mind, it would seem that stage magic is an excellent vehicle by which to instruct catechism. Magic is among the very few art forms that successfully incorporates a variety of different learning styles including the visual, audio, and tactile. As such, Gospel Magic is an appropriate and highly flexible tool in that it can be adapted to a wide range of comprehension levels.

LUKE 4:18-19

The Spirit of the Lord is upon Me, because He has chosen Me to bring good news to the poor. He has sent Me to proclaim liberty to the captives and recovery of sight to the blind, to set free the oppressed and announce that the time has come when the Lord will save His people.

PSALM 131:1-3

Lord, I have given up my pride and turned away from my arrogance. I am not concerned with great matters or with subjects too difficult for me. Instead, I am content and at peace. As a child lies quietly in its mother's arms, so my heart is quiet within me. Israel, trust in the Lord now and forever!

JOHN 16:12-15

I have much more to tell you, but now it would be too much for you to bear. When, however, the Spirit comes, Who reveals the truth about God, He will lead you into all the truth. He will not speak on His own authority, but He will speak of what He hears and will tell you of things to come. He will give Me glory, because He will take what I say and tell it to you. All that My Father has is Mine; that is why I said that the Spirit will take what I give Him and tell it to you.

1 CORINTHIANS 3:1-3

As a matter of fact, my friends, I could not talk to you as I talk to people who have the Spirit; I had to talk to you as though you belonged to this world, as children in the Christian faith. I had to feed you milk, not solid food, because you were not ready for it. And even now you are not ready for it, because you still live as the people of this world live. When there is jealousy among you and you quarrel with one another, doesn't this prove that you belong to this world, living by its standards?

2 CORINTHIANS 3:16-18

But it can be removed, as the scripture says about Moses: "His veil was removed when he turned to the Lord." Now, "the Lord" in this passage is the Spirit; and where the Spirit of the Lord is present, there is freedom. All of us, then, reflect the glory of the Lord with uncovered faces; and that same glory, coming from the Lord, Who is the Spirit, transforms us into His likeness in an ever greater degree of glory.

THE PURPOSE OF THIS BOOK

This book is meant for both the catechist who is interested in using yet one more medium through which he or she may teach catechism (RCIA, sacramental preparation, Eucharist, Reconciliation, Confirmation Classes, Pre-Cana Preparation). It is also for the dedicated Gospel Magician, that is, the person who wishes to be of service to his faith community by specifically performing demonstrations of magic with the aim to instruct in Catholic catechesis. The magic tricks in this book are meant to be supplementary and ancillary to the catechism that you are teaching. They should never supplant regular catechetical classes as it would be disrespectful to the subject at hand and confusing to your classes.

HOW TO USE THIS BOOK

This book has a few standard Gospel Magic tricks but mostly I've used general magic classics and reworked their patter and applicability for Gospel Magic. The instructions in this book are meant for right-handed people. If you are left-handed, simply reverse the instructions.

I sometimes use professional magician's jargon when explaining tricks in this book. For a fuller explanation of magicians' vocabulary, please refer to the glossary located at the back of this book.

This book was developed so that it mirrors the Catholic catechism. The catechism is based on 4 pillars:

THE PROFESSION OF FAITH – The Catholic creed, centered on the ancient Apostles' creed and the Nicene Creed.

THE CELEBRATION OF THE CHRISTIAN MYSTERY – The sacraments of our faith; the salvation of God made present.

LIFE IN CHRIST – The practice of our faith, the Ten Commandments and all that this rule of behavior affects.

CHRISTIAN PRAYER – The prayer of the believer, centered on each line of the Our Father and how all our prayers contain similar forms of praise, petition, and belief.

The magic tricks described here are organized to correspond directly to the Catholic catechism. There is at least one magic trick listed under each catechetical article. Each magic trick listed in this book has several designations:

> The TITLE is the name of the section of the catechism that pertains to the trick.
>
> The NUMBERS IN PARENTHESES are the paragraphs of the catechism that apply to the trick.
>
> The ICONS describe the ease of performing (one hat means easy, 2 hats means moderately difficult) and the time required to prepare for the trick.
>
> The WHAT YOU NEED section describes the materials and tools required to perform the magic trick.
>
> The WHAT THEY SEE section describes how the magic trick will look to your catechetical class.
>
> The WHAT YOU SAY section describes what the magician should say when performing the trick.
>
> The HOW YOU DO IT section explains the actual secret of the trick as known only to the magician/catechist.

PERFORMING MAGIC: A GOSPEL MAGICIAN'S PREPARATION

1) BE PRAYERFUL (MATTHEW 21:22; EPHESIANS 5:20)
Before every performance, I offer my performance to God. I also ask for the special intervention of Sts. Don Bosco and Nicholas Owen, Patrons of Magicians. But, as St. Augustine rightly points out, we should "pray as if all depended upon God and act as if all depended upon us." It is imperative that you are familiar with the tricks you are planning on performing and the theological lesson you are presenting.

2) BE THEOLOGICALLY CORRECT (ACTS 8:27-31, TITUS 2:1)
Take advantage of as much theological and catechetical training as possible. Furthermore, if you are in doubt as to a particular theological issue, do not hesitate to consult your parish priest or a Catholic theologian.

3) BE FAITHFUL (ROMANS 12:6)
A Gospel Magician is not simply an entertainer. He or she is principally a catechist. It's wonderful to have fun while performing but it's more important to be a teacher. Magic is only a vehicle by which you will impart knowledge and understanding.

4) BE JOYFUL (JOHN 17:13)
You are a Gospel Magician. Carry the joy and love of Christ in your heart when you perform before others, especially children. St. Francis of Assisi warns us that "it is not fitting, when one is in God's service, to have a gloomy face or a chilling look."

5) BE A LIGHT UNTO THE WORLD (MATTHEW 5:14)
I wear a crucifix around my neck when I perform Gospel Magic to remind my classes that I am there as a catechist and not as an entertainer. Though, of course, I hope that while they are being entertained, they are being edified. Having a crucifix or icon present in the room is also an excellent way to remember that you are not performing magic for magic's sake. You are there as a minister, an educator and a catechist. It's hoped that your class/audience will be entertained but that is not the final end of your performance. The real goal of your performance is to point to God and to inspire those around you to love and honor Him.

6) BE HUMBLE (LUKE 14:11)
If you are successful during your performance, remember to tell your audience that your skills aren't yours but God's. St. Francis de Sales teaches us that "true progress quietly and persistently moves along without notice."

7) BE CHRISTOCENTRIC (ROMANS 5:17)
Christ must be the main reason for your performance. You are a Gospel magician in order to proclaim God's Word. He is present during your opportunity to teach. Allow Him into your life and He will allow you into His.

PERFORMING MAGIC: MAGICIANS' RULES

1) NEVER TELL SECRETS

> "If A equals success, then the formula is A equals X plus Y and Z, with X being work, Y play and Z keeping your mouth shut." — Albert Einstein

> "I shall be as secret as the grave." — Miguel de Cervantes, Don Quixote de la Mancha

In order to entertain people it is imperative to keep them in the dark as to the mechanisms behind a magic trick. If one reveals a secret, one will no longer be able to entertain that person nor any of the other people with whom that person shares your secret in the future. This point will be driven home to you the moment any of your audience members stands up during your performance and reveals your secret.

Furthermore, once a person has found out the secret to a trick, he is immediately disappointed. The wonder and surprise of a magic trick is by far more important. In a letter to his friend Lucillius, the great orator Seneca wrote about his experience with a street magician. It sums up the disservice one does to a spectator when one reveals a secret to a magic trick: "It is in the very trickery that it pleases me, but show me how the trick is done and I have lost my interest therein."

In addition, a performer's secrets are difficult to come by. They require a tremendous investment of time, energy, money, and resources. To flippantly and callously reveal secrets is tantamount to stealing from other magicians who use the same or similar tricks in their performances. It also shows a blatant contempt for magic as a performing art and for art in general.

2) PRACTICE BEFORE YOU PERFORM

> "The gent who wakes up and finds himself a success hasn't been asleep."
> — Wilson Mizner

> Q: "How do you get to Carnegie Hall?"
> A: "Practice, practice, practice."

It is understandable that one would want to perform a trick immediately after learning it but consider this from the perspective of your audience: it is imperative that you practice a magic trick many times before performing it in front of an audience. Among other reasons, you might inadvertently reveal a secret if you are insufficiently prepared.

Magic is an ancient performing art. It would be very bad form indeed for a dancer to come on stage without a complete knowledge of the dance she is slated to perform. And not many of us would be so forgiving of a stage actor who hadn't committed his lines to memory. No one wants to watch an inept and fumbling magician. The more you practice a trick, the better will be your performance.

3) NEVER LET THEM SEE YOU SWEAT

What happens if you blunder or if a particularly astute audience member figures out a trick? What about if a spectator doesn't wish to cooperate? One can't simply give up the art. The answer is simply this: don't panic. Go on to the next trick or catechetical point if necessary. There's no need to bring undue attention to yourself. You'd be surprised at how quickly your audience will forget your mistakes and concentrate, instead, on your successes. As to unruly volunteers, simply invite them to sit down.

4) TRICKS ARE MEANT TO BE PERFORMED ONLY ONCE

Unless otherwise stated, it is imperative to only perform a trick once. The second time, your audience will more than likely figure out the secret to a trick. This is clearly counterproductive.

5) CONSIDER YOUR PERFORMANCE VENUE

There will be some tricks that you will not be able to perform because of your surroundings. For example, the lighting might be awful or your audience might be sitting much too close to your performance area. It's best to simply replace one trick for another rather than risk destroying an illusion.

6) DEVELOP YOUR REPERTOIRE

A story about Harry Houdini, possibly apocryphal, tells of a young man who approached Houdini and bragged that he knew 500 card tricks. In his arrogance, the young man asked Houdini how many he knew. The great magician paused to think and then responded, "About fifteen." The truth is that Harry knew a few more tricks than fifteen but the point is clear: it is important to build upon your repertoire but it is more important to learn a few tricks correctly rather than hundreds of them poorly.

7) REMEMBER TO HAVE FUN

One can't be an effective magic performer unless one is having at least as much fun as one's audience. Learn to relax and enjoy. Magic is for us also.

8) WE ARE HERE FOR OUR AUDIENCES

Do not make anyone feel embarrassed. It's hard enough for the average person to stand up and assist you in front of a crowd. There's no need to hurt someone's feelings for the sake of your performance.

9) LEAVE THEM WANTING MORE

> "He asked me if I liked card tricks. I said 'No.' He did three."
> — W. Somerset Maugham, "Of Human Bondage"

More is less. Less is more. Magic is meant to be entertaining. "Inflicting" unrequested magic will make one very unpopular and your magic much less appreciated.

10) MAGIC AS PERFORMANCE ART

> "The play is the thing."
> —William Shakespeare, Hamlet, II:2

Magic is a performance art and your audience expects to be entertained. You are an actor in a dramatic and exciting role, that of a magician.

PERFORMING MAGIC FOR CHILDREN

It's understood in the magic fraternity that performing for children is more difficult than performing for adults.

1) Children are by far more perceptive than adults. They perceive the world in an unfettered and uncluttered way. This is not possible for most adults.

2) Children don't have the natural social filters that adults have developed as they mature. For the sake of politeness and sensitivity, adults generally refrain from pointing out a performing magician's errors. Children do not suffer from such social conventions; they instinctively feel the need to let the world know what's on their minds.

3) The physical stature of most children is yet another factor to consider when you perform magic for them. Because of their relative height, they can see "under" your hands. A palmed coin that escapes notice by an average-sized adult is clearly visible to most small children and they have no qualms about pointing it out to the entire audience.

4) Whereas adults might view magic as escapism and as art, children view the same magic as an intellectual challenge and logical puzzle, possibly as a result of many years of games and being "fooled" by adults. Adults are willing to suspend their reason and intellect for the duration of your performance.

THE CATHOLIC MAGICIANS' GUILD

The Catholic Magicians' Guild is an international organization of professional and amateur magicians dedicated to Catholic Gospel Magic. The CMG was started in 1995 for several reasons. First, many Catholic magicians felt constrained, awkward or unwelcomed joining the FCM (Fellowship of Christian Magicians.) Second, many Catholic magicians never really considered doing Gospel Magic. The Catholic Magicians' Guild is an organization of magicians who:

1) Help parishes by augmenting catechetical instructions of children and adults with stage and close-up magic;

2) Spread the devotion of Sts. Don Bosco, Nicholas Owen and Genesius the Actor, three patron saints of magic;

3) Offer our services to Catholic fraternal and philanthropic organizations for fundraising and community;

4) Evangelize and instruct non-Catholics in our faith through the vehicle of stage and close-up magic (ie, Gospel Magic); and

5) Instruct the general public of the tricks and traps of charlatans who present themselves as having magical or psychic powers.

CATHOLIC MAGICIANS' GUILD

RECENT PROJECTS

1) The Catholic Magicians Guild (CMG) has recently helped design a religious medal struck in honor of Don Bosco as Patron Saint of Magicians in partnership with the St. Francis de Sales Religious Art Store (http://www.stfrancisdesales.com).

2) The CMG prepared a hagiography of Don Bosco that was accepted by several Catholic, magic and clowning journals.

3) The CMG developed a cyber-chapel dedicated to St. Don Bosco.

SUGGESTIONS FOR CATHOLIC MAGICIANS

Catholic magicians around the world, principally in Europe (especially southern Europe), the Unites States, Australia and Latin America, seek out many ways to perform Gospel Magic and commemorate the feast days of Sts. Don Bosco, Nicholas Owen, and Genesius the Actor. Here are a few possibilities:

1) Consider offering your services to children's hospitals and homes for the elderly. If during your hospital rounds, you have the opportunity to offer a silent prayer and blessing to the infirm, this is often much appreciated. Even laying on of hands to ask God to heal a child is acceptable.

2) Volunteer time at Catholic schools, catechetical work including Rite of Christian Initiation for Adults (RCIA) and Confraternity of Christian Doctrine (CCD).

3) As to catechetical programs for children, you'd be surprised at how much you do remember from when you were a kid. Catholic theology is admittedly complex ... but not generally so when it comes to teaching children.

4) Offer your services for retreat work with children, prayer groups with adults and school fairs. It offers the most flexible and relaxed settings for children and adults to learn about Catholicism.

5) For those who feel they are truly academically unprepared to teach catechetical classes to children or adults, instead, contact the usual teachers at your parish and ask them for the topic they are about to teach. Instead of teaching the entire course, you might be able to offer a single magic trick or 2 to teach a particular theological point during a single class.

"The more gross the fraud, the more glibly will it go down and the more greedily will it be swallowed, since folly will always find faith wherever imposters will find impudence."
— Christian Nestell Bovee

THE ETHICS OF DECEPTION

Whenever I introduce myself as a Gospel Magician in Christian circles, I immediately bring up St. Don Bosco and how he had used magic as both a teaching tool and a means of attracting the attention of children he hoped to help.

Though scripture specifically admonishes against sorcery (Exodus 22:18, Deuteronomy 18:10-14, Acts of the Apostles, 8:11, 13: 9, 16:16, 19:19, Leviticus 19:26, 19:31, 20:6, 20:27, 2 Kings 21:6, 1 Chronicles 10:13, 2 Chronicles 33:6, Isaiah 2:6, 3:2-3, 3:20, 8:19, 19:3, 47:9-14, 65:4, Jeremiah 27:9, Ezekiel 13:18, Micah 5:12, Malachi 3:5, Hosea 3:4, Galatians 5:19, Revelations 9:21, 18:23, 21:8, 22:15) **and ventriloquism** (Isaiah 8:19), **the idea that stage magic is in some way related to what some deluded individuals think is "real magic" (consorting with spirits) is manifestly illogical. It's obvious to most reasonable and educated people that performance stage magic is a totally different type of "magic" than was envisioned by the authors of the Bible and, as a stage magician, I can assure everyone that there are perfectly logical explanations for all of the "magic" that I perform.**

Despite these admonitions, the Bible is replete with examples of people who relied upon sorcery including Simon, a sorcerer who wanted to buy the Apostles' "power" from them. Coincidentally, the sin of simony is traced back to this Biblical character. (Acts 8:9-24) Saul, despite the very clear warnings, insisted on consulting a witch to conjure up spirits of the dead (1 Samuel 28:5).

This is a long way from the type of magic described in this book and the type of magic tricks used by St. Don Bosco in order to minister to street children. Stage magic is merely a performing art. As it is a very visual and emotionally moving art, it is frequently used as an instructional vehicle. In recent years, magicians have presented any of dozens of topics, including fire safety awareness and drug prevention. Since the ministry of St. Don Bosco in the 19th century, magic has been used to convey Christ's message to others. This book is meant to continue that great tradition.

The magicians' art, like any other, deals in a medium. Some artists work exclusively in oil paints, some in clay, some in words and some in musical notes. Our medium of choice is deception. The major question before us is how does one remain honest and preserve one's Christian integrity in the midst of lies, illusions, and half-truths?

It is imperative that the Gospel Magician be selective in the language he or she uses during catechetical sessions/performances. What we perform in the pursuit of teaching catechism are tricks. We produce illusions that give the impression of something supposedly inexplicable. But clearly, our "magic" is of human origin and in the service of the Divine. Where Christ speaks Truth and produces miracles, we merely perform tricks that have the effect of verisimilitude.

It is very important that Gospel Magicians make it clear that "real magic" doesn't exist and that those people who claim to be able to manipulate the natural and supernatural worlds are either confused, mentally ill, undereducated or lying. In addition, to help avoid any confusion on the part of one's catechism class, we should refer to Gospel Magic as a skill and a performing art.

It is the nature of performance magic that we must deceive our audiences. This is done to assure a sense of mystery required for the tricks presented. This is not meant to take unfair advantage of our audiences. In essence, it is a matter of intention. To say, "I want you to freely select any card" when you are actually forcing a volunteer to take a certain card, is not an instance of deception in the sense of wishing to cause harm or emotionally or financially manipulate the person. It is, instead, an intricate part of our art and required for us to perform the trick at hand. We "deceive" in order to entertain and anyone who has witnessed a magic performance understands that we rely upon guile and illusion to accomplish what we do.

Magic, like all other activities dedicated to Christ, stands the risk of being "misdirected." That is, magicians, just like singers, ushers, and acolytes, for example, could forget that the reason we are in service to our community is to build up Christ's Body for His glory and not our own (Ephesians 4:12). Everything we do or say should be done in the name of the Lord Jesus, as we give thanks through Him to God the Father (Colossians 3:17).

> ### 1 SAMUEL 28:5-15
> When Saul saw the Philistine army, he was terrified, and so he asked the Lord what to do. But the Lord did not answer him at all, either by dreams or by the use of Urim and Thummim or by prophets. Then Saul ordered his officials, "Find me a woman who is a medium, and I will go and consult her." "There is one in Endor," they answered. So Saul disguised himself; he put on different clothes, and after dark he went with 2 of his men to see the woman. "Consult the spirits for me and tell me what is going to happen," he said to her. "Call up the spirit of the man I name." The woman answered, "Surely you know what King Saul has done, how he forced the fortunetellers and mediums to leave Israel. Why, then, are you trying to trap me and get me killed?" Then Saul made a sacred vow. "By the living Lord I promise that you will not be punished for doing this," he told her. "Whom shall I call up for you?" the woman asked. "Samuel," he answered. When the woman saw Samuel, she screamed and said to Saul, "Why have you tricked me? You are King Saul!" "Don't be afraid!" the king said to her. "What do you see?" "I see a spirit coming up from the earth," she answered. "What does it look like?" he asked.
>
> (continued on next page)

(1 SAMUEL 28:5-15 continued)
"It's an old man coming up," she answered. "He is wearing a cloak." Then Saul knew that it was Samuel, and he bowed to the ground in respect. Samuel said to Saul, "Why have you disturbed me? Why did you make me come back?" Saul answered, "I am in great trouble! The Philistines are at war with me, and God has abandoned me. He doesn't answer me any more, either by prophets or by dreams. And so I have called you, for you to tell me what I must do."

ACTS 8:9-24
A man named Simon lived there, who for some time had astounded the Samaritans with his magic. He claimed that he was someone great, and everyone in the city, from all classes of society, paid close attention to him. "He is that power of God known as 'The Great Power,' " they said. They paid this attention to him because for such a long time he had astonished them with his magic. But when they believed Philip's message about the good news of the Kingdom of God and about Jesus Christ, they were baptized, both men and women. Simon himself also believed; and after being baptized, he stayed close to Philip and was astounded when he saw the great wonders and miracles that were being performed. The apostles in Jerusalem heard that the people of Samaria had received the word of God, so they sent Peter and John to them. When they arrived, they prayed for the believers that they might receive the Holy Spirit. For the Holy Spirit had not yet come down on any of them; they had only been baptized in the name of the Lord Jesus. Then Peter and John placed their hands on them, and they received the Holy Spirit. Simon saw that the Spirit had been given to the believers when the apostles placed their hands on them. So he offered money to Peter and John, and said, "Give this power to me too, so that anyone I place my hands on will receive the Holy Spirit." But Peter answered him, "May you and your money go to hell, for thinking that you can buy God's gift with money! You have no part or share in our work, because your heart is not right in God's sight. Repent, then, of this evil plan of yours, and pray to the Lord that He will forgive you for thinking such a thing as this. For I see that you are full of bitter envy and are a prisoner of sin." Simon said to Peter and John, "Please pray to the Lord for me, so that none of these things you spoke of will happen to me."

MAGICAL HAGIOGRAPHIES

It's been said many times that it would seem that St. Jude would have been a more appropriate patron saint of magicians, considering that he is the patron of impossible or desperate situations. Even a thaumaturge such as St. Nicholas might seem to have been a more "appropriate" choice as a patron but stage magic isn't a miracle. St. Don Bosco is the only saint associated with performance magic for the purpose of edifying and inspiring the Faithful. For this reason, he is our patron. In addition, because of the clandestine ministry of British martyr St. Nicholas Owen, it is understandable that stage magicians look to him for inspiration and intercession. Also St. Genesius the Actor, an early martyr of the Church was converted as a result of his dedication to the stage. Catholic magicians, especially Catholic Gospel magicians, will find their hagiographies edifying.

ST. JOHN BOSCO

ST. JOHN BOSCO (DON BOSCO)
Born: 1815 (Becchi, Castelnuovo d'Asti, Piedmont, Italy)
Died: 1888 (Turin, Italy)
Venerated: July 24, 1907 by Pope Pius X
Beatified: June 2, 1929 by Pope Pius XI
Canonized: 1934 by Pope Pius XI
Patronage: Magicians, apprentices, educators, boys, editors, Mexican young people, students, young people, laborers
Communities Founded: Salesians of Don Bosco in 1859, the Daughters of Mary, Help of Christians in 1872 and the Union of Cooperator Salesians in 1875
Feast day: January 31

When most people, Catholics or not, find out that there actually is a Catholic saint whose sphere of influence includes stage and close-up magic, they generally question the fact. January 31st is the day set aside on the Catholic liturgical calendar to honor St. John Bosco, an Italian priest born in Becchi, Castelnuovo d'Asti, Piedmont, Italy.

Many people wonder how the Catholic Church and magic could get together in the first place. During the latter half of the 19th century, as Europe's poor were suffering from the effects of industrialization, John Bosco saw how most of the children in his village remained uneducated and without faith in God.

John's father died when he was only two years old and, as was common at the time, John helped the family's finances with different jobs. Whenever he had an extra penny for himself, little John would go to the many circuses, fairs and carnivals that visited his part of Italy. He watched in rapt attention when magicians performed seemingly impossible, preternatural phenomena. Being a precocious child, he reasoned some of them out; those he could not, he would beg magicians to teach him. With the knowledge he cobbled together, he was able to put on little magic shows free of charge for his friends. Even at that age, he would make sure that the poorest children in his neighborhood would be in attendance. Being devout, he would take the opportunity, in front of his impromptu congregation, to repeat the homily he heard at church on the previous Sunday.

As Don Bosco ("Don" is an Italian honorific equivalent to "Sir" or "Mr.") grew up, he chose to become a priest. He was ordained in 1841 and dedicated his priesthood ministry to teaching and working exclusively with the poor children and youth in the city of Turin. He served as chaplain for a hospice for wayward girls. Feeding and clothing the poor were his main concerns. After meeting the basic needs of the children, he turned his attention to their spiritual development.

Don Bosco needed a way to get children interested in coming to church, returning to school, and accepting the aid he was offering. He remembered his early success as a child with the impoverished children of his neighborhood and decided to use puzzles, gags, riddles, and juggling. But it was the magic that caught the children's attention the best. Stories that have come down from Don Bosco's contemporaries include some specific tricks he used. He was said to be especially good at tying 3 ropes together to form one seamless rope in order to explain the mystery of the Christian Trinity. He also would pull coins from ears and change pebbles into candy delighting the children under his care.

Later in life, Don Bosco started a community of Catholic priests, nuns, brothers and lay people who, to this day, help street children and youth in gangs throughout the world including the largest cities in the United States, South America, Asia, Europe and Africa. Don Bosco was canonized in 1934 by Pope Pius XI. Considering Don Bosco's association with magic during life, it's not a stretch of the imagination to understand why he has been dubbed the "Patron of Magicians" in his afterlife. Catholic magicians in Europe and North and South America still celebrate by performing benefit shows for children on his feast day, January 31.

In January, 2002, hundreds of European and American magicians presented a petition to Pope John Paul II asking him to declare St. John Bosco their patron saint. His Holiness was presented with a magic wand made in India as part of the ceremony. The wand was a present from a young Indian orphan in one of Mother Teresa's orphanages. The wand had belonged to the boy's father, who had been a magician. The magicians all dressed in their stage costumes which greatly added to the festival-like atmosphere of the papal audience.

The principle organizer of the event was Salesian Father Silvano Mantelli, himself an accomplished magician. Fr. Mantelli is very active in the Italian magic community. Each year on Don Bosco's feast day, he celebrates the "Mass of the Conjurers" in Castelnuovo Don Bosco, the homeland of his community's founder. He also is the director of the Magicians Without Frontiers Foundation, which offers magic performances for children in Third World nations. Fr. Mantelli is very clear as to the distinction between stage magic and those supposed powers that "psychics" claim. He sees them as charlatans and opportunists who take advantage of the ignorance and credulity of people. He sees the real purpose of religion, and even stage magic used to promote religious values, as the defeat of superstition.

With the advent of Don Bosco's efforts at teaching spiritual values via the mechanism of stage and close-up magic, we see the birth of Gospel Magic; the altering or tailoring of a magic performance so that it can be used to instruct children or adults on some aspect of Christian theology.

Don Bosco was a man deeply imbued with God's love and inspired by the mysteries with which He surrounds us. When he considered the minds of the children around him, certainly Don Bosco must have seen how they were so much more accepting of God's mysteries than many adults were. It's not so strange to think that Don Bosco responded to God's mysteries with mysteries of his own.

ST. NICHOLAS OWEN
Born: 1Sixth century (Oxford, England)
Died: March 2, 1606 (London, England)
Beatified: December 15, 1929 by Pope Pius XI
Canonized: October 25, 1970 by Pope Paul VI
Feast day: October 25 (one of the Forty Martyrs of England and Wales)

Though St. Nicholas Owen did not use stage magic to promulgate Christ's word, he did use his carpentry and cabinetry skills to help those who did. For this reason, St. Nicholas Owen has become an unofficial patron saint of professional stage illusionists.

On March 22, Catholic magicians around the world honor the Jesuit saint known as "Little John," a man who was small in stature but big of heart. He was the son of a carpenter, whose family was dedicated to the persecuted Church. 2 of his brothers became priests while another brother printed underground Catholic books.

During a time of anti-Catholic persecution in England and Wales (1559-1829) Nicholas, an artisan from Oxford, saved the lives of many priests and Catholic laypersons in the United Kingdom by creating ingenious hiding places for them. Fr. Henry Garnet, Superior of the English Jesuits, directed St. Nicholas and his companion, St. Edmund Campion, to use their cabinetry and masonry skills to construct concealed crannies where priests might be secreted. St. Nicholas used the pseudonym John Owen to conceal his identity while doing this work. Because he was short, he was given the nickname "Little John."

Without his help, hundreds of English Catholics would have been deprived access to their priests and therefore the sacraments. St. Nicholas's gift for spotting unlikely places to hide priests was impressive. Over the course of approximately 20 years he used his carpentry and artistic skills to design at least 200 secret hiding places. In 1577, after years at his life-saving work, he joined the Jesuits as a lay brother but his association was always kept secret because of the times in which he lived. He never had a formal novitiate but received instruction nonetheless.

Every day he worked on normal wood and stone repair jobs so as to not draw undue attention to himself. At night, he would create small hiding places, trap doors, sliding doors, hidden crawl spaces and subterranean passages in order to hide priests and other Catholic fugitives from the priest-hunters. He would use trompe l'oeil, perspective and many of the modern principles of stage illusion-design that magicians today take for granted. Whenever St. Nicholas would design and build such hiding places, he would always begin with prayer and receive the Holy Eucharist. Because of his incredible building skills, he was even able to help 2 Jesuit Catholic priests escape from the Tower of London.

After a number of narrow escapes, he was finally caught by the authorities in 1594 and again in 1606. Both times he was tortured to give up information about the identity and whereabouts of priests and prominent Catholics and his incredible construction secrets. Despite being subjected to torture, and an agonizing death, he never divulged any of his secrets. In 1970, he was canonized with the group known as the Forty Martyrs of England and Wales.

ST. GENESIUS THE ACTOR
Died: c.300
Feast day: August 25

St. Genesius made the laudable mistake of converting to Christianity in front of one of ancient Christianity's worst enemies, Emperor Diocletian. He was a very popular comedic actor at the time; one of Rome's best. Like many pagans, he ridiculed Christ and His followers. The fateful play in which he turned to Christ coincidentally had a scene which mocked the Sacrament of Baptism.

He had infiltrated the underground Christian community in order to learn of their sacraments so as to better mimic them during his performance. In essence, his research was the ancient world's equivalent of method acting. But this method acting would serve to be both his undoing and his salvation.

The irony of the situation was greatest for the Emperor Diocletian himself. The play was specifically written to honor his persecution of the Christians. It was in the midst of the play when St. Genesius realized his faith in the Savior. As the words of the Baptism were spoken and the water fell upon his head, the actor realized his faith. He forsook his patron and, instead, turned to his real Patron. Immediately, the new Christian professed his faith.

At first the Emperor, along with the rest of the audience roared with laughter. It was, after all, a satirical play about Christians and their sacraments, but it soon became apparent to everyone present when St. Genesius offered to catechize Diocletian. "There is no king other than Jesus Christ, and even if you could kill me a thousand times you could not take Him from my lips nor tear Him from my heart," announced the actor, sealing his fate and his faith.

The Emperor ordered Genesius tortured and beheaded. The martyr's iconography depicts him with an actor's mask, a sword, a violin and the baptismal font that he had hoped to mock but ultimately led to his new life. He is considered the patron of actors, converts, and victims of torture.

THE GOSPEL MAGICIAN'S OATH

As a Gospel Magician, I promise never to reveal the secret of any trick to a non-magician, unless he or she, in turn, promises to uphold the Gospel Magician's Oath.

I promise never to perform tricks for non-magicians without practicing, in order to maintain the illusion of the trick.

I promise to increase both my magic repertoire and my knowledge of Catholic theology so that I might be of better service to the Church and to my art.

I promise to be prayerful, to portray an accurate sense of our faith in my magic and to be ever joyful and faith-filled.

I am a catechist and educator and not an entertainer. The goal of my performance is to point to God and to inspire my audience to love and honor Christ. It is only Christ's message that I portray; I must diminish as He grows ever larger.

_____

Cathechist/Gospel Magician

_____

Church

_____

Date

Part 1:
THE PROFESSION OF FAITH

"Christ, like a skillful physician, understands the weakness of men. He loves to teach the ignorant and the erring He turns again to His own true way. He is easily found by those who live by faith; and to those of pure eye and holy heart, who desire to knock at the door, He opens immediately. He does not disdain the barbarian, nor does He set the eunuch aside as no man. He does not hate the female on account of the woman's act of disobedience in the beginning, nor does He reject the male on account of the man's transgression. But He seeks all, and desires to save all, wishing to make all the children of God, and calling all the saints unto one perfect man."

—St. Hippolytus, **On Christ and Antichrist**

THE DESIRE FOR GOD (27-30)

Christ unites us with God.

WHAT YOU NEED:

4 handkerchiefs
an indelible marker
a needle and thread
   or sewing machine
a cigar box

WHAT THEY SEE:

A volunteer is asked to come forward. Two large handkerchiefs are tied together and placed in a small box. The ends of the handkerchief remain out of the box. The catechist holds one end of the handkerchief while the volunteer holds the other. On the count of 3, the catechist and the volunteer pull on the handkerchief. The 2 handkerchiefs are now mysteriously separated by a third handkerchief.

WHAT YOU SAY:

"Man's fall from grace is what separated us from God. Let's use this handkerchief to represent God and this one to represent us. God still loved us even despite our sinfulness. He's always loved us but because of original sin, we needed to repay a debt to God. This debt was so great that no person in the whole world could repay it."

(Place the 2 handkerchiefs into the cigar box but keep the 2 farthest corners sticking out of the box. Have the volunteer hold one these corners.)

"Now, when I say 'Pull!' I want you to pull hard."

(Quickly pull your end and the handkerchief representing Christ will be pulled out of its hidden pocket.)

" ... and that is why God sent His only Son. It was His sacrifice that joined us forever with God our Creator."

MICAH 6:8
No, the Lord has told us what is good. What He requires of us is this: to do what is just, to show constant love, and to live in humble fellowship with our God.

MATTHEW 28:19-20
Go, then, to all peoples everywhere and make them My disciples: baptize them in the name of the Father, the Son, and the Holy Spirit, and teach them to obey everything I have commanded you. And I will be with you always, to the end of the age.

JOHN 1:1-10
In the beginning the Word already existed; the Word was with God, and the Word was God. From the very beginning the Word was with God. Through Him God made all things; not one thing in all creation was made without Him. The Word was the source of life, and this life brought Light to people. The Light shines in the darkness, and the darkness has never put it out. God sent His messenger, a man named John, who came to tell people about the Light, so that all should hear the message and believe. He himself was not the light; he came to tell about the Light. This was the real Light—the Light that comes into the world and shines on all people. The Word was in the world, and though God made the world through Him, yet the world did not recognize Him.

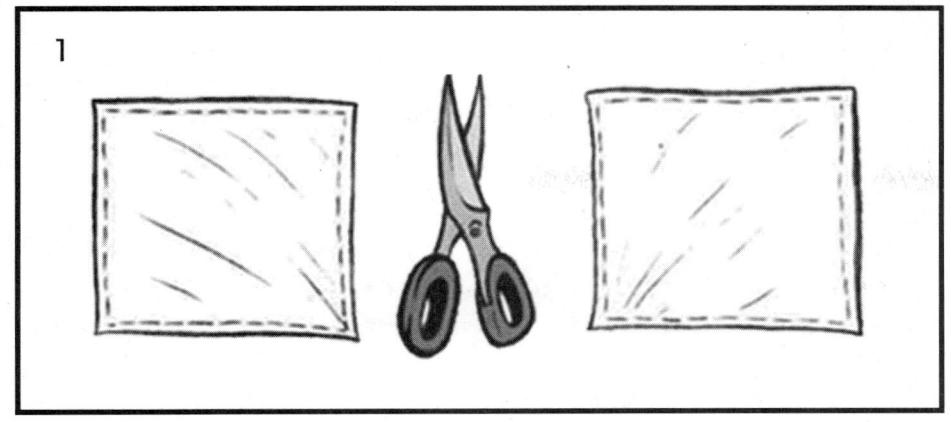

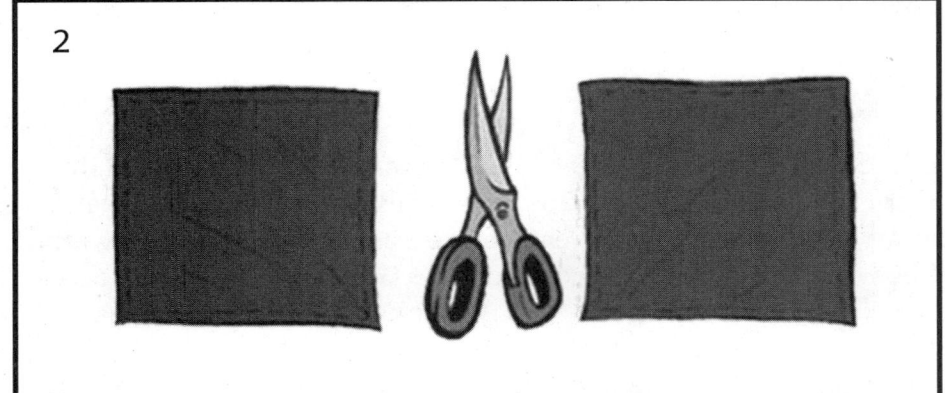

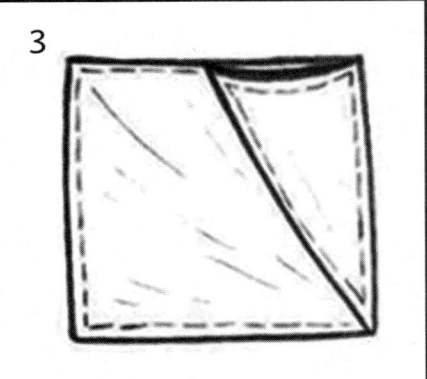

HOW YOU DO IT:

Cut out 2 identical squares of thin white cloth (18-inches square) and hem them. Add a small funnel-shaped pocket to one of these squares. Next, cut out 2 identical squares from red fabric and hem them. Place one white square aside.

Before performing this trick, tie the red square in between the white squares at the corners. Next, stuff the red square into the cone-shaped pocket. The 2 white squares will then look as if they are tied together.

The catechist holds one end of the handkerchief while the volunteer holds the other. On the count of 3, the catechist and the volunteer pull on the handkerchief. The 2 handkerchiefs are now separated by a third handkerchief.

JOHN 15:7-8
If you remain in Me and My words remain in you, then you will ask for anything you wish, and you shall have it. My Father's glory is shown by your bearing much fruit; and in this way you become My disciples.

EPHESIANS 1:10
This plan, which God will complete when the time is right, is to bring all creation together, everything in heaven and on earth, with Christ as head.

THE REVELATION OF GOD (51-73)

God has a plan for us.

WHAT YOU NEED:

a length of rope
4 spring clothes pins
4 handkerchiefs
4 manila envelopes

WHAT THEY SEE:

On a rope strung across the stage, 4 manila envelopes hang by their corners attached by clothes pins. A small bit of colored cloth can be seen protruding from each envelope. A volunteer is given a free choice of any color she wishes. Once she has chosen, the catechist pulls out the other 3 handkerchiefs to show they are completely normal. Finally, the handkerchief she chose is pulled out to show that it is the only one that is knotted.

WHAT YOU SAY:

"Has anyone ever heard of the expression, 'Salvific History?' It means the plan that God has for us and that He has worked throughout human history to show us that plan. God reveals His plan of loving goodness through His Son, Christ Jesus; the mediator and fullness of all revelation. He wants only to give us love and for us to give Him love. But we have free will. We can make choices to answer God's call to us just like Mary did when she accepted God's request for her to bear His Son. We all make choices as to how to live God's Word in our lives. How do we know if we are making the right choice? By listening to our spiritual leaders, praying, never stop learning about our faith, living a Christ-centered life, receiving the sacraments regularly, avoiding sin and consulting our conscience."

"How do you know if you can trust your decision-making? Let's have an experiment. These 4 envelopes all have a handkerchief in them. Three of them are loose and one is in a knot. Choose the one that is knotted. Think about God and His plan for you and choose the correct handkerchief; the one without the knot."

(Have someone choose a handkerchief. Before turning to that one, pull out the handkerchiefs from the other 3 envelopes first making sure you disengage their knots.)

"As you see, when we trust in God and accept Him in our lives, we usually make the right decision."

EXODUS 3:2-6
There the angel of the Lord appeared to him as a flame coming from the middle of a bush. Moses saw that the bush was on fire but that it was not burning up. "This is strange," he thought. "Why isn't the bush burning up? I will go closer and see." When the Lord saw that Moses was coming closer, he called to him from the middle of the bush and said, "Moses! Moses!" He answered, "Yes, here I am." God said, "Do not come any closer. Take off your sandals, because you are standing on holy ground. I am the God of your ancestors, the God of Abraham, Isaac, and Jacob." So Moses covered his face, because he was afraid to look at God.

MATTHEW 14:33
Then the disciples in the boat worshiped Jesus. "Truly You are the Son of God!" they exclaimed.

MATTHEW 16:16
Simon Peter answered, "You are the Messiah, the Son of the living God."

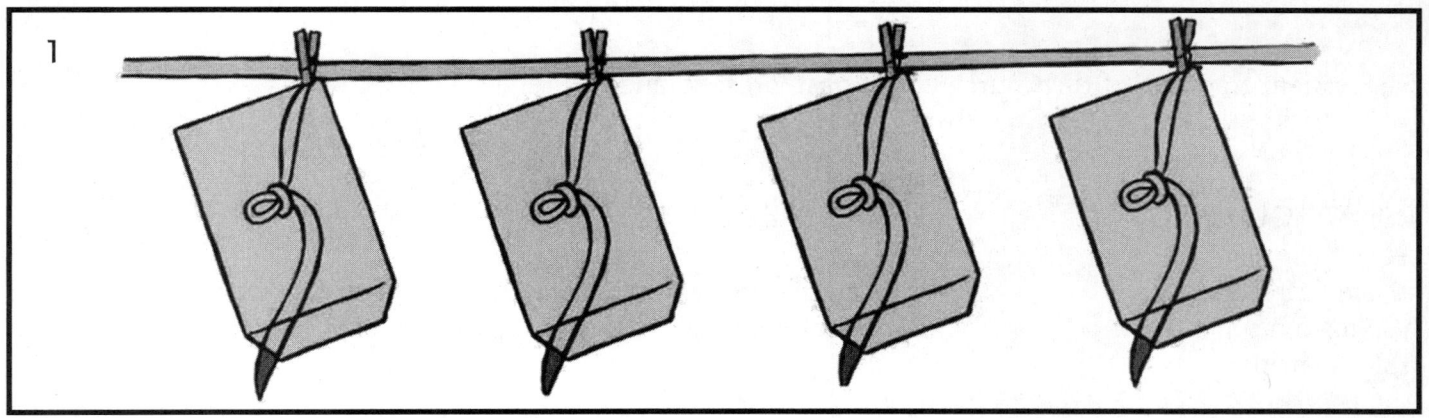

HOW YOU DO IT:

The volunteer has a perfectly free choice. The trick is accomplished by a principle known as a "Four-way Out." This means that no matter which she chooses, she will always be correct.

Consider the diagram as you make the slipknots in your handkerchiefs. Twist the handkerchief so it forms a loop. Pull a bit of the middle of the handkerchief through the loop but don't tighten it. You will know you've tied the knot correctly if a gentle tug can loosen it.

Prepare all 4 handkerchiefs in this manner. When placing the handkerchief inside the envelope, tuck one of the ends of the handkerchief into the corner of the envelope. When the envelope is hung on the clothesline, the clothespin will pinch that corner of the handkerchief. Whichever handkerchief your volunteer chooses, simply disengage the clothespin so as not to disturb the knot. Before showing her the one she selected, pull out the handkerchiefs from the other 3 envelopes making sure you disengage the knots before pulling the handkerchiefs free of their envelopes.

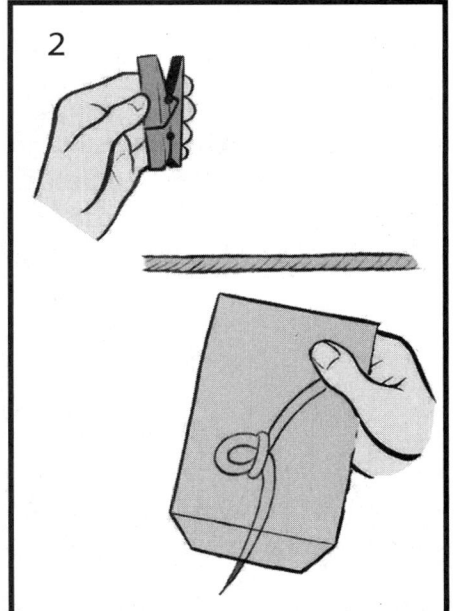

MATTHEW 27:54
When the army officer and the soldiers with him who were watching Jesus saw the earthquake and everything else that happened, they were terrified and said, "He really was the Son of God!"

JOHN 8:12
Jesus spoke to the Pharisees again. "I am the Light of the World," He said. "Whoever follows Me will have the light of life and will never walk in darkness."

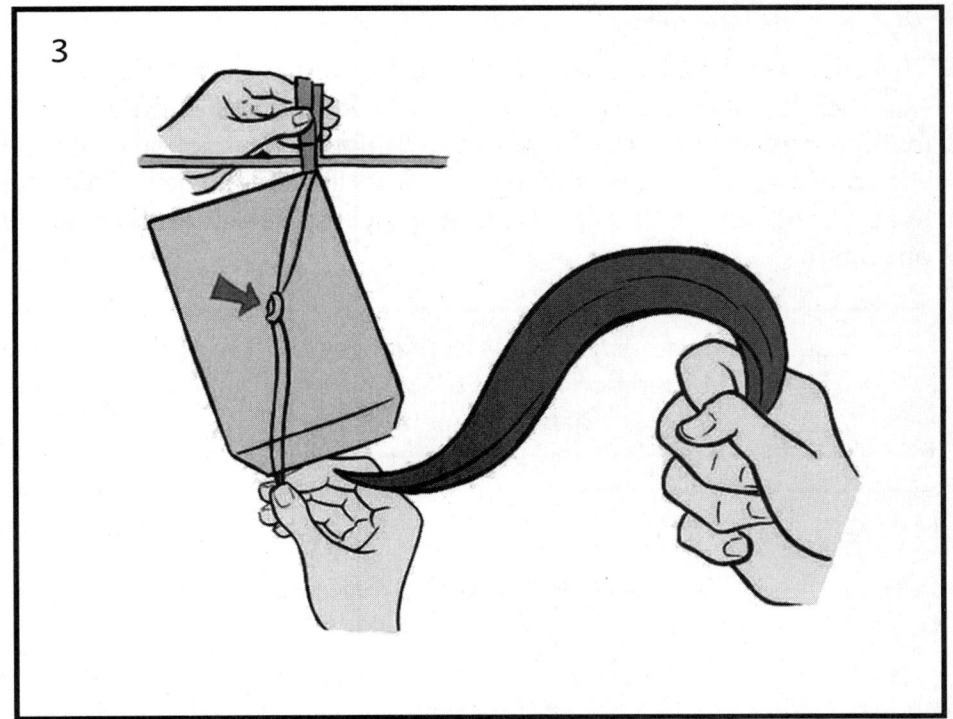

APOSTOLIC TRADITION (75-79)

The ancient tradition of the Church unites past, present, and future.

WHAT YOU NEED:

14 large paperclips
a styrofoam cup
a strong magnet

WHAT THEY SEE:

The catechist places 7 large paperclips into a cup one at a time. He turns the cup over and all of the paperclips are now linked.

WHAT YOU SAY:

"Does anyone know what is 'Apostolic Succession?' When you study the history of the Church, you hear that phrase a lot. It means that we modern Christians are connected through time all the way back to Jesus. Jesus told His Apostles to spread His Word to all the people of the world. St. Peter was in charge of the Apostles and he become the first pope. After him came a long line of popes and bishops all the way until our present pope."

"Imagine that these paperclips are individual Christians."

(Show each paperclip and drop it into the cup.)

"This one is from 2000-years ago. This one is from 1000-years ago. This one is from 500-years ago. This one is from 100-years ago. This one is from today. But how can we be sure that what we believe is what Jesus said?"

(Turn the cup upside down and dump the paperclip chain palmed in your hand.)

"The Church is like a big chain connecting you and me with all of the Christians that have ever lived all the way back to the Apostles and even back to Jesus Himself. When you receive the Holy Spirit during Confirmation or when you receive forgiveness during Reconciliation or share in the Eucharist, you are connected with the historic Christ who died for us. Just like these linked chains. So, as you see, Christ's spirit there at the beginning of the Church, 2000 years ago is still here with us now. We are one church united by the one Spirit."

> Tradition means giving votes to the most obscure of all classes, our ancestors. It is the democracy of the dead. Tradition refuses to submit to the small and arrogant oligarchy of those who merely happen to be walking about. — G. K. Chesterton, Orthodoxy

CATECHETICAL TIP

St. Don Bosco was the world's first Gospel Magician. Even now, many Salesian priests, brothers, nuns and lay people dedicated to Don Bosco's work, continue in his tradition of performing magic for poor and sick children.

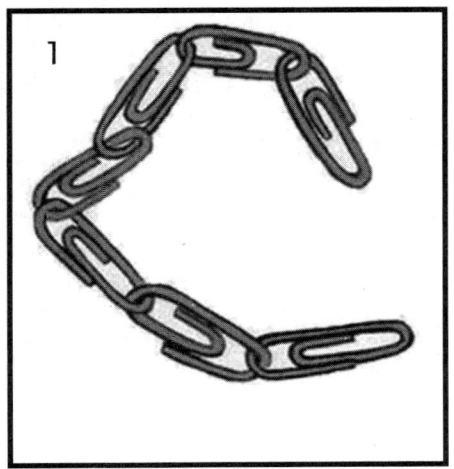

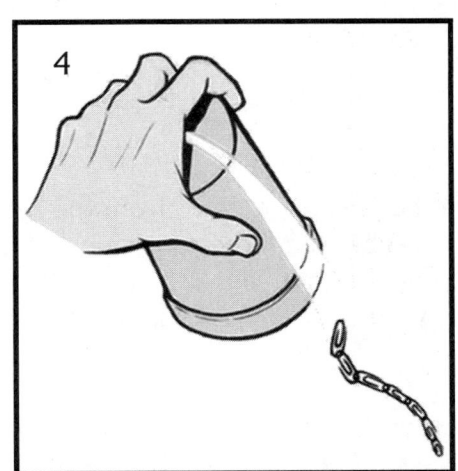

HOW YOU DO IT:

Glue a strong magnet to the bottom of a styrofoam cup. Prepare a chain of 7 large paperclips and hide them in the palm of the hand that holds the cup. During your performance, openly drop the 7 large paper clips into the cup one at a time making sure they engage the magnet. When you turn over the cup to pour out the paperclips, the magnet will grab hold of the individual clips. At the same moment, release the paperclip chain in your palm. This will give the illusion that the paperclips have fallen out of the cup and have linked together.

TEACHING TIP
Use 2 tables as you perform. One to set up your props and the other to perform upon.

MATTHEW 4:19
Jesus said to them, "Come with Me, and I will teach you to catch people."

MATTHEW 11:1
When Jesus finished giving these instructions to his twelve disciples, He left that place and went off to teach and preach in the towns near there.

MATTHEW 28:20
And teach them to obey everything I have commanded you. And I will be with you always, to the end of the age.

MARK 6:2
On the Sabbath He began to teach in the synagogue. Many people were there; and when they heard Him, they were all amazed. "Where did He get all this?" they asked. "What wisdom is this that has been given Him? How does He perform miracles?

MARK 6:34
When Jesus got out of the boat, He saw this large crowd, and His heart was filled with pity for them, because they were like sheep without a shepherd. So He began to teach them many things.

SACRED SCRIPTURE (101-141)

The Bible is the source of our knowledge of God.

WHAT YOU NEED:

cardboard or plywood
duct tape or carpentry
　　tools and screws
production items such as feather
　　boas, goldfish bowls and
　　bowling balls

WHAT THEY SEE:

A box is tilted over to show that it is completely empty. It is righted once again and immediately a tremendous amount of items, more than one would think could possibly fit inside, are produced from it.

WHAT YOU SAY:

"When we go to Mass, the lectors and the priest read to us from the Bible. Whenever we learn about Jesus and Mary we hear about them from the Bible. Even the songs we sing in church are based on the Bible. The Bible is our main source of information about God. The Bible is like this box; every time we look into it, we receive a new treasure. If you don't know how to read and understand the Bible, it will seem empty to you like this."

(Demonstrate that the box is empty by tipping it over.)

"But, if the lectors or presiding priest at Mass teaches you about God's Word, you will find many treasures and surprises in it."

(Right the box, flip open the top lid and produce the items you've stored in it.)

ACTS 8:27-31

So Philip got ready and went. Now an Ethiopian eunuch, who was an important official in charge of the treasury of the queen of Ethiopia, was on his way home. He had been to Jerusalem to worship God and was going back home in his carriage. As he rode along, he was reading from the book of the prophet Isaiah. The Holy Spirit said to Philip, "Go over to that carriage and stay close to it." Philip ran over and heard him reading from the book of the prophet Isaiah. He asked him, "Do you understand what you are reading?" The official replied, "How can I understand unless someone explains it to me?" And he invited Philip to climb up and sit in the carriage with him.

HEBREWS 5:12

There has been enough time for you to be teachers—yet you still need someone to teach you the first lessons of God's message. Instead of eating solid food, you still have to drink milk.

HOW YOU DO IT:

The Tilt-over Box has a pivoting load chamber and can have all of its sides shown, including its bottom, as long as the pivot chamber is closed. You may make the box out of wood or cardboard. If you hope to make a rabbit appear, I would suggest making this prop out of wood as cardboard won't stand up to the rigors of containing a live rabbit.

The Tilt-over box is composed of 2 elements. Figure 1 shows the individual pieces. Figures 2 and 3 show the assembled version.

To construct a corrugated cardboard version of Tilt-over Box cut out a piece of cardboard following the pattern (you can enlarge the pattern with a photocopier). Using duct tape, affix the panels together to form a box. Repeat these instructions to create the pivot chamber. You will need to create the hinge with duct tape. If you are handy with tools, a wooden Tilt-over Box will last for many years and will allow you a great deal of flexibility in your performance. You can load the box with any production item that is compressible and showy. I've made bowling balls, feather boas, and fishbowls with live fish appear using this type of prop. You are limited only by the available space and your imagination.

If you decide to make the Tilt-over Box out of wood, use half-inch plywood and wood screws rather than brads or nails.

When you are ready to perform this trick, simply tip over the box and lift the hinged lid. As you tip the box allow the bottom of the box (which is the outer portion of the pivot chamber) to stay on the table. Keep the protruding pivot chamber hidden behind the box so that audience cannot see it. The inside face of the pivot chamber will move, and seem to the audience to be the back of the inside of the box. The contents of the pivot chamber will be hidden and the audience should be convinced that the box is empty. Return the box to its upright position (sliding it back onto the pivot chamber) and open the top lid once again to remove the production items from inside.

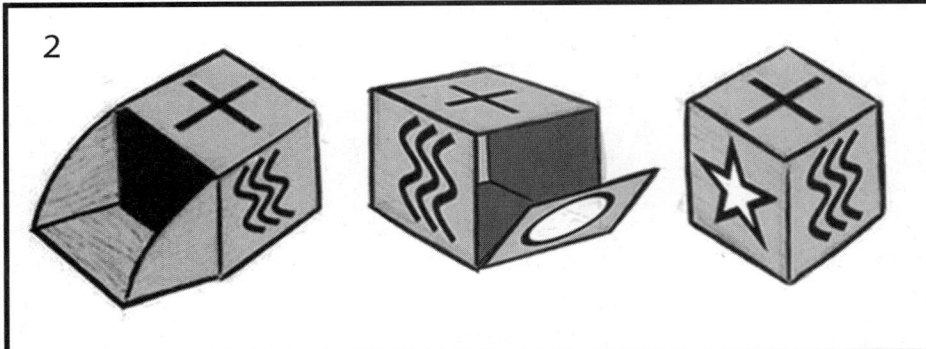

TEACHING TIP

Let me introduce my lovely assistant, Miss Direction. Ninety percent of any magic trick is psychological. The last thing you want people to do is think about what you're doing. If you don't want your audience to look at your hand, DON'T LOOK AT YOUR HAND!!!

I BELIEVE (144-165)

Belief in God means trusting Him.

WHAT YOU NEED:

two 3-foot pieces of rope

WHAT THEY SEE:

The catechist asks a volunteer to join him and offers her a length of rope. He challenges her to make a knot simply by whipping the rope. She fails but the catechist deftly shows her how a knot can be produced quickly and easily.

WHAT YOU SAY:

"What do you think it means when we say we believe in something? Do you believe in God? Do you believe I am standing here right now and speaking to you? When we say we believe in God, it means that we know He exists and that He loves us. We really believe it just like you believe I'm here right now. Do you believe that someone can make a knot in a rope without actually tying it? Let's find out. Can you spin this rope? Once you get it spinning, try snapping it. Can you make a knot while holding only one end? It's hard to do, right? Do you believe I can do it? If you believe it can be done, it will be possible. This is what is meant by belief."

(Flip the rope over and release the knotted end.)

"It means trust, respect and acceptance. When we believe in God, it means that we have trust and respect, and accept God in our lives. Just like making a knot in this rope, if we believe and trust in God's love, He will bless us and make all things possible."

TEACHING TIP

There will inevitably be many dozens of children who will yell out in the middle of the performance that they, in fact, know the secret to your next trick. Ask them to step up to the stage so that they can perform in your place. This usually makes them a lot more humble and quiet for the duration of your performance.

MATTHEW 8:5-13

When Jesus entered Capernaum, a Roman officer met Him and begged for help: "Sir, my servant is sick in bed at home, unable to move and suffering terribly." "I will go and make him well," Jesus said. "Oh no, Sir," answered the officer. "I do not deserve to have You come into my house. Just give the order, and my servant will get well. I, too, am a man under the authority of superior officers, and I have soldiers under me. I order this one, 'Go!' and he goes; and I order that one, 'Come!' and he comes; and I order my slave, 'Do this!' and he does it." When Jesus heard this, He was surprised and said to the people following Him, "I tell you, I have never found anyone in Israel with faith like this. I assure you that many will come from the east and the west and sit down with Abraham, Isaac, and Jacob at the feast in the Kingdom of heaven. But those who should be in the Kingdom will be thrown out into the darkness, where they will cry and gnash their teeth." Then Jesus said to the officer, "Go home, and what you believe will be done for you." And the officer's servant was healed that very moment.

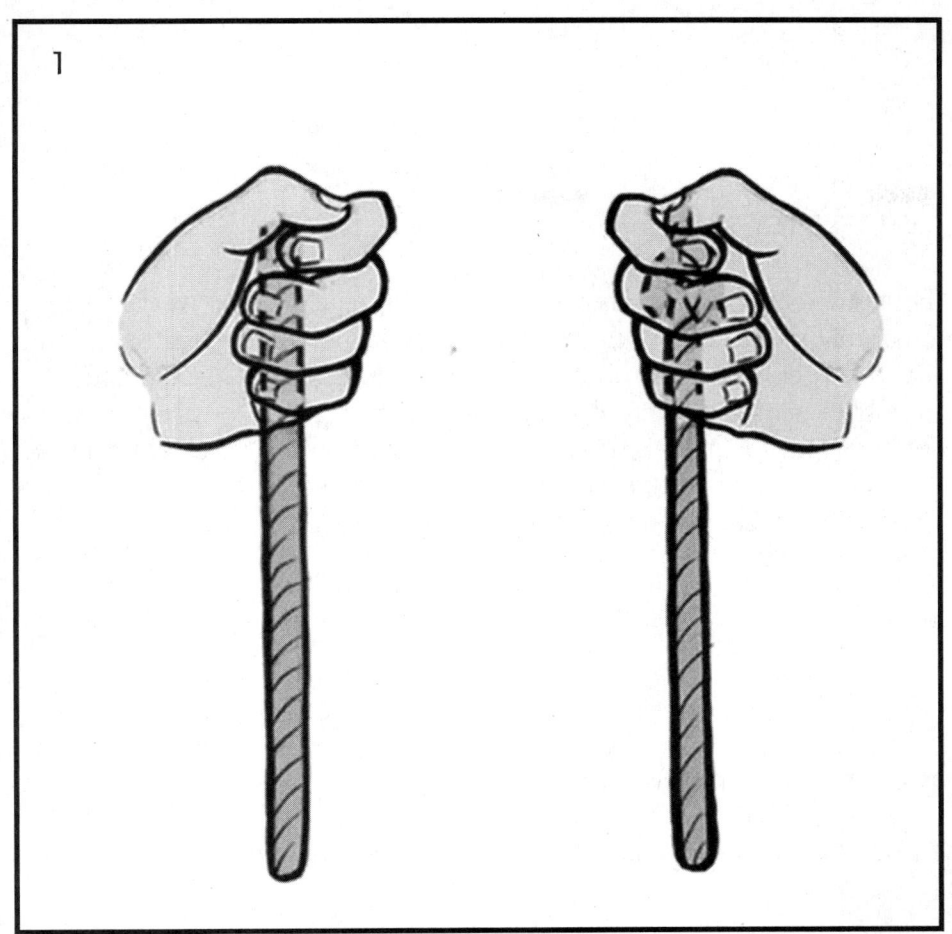

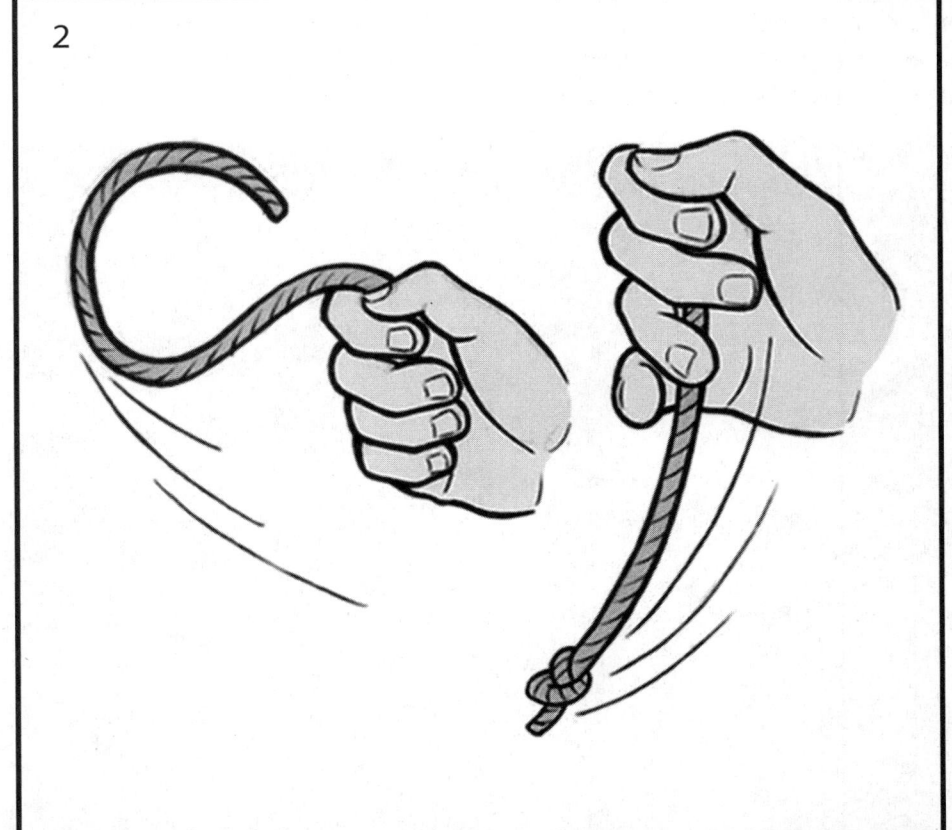

HOW YOU DO IT:

Tie a knot near the end of one of the ropes and close your hand over the knot. Take another unprepared rope in your other hand. Ask your volunteer to choose one. If she chooses the unprepared rope, hand it to her. If she chooses the prepared one, tell her that you'll take that one and offer her the other one. Either way, you get the prepared rope and she gets the unprepared one. To produce the knot, simply flip the dangling end of your rope and catch it in the same hand while simultaneously dropping the knotted end (see illustration). It might take a bit of practice but it's pretty stunning when done correctly.

> **MARK 8:29; MATTHEW 16:16; LUKE 9:20**
> "What about you?" He asked them. "Who do you say I am?"
> Peter answered, "You are the Messiah."
>
> **MARK 12:37**
> David himself called Him 'Lord'; so how can the Messiah be David's descendant? A large crowd was listening to Jesus gladly.
>
> **MARK 14:61**
> But Jesus kept quiet and would not say a word. Again the High Priest questioned Him, "Are You the Messiah, the Son of the Blessed God?"
>
> **JOHN 1:41**
> At once he found his brother Simon and told him, "We have found the Messiah." (This word means "Christ.")

ONLY ONE FAITH (172-175)

God acts in our lives every day.

WHAT YOU NEED:

access to a lamination machine
8-inch x 8-inch foam core, colored construction paper
   (blue, yellow, green, and red)
glue

WHAT THEY SEE:

Four different colored cards are laid facedown on a tabletop. A volunteer randomly selects a number between 1 and 16. She is then directed to count up to her selected number on a large multicolored card. The volunteer counts to her selected number and thereby chooses a color. It will always be blue. The volunteer is directed to the 4 cards on the table before her and is asked to select the blue card. A card is turned over to reveal the words, "The Catholic Church" on a blue background. The yellow, green, and red cards, once turned over, are all shown to be blank.

WHAT YOU SAY:

"God chose to reveal Himself as fully as we humans can possibly understand Him."

    (Ask your volunteer to choose a number between 1 and 16 and hand the prepared card to her positioning as described in the How You Do It section.)

"Choose any number between 1 and 16. Take this card and count to the number you've freely chosen. Name that color and turn over the paper with that color. Now, turn over the others. As you see, God has guided us to through the patriarchs, the prophets, and finally to Christ who, in turn, established the Catholic Church with St. Peter as its first Pope. The paper you chose says the words "The Catholic Church" while the others are blank. In this same way, God leads those who believe into faith."

JOHN 4:29
"Come and see the man Who told me everything I have ever done. Could He be the Messiah?"

JOHN 11:27
"Yes, Lord!" she answered. "I do believe that You are the Messiah, the Son of God, Who was to come into the world."

ACTS 9:22
But Saul's preaching became even more powerful, and his proofs that Jesus was the Messiah were so convincing that the Jews who lived in Damascus could not answer him.

ACTS 17:3
And explaining the Scriptures, and proving from them that the Messiah had to suffer and rise from death. "This Jesus Whom I announce to you," Paul said, "is the Messiah."

ACTS 18:28
For with his strong arguments he defeated the Jews in public debates by proving from the Scriptures that Jesus is the Messiah.

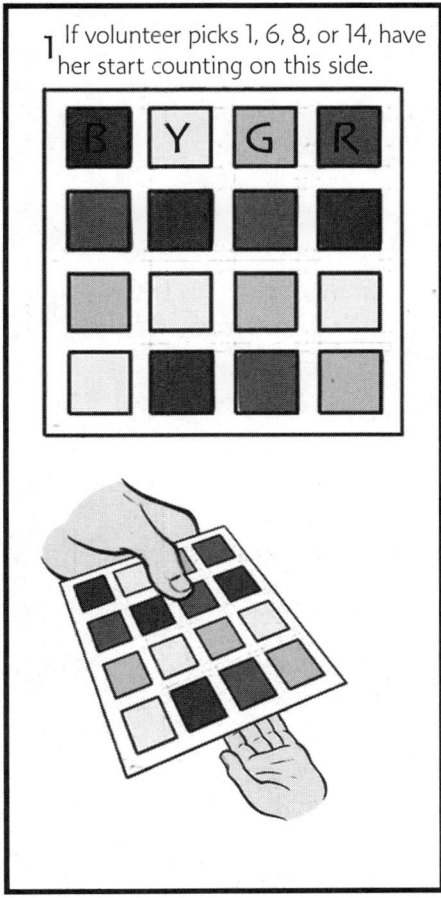

1. If volunteer picks 1, 6, 8, or 14, have her start counting on this side.

2. If volunteer picks 4, 5, 7, or 15, have her start counting on this side.

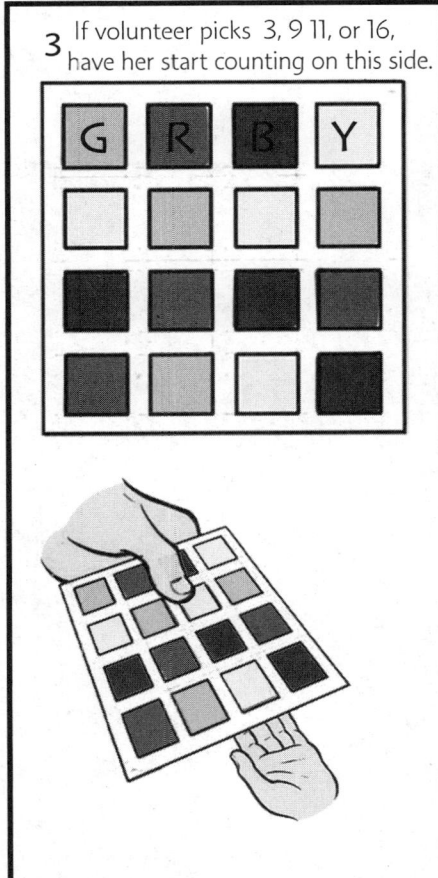

3. If volunteer picks 3, 9, 11, or 16, have her start counting on this side.

4. If volunteer picks 2, 10, 12 or 13, have her start counting on this side.

HOW YOU DO IT:

Create a color forcing card by cutting out squares of construction paper and affixing them to the foam board in the pattern of the diagram. Next, write the words "The Catholic Church" on a sheet of blue paper or use a laser printer. Place the blue paper with writing as well as the blank yellow, red, and green papers facedown on a table top. The color of paper is obvious from the back but writing should not show through.

Ask your volunteer to randomly choose a number between 1 and 16. Ask her count the squares (from left to right, and top to bottom as you would read words in a book). If she chooses the numbers 1, 6, 8 or 14, hand her the card oriented as shown in the diagram. If she chooses 3, 9, 11 or 16, reverse the chart before handing it to her. If she chooses 2, 10, 12 or 13, rotate the card 90-degrees to the right before handing it to her. If she chooses 4, 5, 7 or 15, rotate the card 90-degrees to the left before handing it to her. By so orienting the card, your volunteer will be forced to always land on a blue square. You can pencil in the numbers very lightly along the edge of the paper to help you remember how to orient the card as you hand it to your volunteer. When she chooses blue, direct her to turn over the blue paper.

CATECHETICAL TIP

Jesus is the cause, the heart and the goal of all catechesis. Catechesis can never be simple communication of abstract ideas but the proclamation of Christ's living Gospel for the strengthening of faith among the Faithful.

I BELIEVE IN ONE GOD (200-202)
The One, Eternal God is our Father and Creator.

WHAT YOU NEED:

a 3 1/2-foot length of rope
a pair of scissors

WHAT THEY SEE:

A rope is shown to have 3 knots on it. The catechist runs his hand along it and seemingly pulls off the knots in his hand. Both the rope and the knots may be examined.

WHAT YOU SAY:

"We often talk about The Father, the Son and the Holy Spirit. But though we describe God as being a Trinity, He is One. We use a special word to describe Him. We say that He is 'Triune.'"

(Hold one end of the rope in the air and slide your other hand along the rope and dislodge the first knot.)

"He is not 3 gods."

(Continue to slide your hand along the rope and dislodge the second knot.)

"Even though we see 3 knots on this rope to represent the Trinity, we understand that He is One."

(Continue to slide your hand along the rope and dislodge the third knot. Open your hand and show the knots. Toss them out into the audience.)

MATTHEW 5:16
In the same way your light must shine before people, so that they will see the good things you do and praise your Father in heaven.

MATTHEW 5:45
So that you may become the children of your Father in heaven. For He makes His sun to shine on bad and good people alike, and gives rain to those who do good and to those who do evil.

MATTHEW 5:48
You must be perfect—just as your Father in heaven is perfect.

MATTHEW 6:9
This, then, is how you should pray: "Our Father in heaven: May Your holy name be honored."

MATTHEW 6:14
If you forgive others the wrongs they have done to you, your Father in heaven will also forgive you.

1

HOW YOU DO IT:

Prepare a rope by forming 3 slip knots along it at equal distances from each other. A slip knot is created by looping the rope and then pulling a small bit of the same rope through the newly formed loop. You should tighten these fake knots as much as possible. Remember that the slightest bit of pressure on them will dislodge them.

Also, create 3 separate fake knots. To do so, simply tie a knot in a rope and cut it off the rope as closely as possible. Hide these 3 knots in your right palm.

As you run your hand across the rope, the slipknots will dissolve. When you get to the end of the rope, open your hand to reveal the 3 fake knots. Toss them out to the audience. Everyone will presume you pulled the knots off the rope.

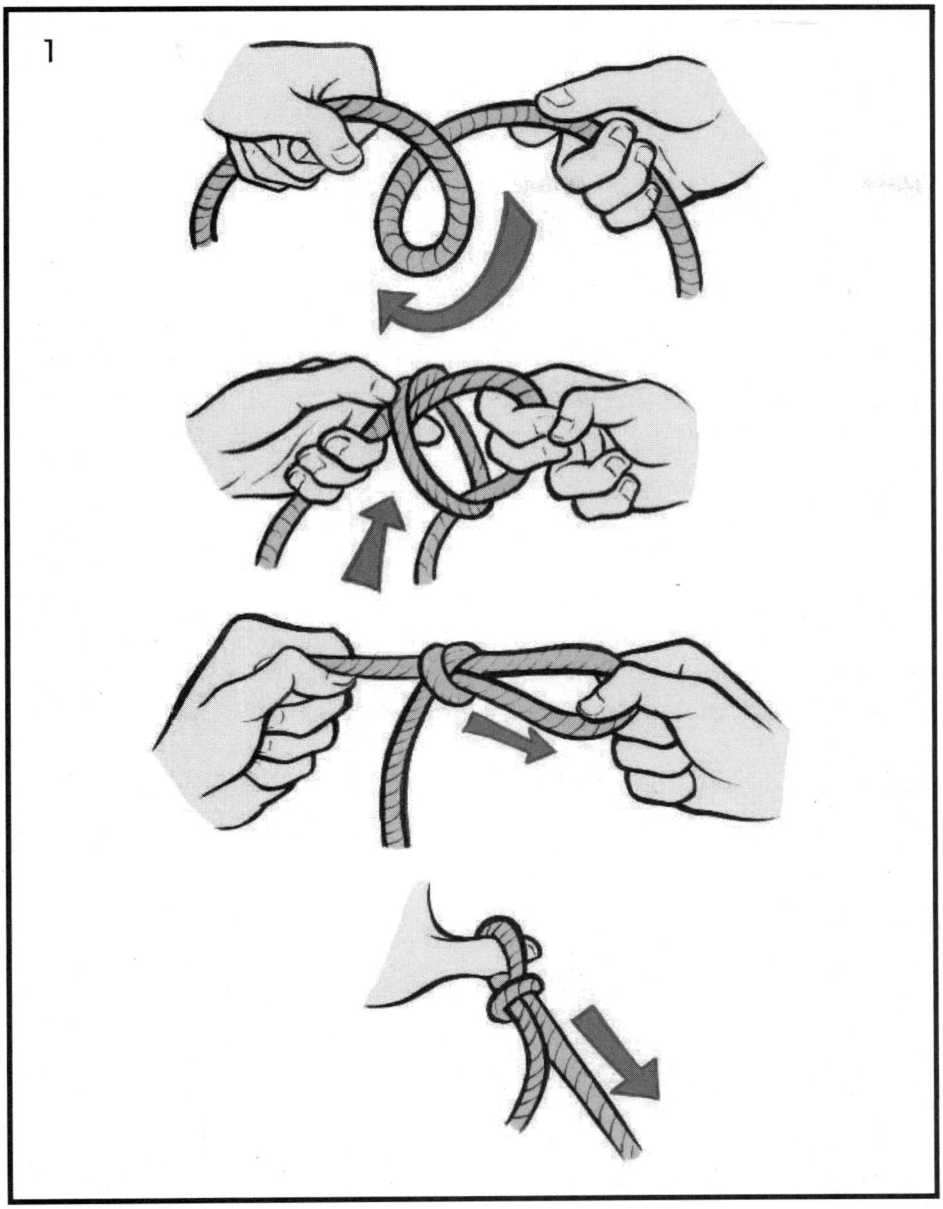

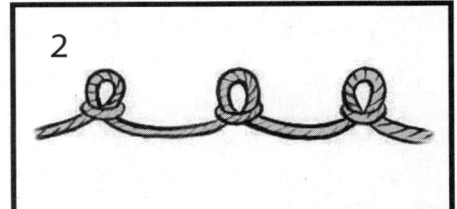

2

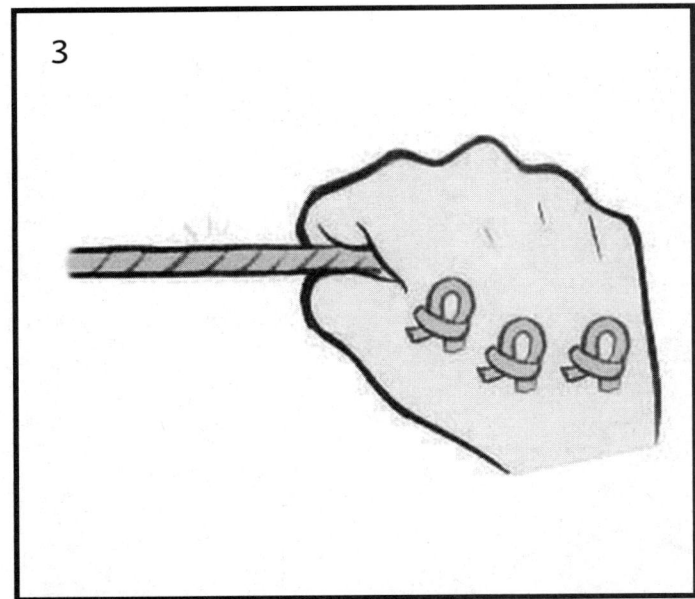

3

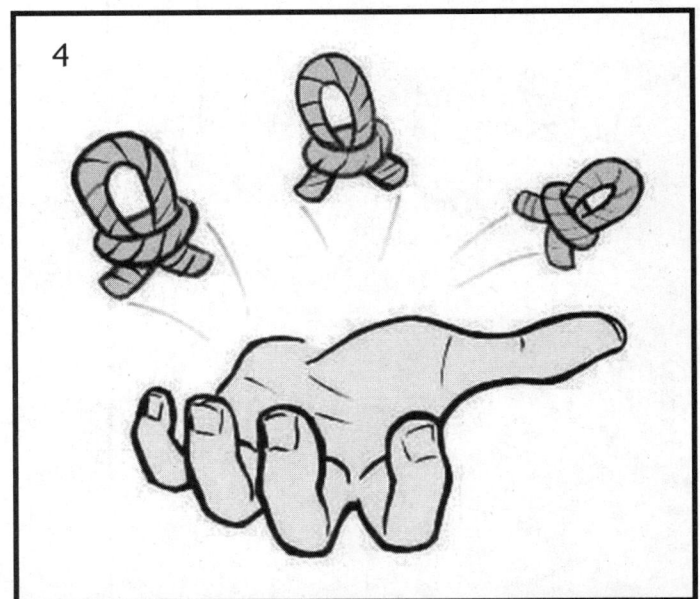

4

57

THE FATHER (232-267)

The Father, Son, and Holy Spirit are one.

WHAT YOU NEED:

a yard of fabric
needle and thread
   or sewing machine
one 3-foot piece of rope
three 1-foot pieces of rope
two 4-inch pieces of ropes

WHAT THEY SEE:

The catechist shows 3 short pieces of ropes. A volunteer places these ropes into a cloth bag. The catechist immediately takes the rope out of the bag and shows that they were magically tied together. He rolls up the rope and hands it out for examination. The volunteer opens the rope to find the knots have disappeared and that the rope is now one long continuous piece.

WHAT YOU SAY:

"I have 3 ropes here. They represent the Father, Son, and the Holy Spirit. Three persons in one God. But this is not the real Trinity ... because you can see the individual parts. Would you please put the ropes into this bag? Oh! Not all the way. I want an end of it to stick out so that you can keep an eye on it at all times."

"Even though we speak about the Father, Son, and Holy Spirit as if they were separate, they aren't. At all times and in all places, the Trinity is always present to us. Here ... I'll show you. Would you please pull on this rope very slowly?"

(Rope with knots tied on is revealed.)

"As you see, 3 ropes are now tied together, but in truth they were never really separate."

(Pull the knots off the rope to show a single, complete length of rope.)

"They are really one, unified ... just as the Trinity is Triune. Three in One."

MATTHEW 6:26
Look at the birds: they do not plant seeds, gather a harvest and put it in barns; yet your Father in heaven takes care of them! Aren't you worth much more than birds?

MATTHEW 6:31-32
So do not start worrying: "Where will my food come from? or my drink? or my clothes?" (These are the things the pagans are always concerned about.) Your Father in heaven knows that you need all these things.

MATTHEW 7:11
As bad as you are, you know how to give good things to your children. How much more, then, will your Father in heaven give good things to those who ask him!

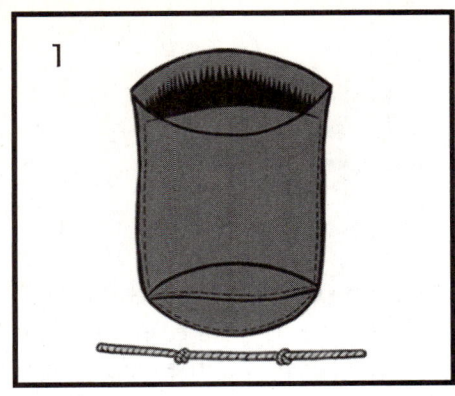

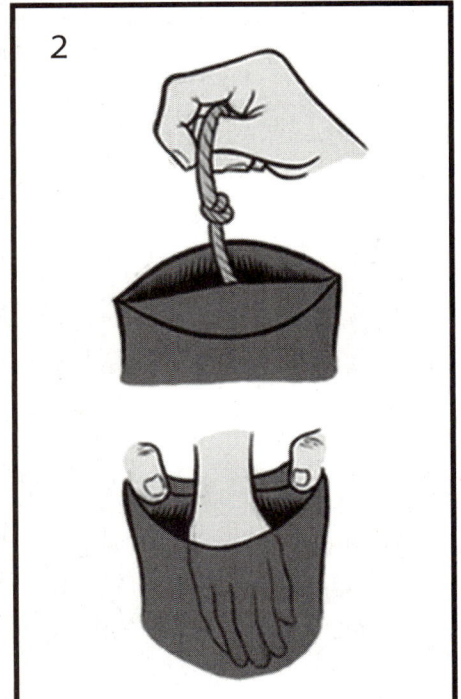

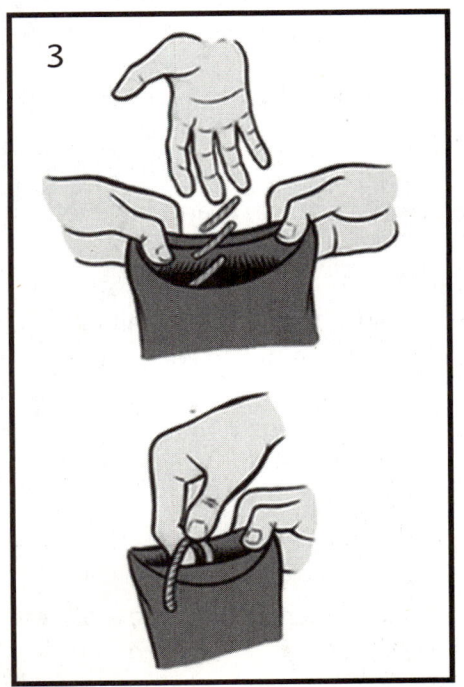

HOW YOU DO IT:

For this trick you need a common piece of magic equipment called a Change Bag that is easy to make and extremely useful. Take 3 pieces of fabric, 10-inch by 10-inch, preferably plaid or flat black and sew them together on 3 sides to make a double pocket as shown. Turn the pocket inside out to hide the seams. This will create a bag with 2 inner compartments. Plaid is frequently used for this device because it best hides any bulge in the bag. Experiment with different types of fabric, colors, and patterns to find which works best for you.

Take one of the 3-foot ropes and tie the 2 small pieces of rope along the length of the 3-foot rope. Space these 2 knots out at the 1-foot and 2-foot mark as described in the accompanying diagram. On cursory inspection, the rope will give the impression that it is 3 ropes tied together to form one long length.

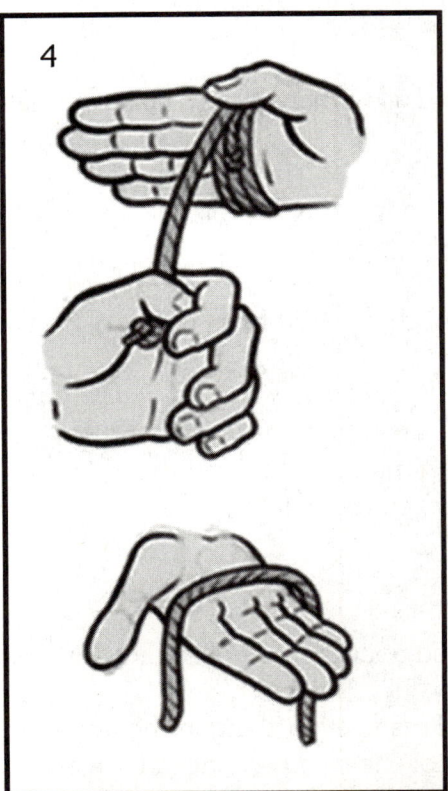

Hide this prepared rope in one of the pockets of the Change Bag. To begin the performance, ask a volunteer to place her hand into the bag's empty pocket. Avoid allowing her to touch the secret pocket. Have her place the 3 ropes into the pocket she just examined.

Once she has done this, explain that you actually wanted a small bit of the rope to hang out of the bag. Place your hand into the other pocket and pull out a few inches of the prepared rope and allow it to hang out of the bag.

After explaining the mystery of the Trinity, ask the volunteer to pull the rope out completely. Point out that the ropes are now tied end-to-end. Take the rope from her and as you speak about the Trinity, roll the rope around your hand. As you do so, you will note that the little pieces of rope that have been tied on to the longer rope will be easy to pull off. Do not make a great show of this. Instead, simply look at your audience and disregard the fact that the knots are coming off your hand. As you hand the now rolled up rope to your volunteer, pocket the 2 knots in your hand. When the volunteer unrolls the rope, she will see that the 3 tied ropes have now transformed into a single, long piece.

> **MATTHEW 10:32**
> Those who declare publicly that they belong to me, I will do the same for them before my Father in heaven.

THE ALMIGHTY (268-274)
Out of nothing, God created the universe.

WHAT YOU NEED:

2 broad-rimmed Asian-style bowls (plastic, ceramic or lacquered) approximately 5-6 inches in diameter
sandpaper
one 8-inch by 10-inch by 3/64-inch flexible transparent plastic sheet (a kid's book report cover works well)
petroleum jelly
enough uncooked rice to fill one of the bowls

WHAT THEY SEE:

The catechist introduces 2 rice bowls. He fills one with rice, covers it with the other bowl, and then flips them over. When the bowls are separated, the rice has seemingly doubled. The catechist scrapes away the excess rice and covers the bowl once again and immediately separates them only to find that all of the rice has disappeared and has been changed into water.

WHAT YOU SAY:

"We call God 'The Almighty' because He created the whole universe. He created us and everything else that's around us."

(Two bowls are stacked upside down on a table. Pick up the top bowl and show it to be empty. Fill it with rice.)

"You have to be pretty powerful and important to be able to create one star or one person."

(Keeping the water bowl facing downwards, place it over the bowl of rice in your other hand and turn the entire assemblage over.)

"To be able to create all of the stars and all humans beings that ever have been means that God is all-powerful. He can do anything."

(When you remove the bowl on top, the rice will spill over, giving the impression that the rice has unexpectedly doubled.)

"He made the whole universe out of nothing. And from nothing, He created the whole world and He even made food for us."

(Take the empty top bowl with your right hand and hold both bowls out in front of you. Spin around and, as you do so, use your left thumb to push off the circular plastic piece that holds the water in its bowl and allow it to fall unnoticed to the floor.)

"He made water for us too!"

(Turn towards the audience and pour the water back and forth from one bowl to the other.)

"He did this because He loves us. God made everything in the universe for us. He made the universe a place for us to live and love. He gives us all of the things we need to live. For this we should be grateful to Him."

HOW YOU DO IT:

Most magic stores will sell a very inexpensive but plain set of rice bowls that are perfectly suited for this trick. If you prefer a more attractive set of rice bowls, you can prepare your own. This trick is messy so be prepared for the rice to spill over.

Sand the rims of the bowls with sandpaper to roughen them a bit. Lay one bowl over a transparent plastic sheet and trace its outline. Allow for a slight overhang and cut out the circle that is formed.

Rub a thin coating of petroleum jelly over the rim of one bowl and fill it to the brim with water. Place the flexible plastic circle over this bowl and make sure a seal forms. Turn the bowl upside-down (don't worry, the seal will hold). Place this bowl upside down on your tabletop. Stack the empty bowl upside down over the water-filled bowl.

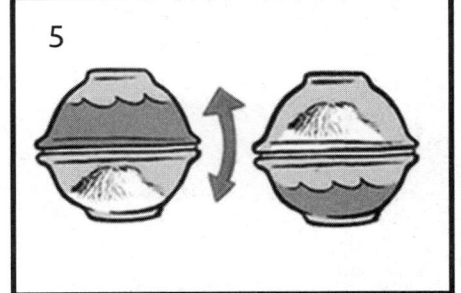

When you are ready to perform this trick, pick up the top bowl and show it to be empty. Fill it with rice. Keeping the water bowl facing downwards, place it over the bowl that is filled with rice. Turn the entire assemblage over. When you remove the bowl on top, the rice will spill over, giving the impression that the rice has unexpectedly doubled.

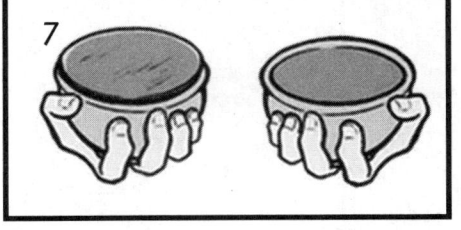

Take the empty top bowl with your right hand and hold both bowls out in front of you. Spin around and as you do so, use your left thumb to push off the circular plastic piece that holds the water in its bowl and allow it to fall to the floor. Once you've oriented yourself towards your audience, pour the water from one bowl to the other several times.

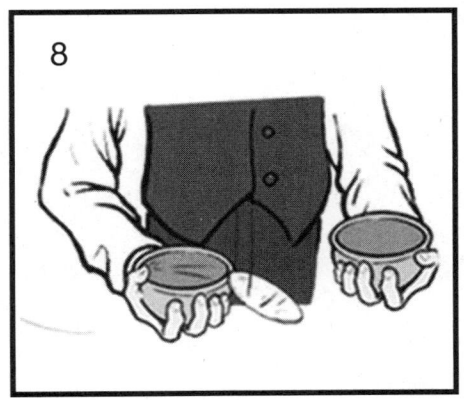
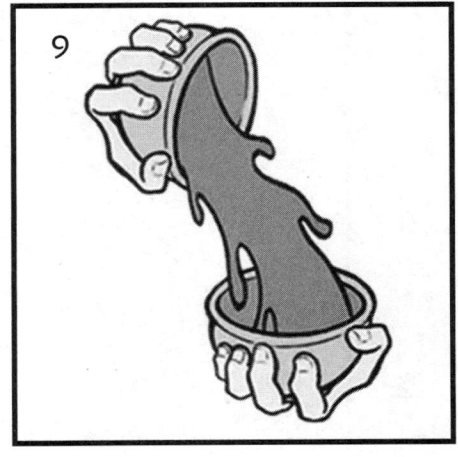

61

THE ALMIGHTY (268-274)
(continued)

(Scripture for preceding trick)

MATTHEW 16:17
"Good for you, Simon son of John!" answered Jesus. "For this truth did not come to you from any human being, but it was given to you directly by My Father in heaven.

MATTHEW 18:10
See that you don't despise any of these little ones. Their angels in heaven, I tell you, are always in the presence of My Father in heaven.

MATTHEW 18:14
In just the same way your Father in heaven does not want any of these little ones to be lost.

MATTHEW 18:19
And I tell you more: whenever 2 of you on earth agree about anything you pray for, it will be done for you by My Father in heaven.

MATTHEW 18:35
And Jesus concluded, "That is how My Father in heaven will treat every one of you unless you forgive your brother from your heart."

THE CREATOR (279-324)
The creative force of love illuminates us.

(Scripture for following trick)

MARK 11:25
And when you stand and pray, forgive anything you may have against anyone, so that your Father in heaven will forgive the wrongs you have done.

LUKE 11:13
As bad as you are, you know how to give good things to your children. How much more, then, will the Father in heaven give the Holy Spirit to those who ask Him!

JOHN 6:32
"I am telling you the truth," Jesus said. "What Moses gave you was not the bread from heaven; it is My Father Who gives you the real bread from heaven."

JOHN 7:16
Jesus answered, "What I teach is not My own teaching, but it comes from God, Who sent Me.

THE CREATOR (279-324) (continued)

The creative force of love illuminates us.

WHAT YOU NEED:

a lemon
a knife, glue
a knitting needle
a dollar bill
a lighter
an ashtray
a pay envelope
a dollar bill

WHAT THEY SEE:

The catechist asks for a dollar bill from the audience. He reads out the serial number and asks a volunteer to write it down. He rips off a corner of the bill and gives it to the volunteer. The remainder of the bill is folded and placed in a small pay envelope. This envelope is, in turn, burned completely destroying it and the bill inside it. When this is completed, the catechist cuts through a lemon that has been in plain sight the entire performance. Bizarrely, a rolled-up bill is found in the very center of the lemon. The bill is removed and the serial number is checked. It is found to match the recorded one exactly. The catechist then retrieves the torn-off corner from the volunteer which is found to be a perfect match for the embedded bill.

WHAT YOU SAY:

"We call God the Creator because He made us from nothing. It must be very hard to make something from nothing. You can probably make a lemon if you had a seed but it would be really hard to make a seed."

(Borrow a dollar bill and while pretending to read out its serial number, read out the number of the bill you've secreted in the lemon.)

"Imagine ... there was nothing ....and then there was something ... the whole universe ... a lot of people and even lemons. Let me show you how hard it is to make something from nothing."

(Burn the pay envelope in the ashtray.)

"I've just destroyed the envelope with the dollar bill in it. It will never be able to reappear. Imagine doing this in reverse ... just like God did when He made the universe."

(Take the knife, cut open the lemon, and reveal the rolled up bill. Have a spectator remove the bill, examine the serial number, and match the bill to the corner that she has retained.)

"This is a little like how God made something out of nothing. Of course, He did it much better than I did. He can make lemons and all I can do is make a magic trick!"

FINGER PALMING

Finger palming is what magicians call hiding a small object like a coin or a billet in the crook of the fingers or between the fingers, depending upon the object. Keep your fingers relaxed. If you strain your fingers, it will draw attention to your hand and destroy the illusion.

64

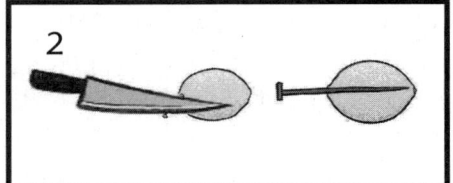

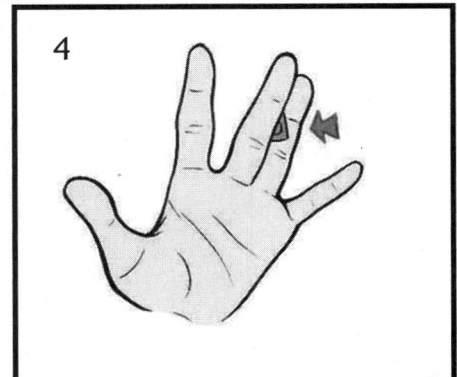
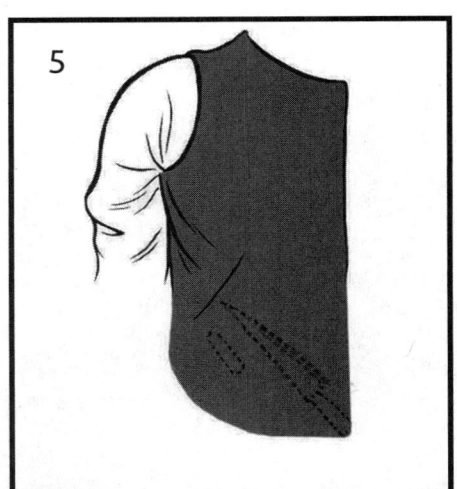

HOW YOU DO IT:

This trick is accomplished with a prepared lemon and a little sleight-of-hand. Carefully remove the stem remnant from the tip of a lemon and place it aside. Using a medium gauge knitting needle, create a space in the lemon's center. Tear off a corner of a dollar bill and place it aside. Record its serial number on the gummed part of the pay envelope using a very light pencil. Alternatively, you can lightly write the number on the side of your finger with a fine-line marker. Tightly roll up the remainder of the bill and gently work it into the space you've created in the lemon's center. Once completed, glue the tip back on the lemon.

Before performing this trick, place the knife and the lighter in your jacket pocket. Hide the ripped-off bill corner in the space between your ring and middle fingers (see Finger Palming, page 63).

Borrow a dollar bill from a trusting volunteer and instead of reading out loud its serial number, read out the number of the bill you've embedded in the lemon (the number you've written on the pay envelope.) Openly rip off the corner of the borrowed bill. When you retrieve the envelope from your pocket, put the borrowed bill and its ripped-off corner in your pocket. Hold the envelope up and pretend to place the borrowed bill in it. Hand the torn-off corner hidden between your fingers to the volunteer. She will think it's the corner of her dollar bill. Burn the envelope over the ashtray. People will presume the borrowed bill is destroyed along with the burning envelope.

Next, cut the lemon in half but avoid destroying the embedded bill. Instead, simply cut the lemon around the bill and twist the end off. Show your hands to be empty and invite your volunteer to extract the bill and unroll it. Have her check the wet, lemon-scented bill with the serial number she wrote down earlier. Have her confirm that the corner she had retained since the beginning of the trick fits the bill from the lemon exactly (as well it should since this is the bill from which it came in the first place!).

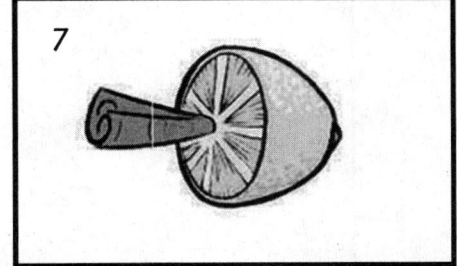
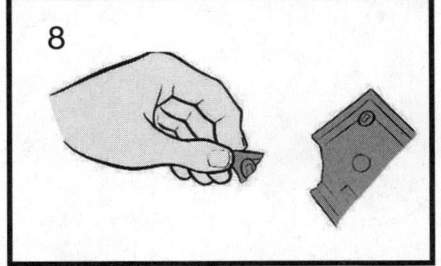

THE ANGELS (328-336)

Angels are signs of God's love.

WHAT YOU NEED:

an opaque piece of cloth
a needle and thread
   or sewing machine
a piece of wire
   (a wire coat hanger works well)
a wire cutter

WHAT THEY SEE:

A small piece of cloth is introduced. The catechist folds the 4 corners in toward the center. He then places his hands over the cloth and closes his eyes. Momentarily, the fabric seems to leap from the table. This happens several more times. The cloth is then held out for examination.

WHAT YOU SAY:

"Jesus taught us how to pray and reminded us that God already knows what we need before we ask for it. What is the purpose of prayer? It's meant to bring us closer to God; to ask God to be a part of all of our lives and to bless all of our endeavors."

(Hand your volunteer a piece of paper and take the gimmicked one for yourself. Rip up the gimmicked paper as she rips up hers.)

"If God isn't involved with building the house, it's useless to try building it on your own. We all have to orient ourselves to God."

(Restore your paper. Your volunteer won't be able to do so.)

"Don't worry ... let's try something else."

(Place her ripped pieces into the Change Bag.)

"Now, you've tried once to restore what was broken and what happened? It didn't work. But if you try again, if you place yourself in God's hands, everything is possible. That which was wounded is healed. That which was lost is found. That which was torn up can become whole, just like this piece of paper."

(Let your volunteer reach into the Change Bag to retrieve and open the intact piece of paper that was hidden in the other compartment.)

LUKE 10:21
At that time Jesus was filled with joy by the Holy Spirit and said, "Father, Lord of heaven and earth! I thank You because You have shown to the unlearned what You have hidden from the wise and learned. Yes, Father, this was how You were pleased to have it happen."

JOHN 6:32
"I am telling you the truth," Jesus said. "What Moses gave you was not the bread from heaven; it is My Father who gives you the real bread from heaven."

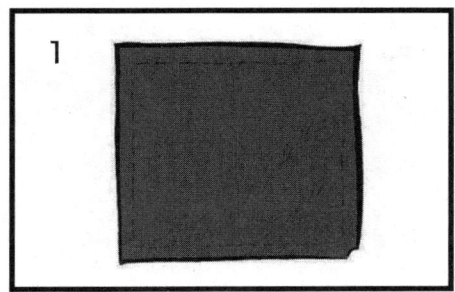

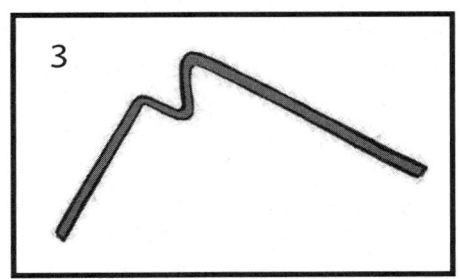
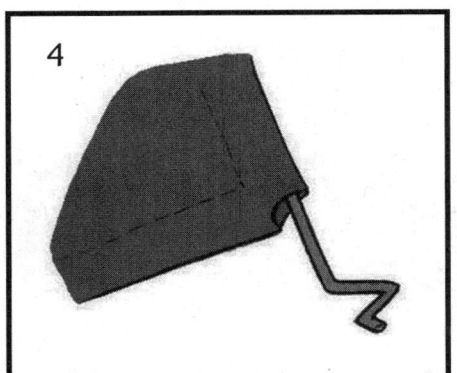

HOW YOU DO IT:

The advantage to this magic trick is that the cloth can be fully examined by anyone. Cut a one-foot square piece of cloth and create a hem on all 4 sides. Cut a 5-inch piece of wire from a coat hanger with a wire cutter. Using a pair of pliers, bend the wire into a right angle at about 3 1/2 inches from one end. Near the right angle, produce a small bump in the wire so that a bit of the wire lifts off the table while the rest of it lies flat. Next, cut a hole in the cloth's hem, near the corner. Make the hole just large enough to allow the wire to poke through. Work the whole length of the wire into the hole so that the 90-degree bend matches the corner of the handkerchief. A tiny bit of the wire should remain poking out of the hole.

To perform this trick fold the corner of the cloth that conceals the wire in towards the center. To make sure that the wire isn't detected, quickly fold in the other corners. Place your hands slightly above the folded packet of fabric and smooth it down. This will help you to locate the wire. You will note that the shape of the wire will allow you to make one end of it (and therefore the fabric) "jump" as you press the lifted end downwards. Experiment with the shape of the wire until you are comfortable with the cloth's movement. When you are done with the trick, hand the cloth to the audience members to be examined and keep hold of the wire. It should slide out easily as your spectator pulls the cloth from your hands. Once you're left with the wire, simply turn slightly away from your audience so you can place it in your pocket undetected.

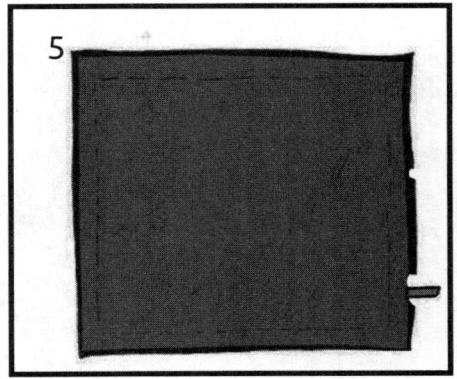
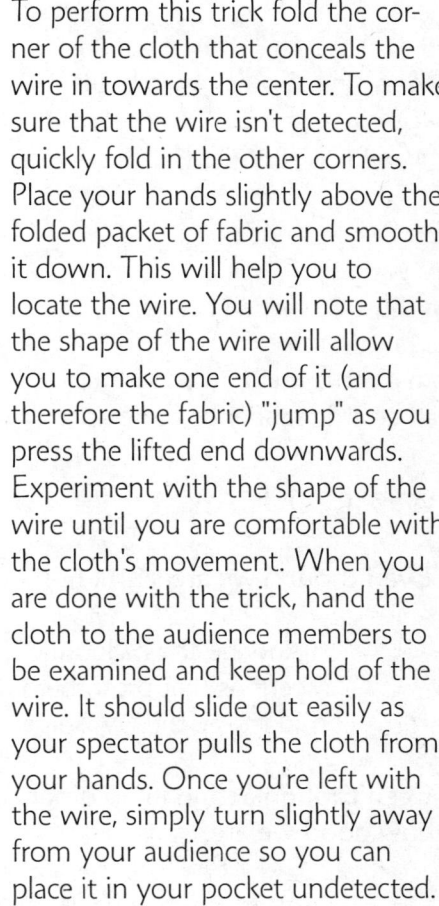
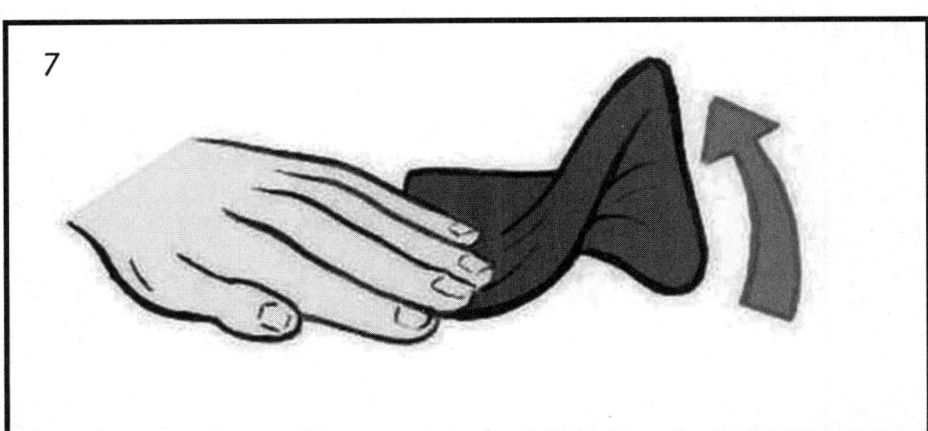
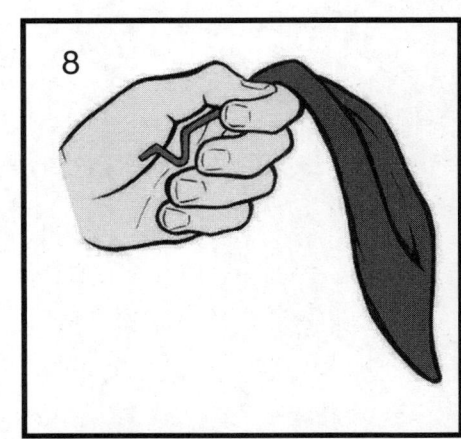

WHERE SIN ABOUNDED, GRACE ABOUNDED ALL THE MORE (386-389)

Man sins, God's grace heals.

WHAT YOU NEED:

an 8-inch length of
  wide PVC piping
a sausage-shaped balloon
a knitting needle
an electric drill
an electric sander or sandpaper

WHAT THEY SEE:

A balloon is inflated and placed inside a plastic tube. A needle is introduced and seemingly pierces the balloon but doesn't destroy it.

WHAT YOU SAY:

"Even though we are sinful human beings, it is through God's grace that we are saved.

(Blow up the balloon in PVC pipe. Just before completely filling the balloon, turn the top and bottom sections that protrude out of the pipe in opposite directions so that a twist is formed. This twist is hidden by the PVC pipe.)

"Even though acting in accordance with God's will is very important, we can not save ourselves, no matter how good we are."

(Introduce the needle into the hole in the pipe.)

"But with His grace, even the impossible can be accomplished. Just like this needle passing through this balloon, God's grace preserves us and guides us."

GENESIS 3:1-24

Now the snake was the most cunning animal that the Lord God had made. The snake asked the woman, "Did God really tell you not to eat fruit from any tree in the garden?"

"We may eat the fruit of any tree in the garden," the woman answered, "except the tree in the middle of it. God told us not to eat the fruit of that tree or even touch it; if we do, we will die." The snake replied, "That's not true; you will not die. God said that because He knows that when you eat it, you will be like God and know what is good and what is bad." The woman saw how beautiful the tree was and how good its fruit would be to eat, and she thought how wonderful it would be to become wise. So she took some of the fruit and ate it. Then she gave some to her husband, and he also ate it. As soon as they had eaten it, they were given understanding and realized that they were naked; so they sewed fig leaves together and covered themselves."

That evening they heard the Lord God walking in the garden, and they hid from Him among the trees. But the Lord God called out to the man, "Where are you?" He answered, "I heard You in the garden; I was afraid and hid from You, because I was naked." "Who told you that you were naked?" God asked. "Did you eat the fruit that I told you not to eat?" The man answered, "The woman you put here with me gave me the fruit, and I ate it." The Lord God asked the woman, "Why did you do this?"

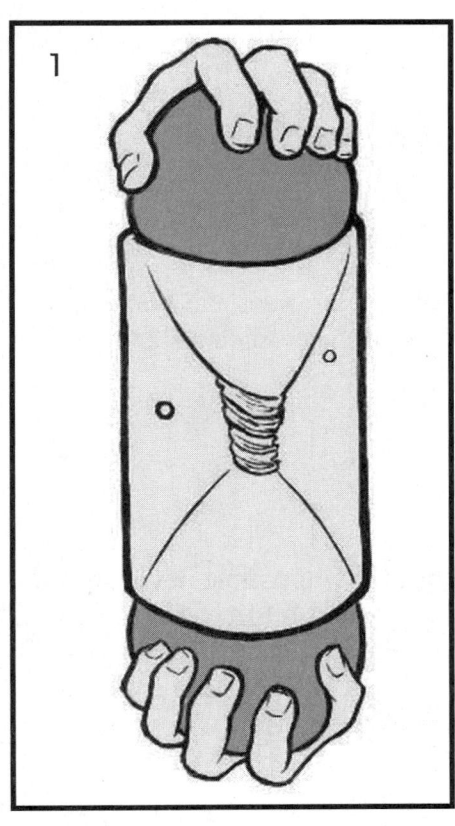 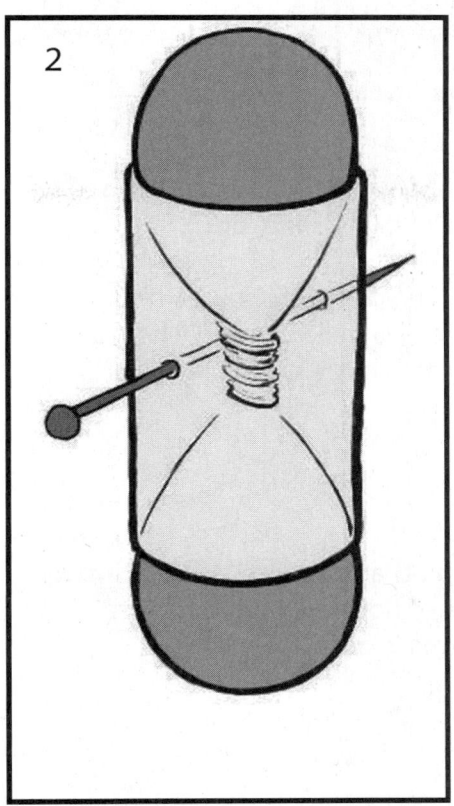

HOW YOU DO IT:

The reason the needle doesn't destroy the balloon is because just before the balloon is totally inflated the magician twists it, which moves it away from where the needle pokes through the hole in the pipe (see diagram).

Drill a hole though the piping midway between the 2 ends. A cross-section of the tube would show the needle piercing it on the upper part of the circle rather than through the center so that the needle clears the balloon. Sand the ends of the PVC piping so the balloon doesn't pop on the rough edges accidentally.

TEACHING TIP
Remember: As a Gospel Magician, you are a catechist. As a catechist, you are a teacher. This is your ministry.

(GENESIS 3:1-24 continued)

She replied, "The snake tricked me into eating it." Then the Lord God said to the snake, "You will be punished for this; you alone of all the animals must bear this curse: From now on you will crawl on your belly, and you will have to eat dust as long as you live. I will make you and the woman hate each other; her offspring and yours will always be enemies. Her offspring will crush your head, and you will bite her offspring's heel." And He said to the woman, "I will increase your trouble in pregnancy and your pain in giving birth. In spite of this, you will still have desire for your husband, yet you will be subject to him."

And He said to the man, "You listened to your wife and ate the fruit which I told you not to eat. Because of what you have done, the ground will be under a curse. You will have to work hard all your life to make it produce enough food for you. It will produce weeds and thorns, and you will have to eat wild plants. You will have to work hard and sweat to make the soil produce anything, until you go back to the soil from which you were formed. You were made from soil, and you will become soil again." Adam named his wife Eve, because she was the mother of all human beings. And the Lord God made clothes out of animal skins for Adam and his wife, and He clothed them. Then the Lord God said, "Now these human beings have become like one of us and have knowledge of what is good and what is bad. They must not be allowed to take fruit from the tree that gives life, eat it, and live forever." So the Lord God sent them out of the Garden of Eden and made them cultivate the soil from which they had been formed. Then at the east side of the garden he put living creatures and a flaming sword which turned in all directions. This was to keep anyone from coming near the tree that gives life.

THE SON OF GOD BECAME MAN (456-483)

The loving power of God shines in our lives.

WHAT YOU NEED:

a colorful handkerchief
an 8-inch by 11 1/2-inch sheet of opaque white paper
black thread

WHAT THEY SEE:

The catechist shows a piece of blank paper on both sides and from every other angle. Suddenly he crumples it and from the crushed ball of paper, he pulls out a large handkerchief.

WHAT YOU SAY:

"A virgin AND pregnant? Do you think that's impossible? It is impossible ... but the impossible never stopped God. If He can make the universe out of nothing, he can make a virgin pregnant. He can turn our loveless and cold hearts into warm, compassionate ones."

(Demonstrate a piece of paper. While doing so, grab the thread attached to the balled up handkerchief in your pocket. Hide the handkerchief behind the paper.)

"He can take us as we are, not capable of anything on our own, just like this sheet of paper."

(Crumple the paper around the hidden handkerchief.)

"By molding us, changing us, guiding us ...."

(Rip open the paper ball and pull out the hidden handkerchief.)

"He can produce beautiful things inside our hearts. Just like this little handkerchief appearing and showing itself, so too did Christ come into the world and into our hearts."

LUKE 1:27-38

He had a message for a young woman promised in marriage to a man named Joseph, who was a descendant of King David. Her name was Mary. The angel came to her and said, "Peace be with you! The Lord is with you and has greatly blessed you!" Mary was deeply troubled by the angel's message, and she wondered what his words meant. The angel said to her, "Don't be afraid, Mary; God has been gracious to you. You will become pregnant and give birth to a son, and you will name him Jesus. He will be great and will be called the Son of the Most High God. The Lord God will make him a king, as his ancestor David was, and he will be the king of the descendants of Jacob forever; his kingdom will never end!" Mary said to the angel, "I am a virgin. How, then, can this be?" The angel answered, "The Holy Spirit will come on you, and God's power will rest upon you. For this reason the holy child will be called the Son of God. Remember your relative Elizabeth. It is said that she cannot have children, but she herself is now 6 months pregnant, even though she is very old. For there is nothing that God cannot do." "I am the Lord's servant," said Mary; "may it happen to me as you have said." And the angel left her.

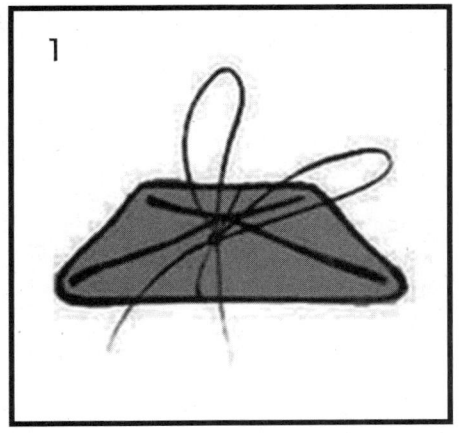

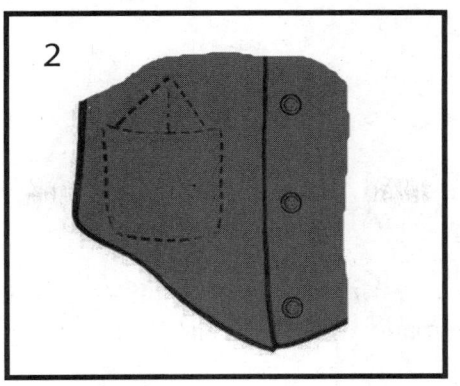

HOW YOU DO IT:

If you are doing a full evening's Gospel Magic show, then it's best to perform this trick as an opener. Fold your handkerchief into as small a package as possible and tie it with a 12-inch piece of black thread. Place this small bundle into your breast pocket but keep the thread sticking out of your pocket.

Roll up your sleeves before performing this trick in order to waylay suspicions. Show the front and back of the piece of paper in your hand. As you show the back, grab hold of the thread and use it to pull the folded handkerchief to the paper. At that point, crumble the paper making sure the handkerchief bundle gets crumbled inside the paper. Toss the ball into the air a few times. Hold it openly in your hand and poke a finger into it to tear a small hole. Carefully pull out the handkerchief.

ISAIAH 7:14

Well then, the Lord Himself will give you a sign: a young woman who is pregnant will have a son and will name Him "Immanuel."

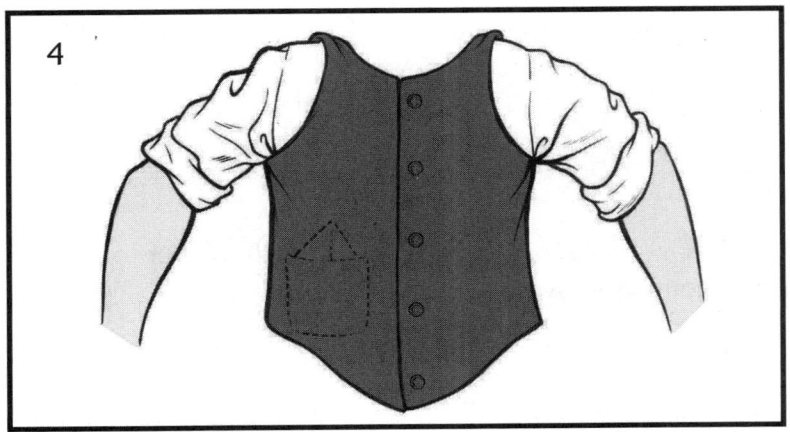

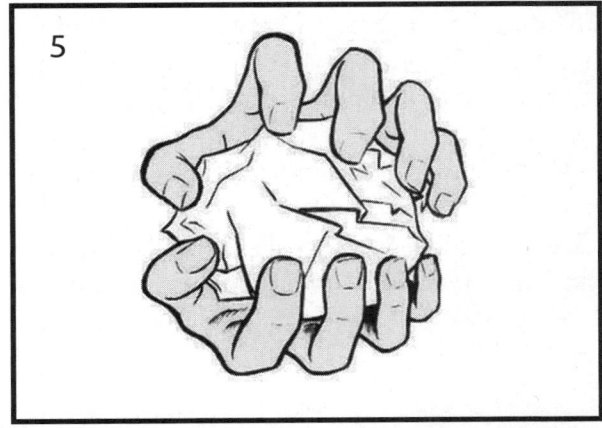

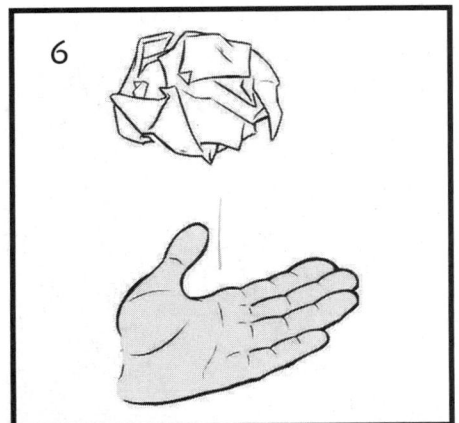

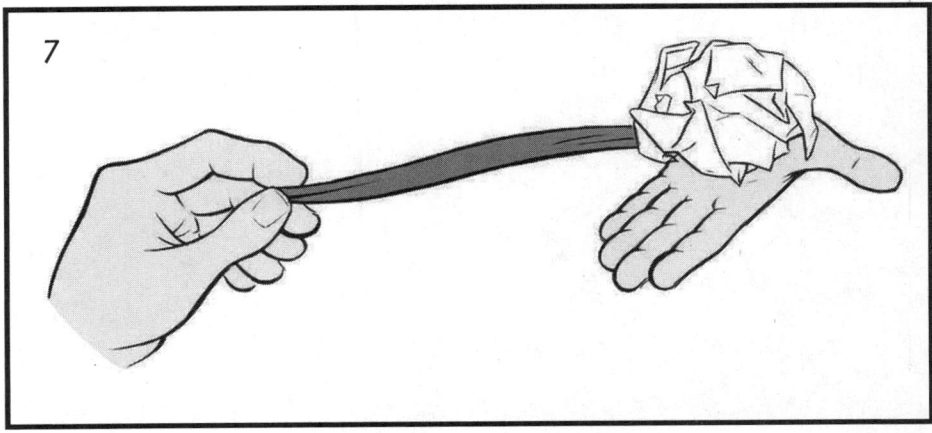

71

THE INCARNATION (461-463)

We offer ourselves to God.

WHAT YOU NEED:

a wooden or plastic ball
an electric drill
a 2-foot length of cord, superglue
2 yards of invisible thread

WHAT THEY SEE:

A wooden ball strung on a cord moves up and down and stops on command as it travels along the cord.

WHAT YOU SAY:

"All of Creation was made for Jesus. He was there before the universe was created. A Creation that was good but allowed for Man's free will."

> (Hold the assemblage upright in your hands. Hold the ball lightly in your right hand. Allow the invisible cord to pass over the back of your right hand.)

"And, with free will, came the possibility for evil."

> (Allow the ball to fall down to your left hand.)

"That means that God knew and accepted us as free beings even before He created the universe and yet He works to convince us to come back to Him. What does it mean to be 'obedient to God'? It means not only to follow His law but also to go further and to give ourselves, our wills, over to the Lord of Creation."

> (Twist your body so that the ball rises along the cord.)

"Just like this ball, our wills can follow God's will if we allow them to. We must give ourselves over to Him and, in this way, He will guide us and show us His extraordinary love."

ROMANS 6:16
Surely you know that when you surrender yourselves as slaves to obey someone, you are in fact the slaves of the master you obey—either of sin, which results in death, or of obedience, which results in being put right with God.

PHILIPPIANS 2:8
He was humble and walked the path of obedience all the way to death—His death on the cross.

MATTHEW 7:26
But anyone who hears these words of mine and does not obey them is like a foolish man who built his house on sand.

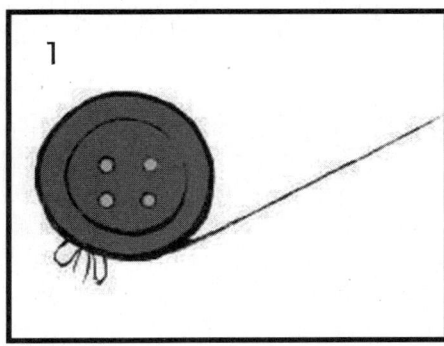

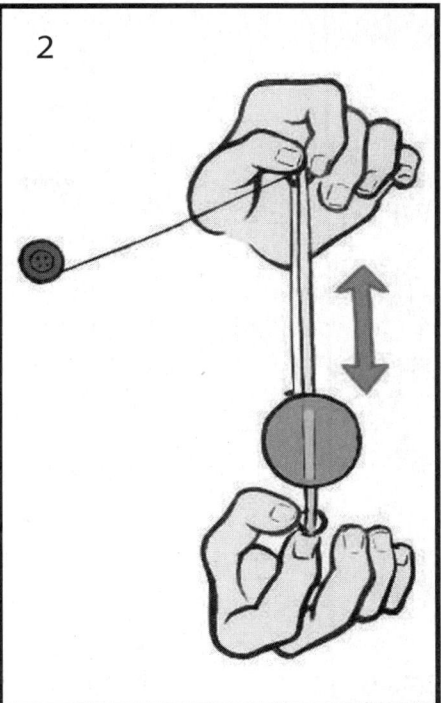

TEACHING TIP
When performing for children, enlist the help of other adults in keeping order.
This is your ministry.

HOW TO MAKE INVISIBLE THREAD

Tape a sheet of white paper to your work table. You will need a brightly lit work area, a pair of tweezers, and a small sharp knife. Cut the hem off an old pair of nylon stockings. This will expose many individual threads. By carefully working these threads, you will be able to loosen several of them to produce a long individual thread. Each thread will be connected by a cross stitch that runs horizontally. Carefully cut the horizontal thread.

Once you've worked out a single thread of approximately 6 inches, use some scotch tape to attach it to the table so you won't lose it.

The individual threads that you isolated are actually made up of many even thinner, barely visible threads. Disassemble these threads, taping each one to the table top or anchoring them around your shirt button as you pull them apart. These individual threads are fragile so you must tease them apart gently.

These threads are hard to see against a white surface but against a dark background they will not be visible at all.

HOW YOU DO IT:

Drill a hole through a large, colorful wooden or solid plastic ball. You will need to experiment with the diameter of the hole, the diameter and smoothness of the cord and the weight and density of the ball you've selected. Start with a small hole; you can always make it bigger. Glue one end of the invisible thread to the ball near the hole at the top. Tie the other end to a shirt or jacket button leaving approximately 2 feet of invisible thread in between. Thread the cord through the hole and hold the cord vertically with one hand on top and one on the bottom. The ball's motion is controlled by the length of invisible thread. The ball is engaged simply by passing the invisible thread lightly over the knuckles of the top hand. The ball can be made to move upwards on the cord by increasing tension on the invisible thread by subtly twisting your body and moving the cord and ball away your body. As you release tension the ball will fall because of gravity. You may need to adjust the length of the invisible thread.

JOHN 4:34
"My food," Jesus said to them, "is to obey the will of the One who sent Me and to finish the work He gave Me to do."

MATTHEW 6:14
If you forgive others the wrongs they have done to you, your Father in heaven will also forgive you.

BORN OF THE VIRGIN MARY (487-507)

In God, the impossible is possible.

WHAT YOU NEED:

prepared rope
ungimmicked rope of the same length
a spool of thread the same color as the rope
a ping-pong ball

WHAT THEY SEE:

The catechist swings a rope over his head and then holds it taut between his hands and rests a ping-pong ball deftly at one end. Slowly, the ball starts to roll from one end of the rope to the other. The ball and the rope can be handed out for examination.

WHAT YOU SAY:

"How can we say that Mary was a virgin and pregnant? That sounds impossible, doesn't it? When one is one, one can't be the other. But, if God can make the universe with all of the beautiful and wonderful things around us, certainly He can ask the Virgin Mary if she would carry His Son and give birth to Him. Since God made the universe, He can change the laws when the need arises. For example how would you describe this piece of rope? It's soft, not rigid. It's flexible. It can't be used to push something heavy, for example. It can't be used to hold something up."

(Attempt at balancing the ball on the rope. Allow it to fall.)

"A ball could never balance on it because it's round. But, let's see if the impossible can be done."

(Pretend to concentrate. Engage the secret thread and balance the ball in this groove.)

"This is just an example of things that might seem impossible to you and me. For God, nothing is impossible."

DOGMATIC CONSTITUTION ON THE CHURCH, 68

In the bodily and spiritual glory which she possesses in heaven, the Mother of Jesus continues in this present world as the image and first flowering of the Church as she is to be perfected in the world to come. Likewise, Mary shines forth on earth, until the day of the Lord shall come (cf. 2 Peter 3:10), as a sign of certain hope and comfort for the pilgrim People of God.

DOGMATIC CONSTITUTION ON THE CHURCH, 69

Let the entire body of the faithful pour forth persevering prayer to the Mother of God and Mother of men. Let them implore that she who aided the beginnings of the Church by her prayers may now, exalted as she is in heaven above all the saints and angels, intercede with her Son in the fellowship of all the saints. May she do so until all the peoples of the human family, whether they are honored with the name of Christian or whether they still do not know their Savior, are happily gathered together in peace and harmony into the one People of God, for the glory of the Most Holy and Undivided Trinity.

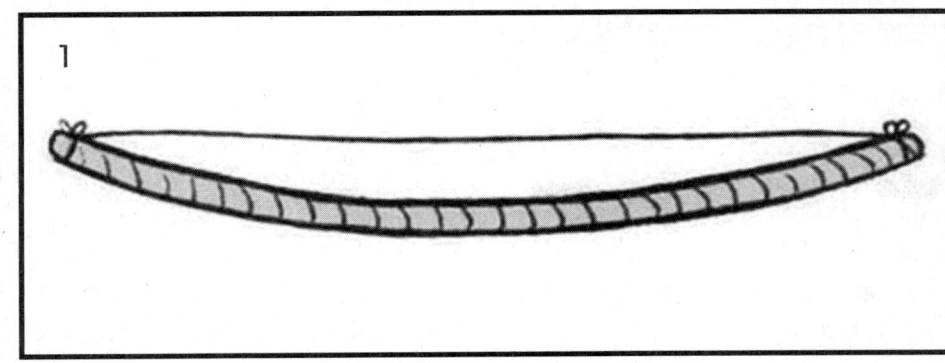

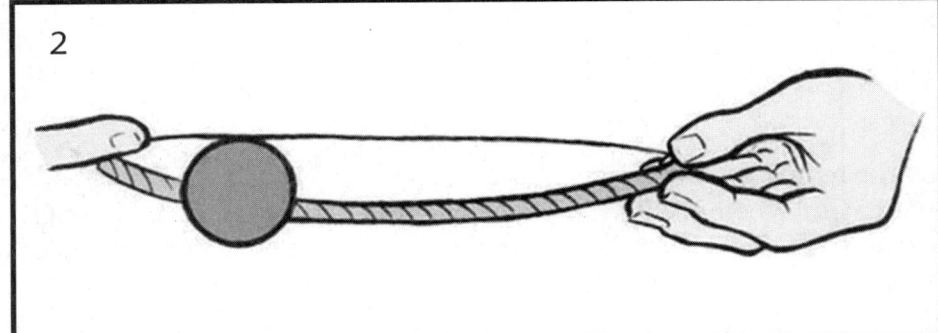

HOW YOU DO IT:

Tie one end of the thread to one end of the rope and the other end of the thread to the other end of the rope. When the rope is held taut, the thread should be taut as well.

Prepare a second rope, identical to the first except without the string. You can use this to hand out for examination. Switch this for the gimmicked one after you perform the trick.

Joke with your audience about balancing the ball on the rope. Clearly it will be impossible. Pull the rope taut and, with your index fingers, simultaneously pull the string tautly so that it rests a half-inch away from the rope. Rest the ball on this groove and allow the ball to roll from one end to the other. Say, "Stop!" and allow the ball to come to rest. Allow it start again and continue on its way. Allow it to roll back in the opposite direction. Place the rope down next to the ungimmicked rope and immediately pick up the ungimmicked one in order to hand it out for inspection. Hand out the ball if you wish.

CATECHETICAL TIP

Catechesis is not merely an intellectual pursuit. It is more appropriately a spiritual development whose end is a greater acceptance of Christ's salvation and submission to His will. Though an academic understanding is essential to this development, the main goal of catechesis is growth in faith.

SALVE REGINA (HAIL, O QUEEN)

Salve Regina, Mater Misericordiae Vita dulcedo et spes nostra salve
Ad te clamamus, exsules filii Hevae
Ad te suspiramus, gementes et flentes in hac lacrimarum valle
Eia, ergo, advocata nostra illos tuos misericordes oculos ad nos converte
Et Iesum, benedictum fructum ventris tui, nobis post hoc exsilium ostende
O clemens, O pia, O dulcis, Virgo Maria

Hail, O Queen, Mother of mercy: our life, our sweetness, and our hope, hail.
To thee do we cry, exiles; sons of Eve.
To thee do we sigh, moaning and weeping in this valley of tears.
Ah then, our Advocate, those merciful eyes of thine turn towards us.
And Jesus, the blessed fruit of thy womb, after this exile show unto us.
O clement: O holy: O sweet Virgin Mary.

JESUS CHRIST SUFFERED UNDER PONTIUS PILATE, WAS CRUCIFIED, DIED AND WAS BURIED (571-630)

Jesus died for our sins.

WHAT YOU NEED:

the cutout on page 229
an envelope
a pair of scissors

WHAT THEY SEE:

The catechist asks a volunteer to examine a cutout figure of Jesus. The catechist slips the figure into a long envelope and cuts it in half. The figure is then shown to be unharmed.

WHAT YOU SAY:

"When Jesus said that He would destroy the temple and, in 3 days, would rebuild it, He wasn't speaking about the actual Temple in Jerusalem dedicated to God where the Jews would make their sacrifices to God. Instead, Jesus was referring to His body, which would be crucified and then resurrected. Let me show you an example of what Jesus meant."

(Slide the cutout figure into the slits of the envelope.)

"When Jesus was killed, His body stayed in the tomb for 3 days."

(Cut the envelope without damaging the cutout.)

"But do you know what happened after those 3 days?"

(Show the cutout hasn't been destroyed.)

"This is what Jesus meant. His body might have been destroyed, but He lives forever with us and the Father."

MALACHI 3:1
The Lord Almighty answers, "I will send My messenger to prepare the way for Me. Then the Lord you are looking for will suddenly come to His temple. The messenger you long to see will come and proclaim My covenant."

HAGGAI 2:9
The new temple will be more splendid than the old one, and there I will give My people prosperity and peace." The Lord Almighty has spoken.

1 KINGS 8:13
Now I have built a majestic temple for you, a place for you to live in forever.

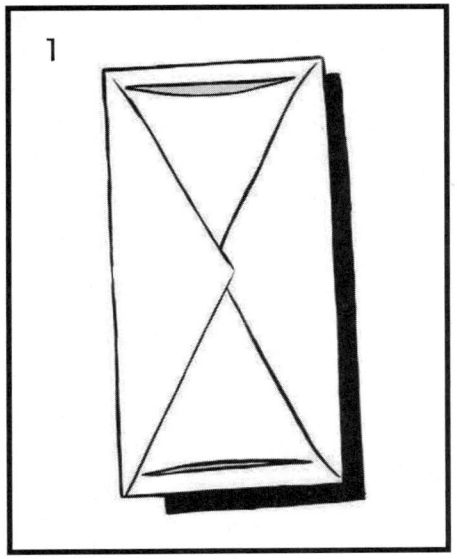

HOW YOU DO IT:

I prefer to have an outline of Jesus cut out and have a child color it before I give my magic presentation. Prepare the envelope by sealing it closed and slicing open its short ends. This will make it easier to maneuver the cut-out Jesus into the envelope's slit.

Prepare 2 slits that penetrate through only the back of an envelope. The slits should each be an inch or 2 from the ends and run perpendicular to the normal opening of the envelope. The slits should be large enough to let the cutout figure pass through unimpeded. As you place the doll in through one end of the envelope, you will actually be passing it out of the first slit and back in again through the second one. Make sure that you don't flash the back of the envelope or the illusion will be destroyed.

Maneuver the scissors so that they cut the envelope but not the Jesus figure. Once you've cut the envelope in half, overlap the 2 pieces slightly and pull out the cutout figure. Hand it out for examination and rip up the envelope so as to destroy any evidence of the trick.

JOHN 2:18-22

The Jewish authorities came back at Him with a question, "What miracle can you perform to show us that You have the right to do this?" Jesus answered, "Tear down this temple, and in 3 days I will build it again." "Are you going to build it again in 3 days?" they asked Him. "It has taken 46 years to build this temple!" But the temple Jesus was speaking about was His body. So when He was raised from death, His disciples remembered that He had said this, and they believed the scripture and what Jesus had said.

JESUS CHRIST WAS BURIED (624-628)

The emptiness of Christ's tomb brings forth great blessings.

WHAT YOU NEED:

a cigar box
a box-cutter
a small cardboard box
handkerchiefs
a small crucifix

WHAT THEY SEE:

A small box is shown to be completely empty. It is closed, and immediately handkerchiefs and a crucifix are produced from within it.

WHAT YOU SAY:

"There are those in the modern world who don't believe in Jesus and in His Resurrection. They see our claims and those of the Apostles of experiencing the Risen Lord as empty ... just like this box. They say, 'Show me proof!' and 'Where is this God of yours?' We, who are Believers, know that God speaks to us in the quiet of our hearts. He guides us and we can feel His love."

"St. Thomas the Apostle couldn't or wouldn't believe his friends when they told him that they had seen Christ resurrected from the dead. Finally he believed. Christ saw his disbelief and offered proof. He said, 'Touch My wounds so that you might believe.' As you see, the Lord greets confusion and doubt with love and compassion."

> (Open both flaps of the box and show it to be empty. The flaps should hang downwards with the empty frame of the cigar box on top like an open window that the audience can look through. The audience should see the inside of the top lid. Keep the side with the small box hidden by opening it first, towards yourself.)

"If you have doubts, ask God and He will give you the answers you need. Touch Him in your mind and heart and you will find many treasures."

> (Close the box, closing the ungimmicked lid first, and then flip it over so that inner box with the handkerchiefs and crucifix is on the bottom. Lay the box on the table.)

"And when you do, you will come to understand the great sacrifice that He made for you and me."

> (Open the box and produce the handkerchiefs and crucifix from the smaller inner box.)

"Christ died for our sins."

> (Point to the crucifix.)

"He loves us so much that He would go through horrible pain and death to redeem us."

MATTHEW 27:26
Then Pilate set Barabbas free for them; and after he had Jesus whipped, he handed Him over to be crucified.

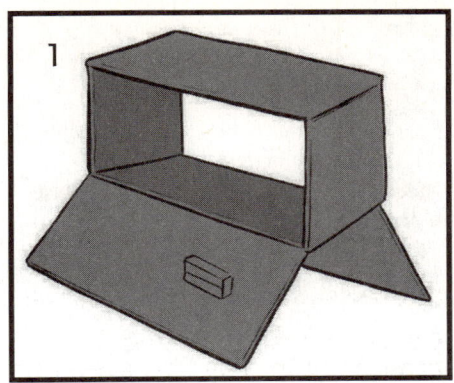

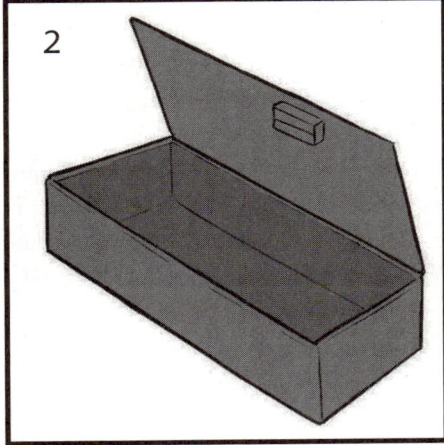

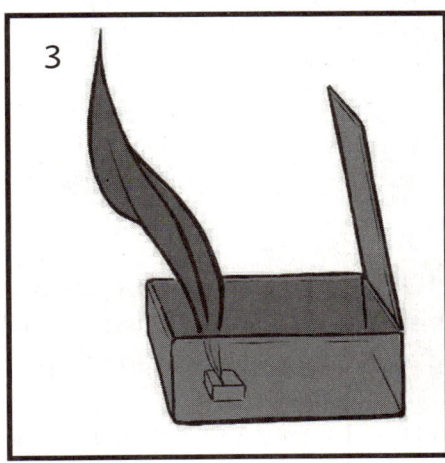

HOW YOU DO IT:

Carefully cut out the bottom of a cigar box. Make a swinging opening that mirrors the top lid by attaching one side of the bottom in place with duct tape. Create this hinge with the duct tape on the side that is directly underneath the top lid's hinge. Decorate the box if you wish. Glue a smaller box to the top lid in the position described in the diagram. The smaller box should be closed on the side that faces the inside of the cigar box, but should have a slit in its lid so that you can stuff in the handkerchiefs and a crucifix.

EXODUS 17:9-13
Moses said to Joshua, "Pick out some men to go and fight the Amalekites tomorrow. I will stand on top of the hill holding the stick that God told me to carry." Joshua did as Moses commanded him and went out to fight the Amalekites, while Moses, Aaron, and Hur went up to the top of the hill. As long as Moses held up his arms, the Israelites won, but when he put his arms down, the Amalekites started winning. When Moses' arms grew tired, Aaron and Hur brought a stone for him to sit on, while they stood beside him and held up his arms, holding them steady until the sun went down. In this way Joshua totally defeated the Amalekites.

LUKE 23:33
When they came to the place called "The Skull," they crucified Jesus there, and the 2 criminals, one on His right and the other on His left.

JOHN 19:38-42
After this, Joseph, who was from the town of Arimathea, asked Pilate if he could take Jesus' body. (Joseph was a follower of Jesus, but in secret, because he was afraid of the Jewish authorities.) Pilate told him he could have the body, so Joseph went and took it away. Nicodemus, who at first had gone to see Jesus at night, went with Joseph, taking with him about 100 pounds of spices, a mixture of myrrh and aloes. The 2 men took Jesus' body and wrapped it in linen cloths with the spices according to the Jewish custom of preparing a body for burial. There was a garden in the place where Jesus had been put to death, and in it there was a new tomb where no one had ever been buried. Since it was the day before the Sabbath and because the tomb was close by, they placed Jesus' body there.

HE DESCENDED INTO HELL. ON THE THIRD DAY HE ROSE AGAIN (631-658)

Do not look here, He has risen.

WHAT YOU NEED:

2 white plastic disks approximately the size of a US half-dollar
a grease pencil that will mark the plastic disks
a small handkerchief.

WHAT THEY SEE:

The catechist shows both sides of a small, white plastic disk. Suddenly, on a previously blank side are the words, "Do Not Look Here!" The coin is handed out for examination. The catechist retrieves the coin and shows that it has become blank on both sides once again. Then, the words "He Has Risen!" appear on a previously blank side. The coin can be handed out for examination.

WHAT YOU SAY:

"I think you can imagine the sadness of Jesus's disciples when they saw their Friend and Savior die. Many of them weren't strong enough even to visit Jesus's tomb. When Mary Magdalene visited His tomb she was shocked to find the stone door pushed aside and an angel standing in front of it."

>   (Flip the disk in your hand using the Turn/No-Turn maneuver.)

"Do you remember what the angels told her? That's right! They told her not to bother looking here."

>   (Expose the "Do Not Look Here" side of the disk and hand it out for inspection. Remove the handkerchief and other disk from your pocket and lay them on your hand making sure no one can see the newly introduced coin.)

"The angels told her this because they knew Jesus had risen."

>   (Remove the handkerchief and take away the first disk—the one that reads "Do Not Look Here"—and return both of them to your pocket.)

>   (Flip the disk in your hand using the Turn/No-Turn maneuver.)

"As Mary Magdalene listened to the angels, she realized what they were talking about."

>   (Expose the "He Has Risen" side of the disk and hand it out for inspection.)

"Jesus rose from the dead because His love for us and His Father was so great. He wanted to share eternal life with us all. Through His death, we have eternal life."

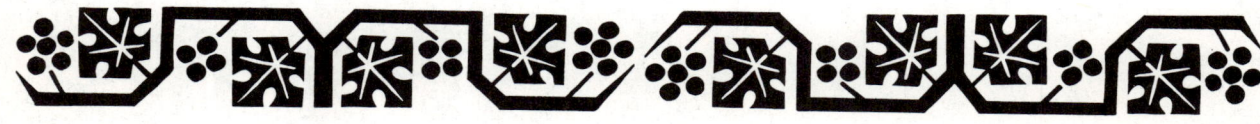

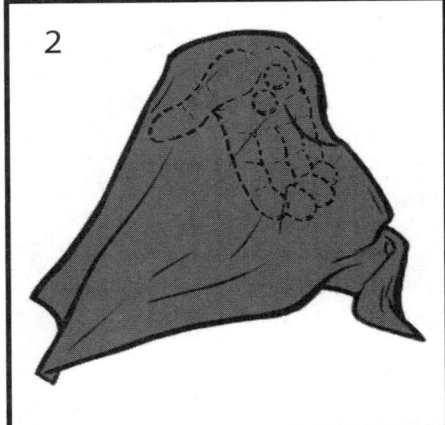

HOW YOU DO IT:

This magic trick is accomplished with a sleight-of-hand maneuver called "Turn/No-Turn." On one of the white disks that you've procured from a plastic supply store, write the words, "Do Not Look Here!" On the other white disk, write the words, "He Has Risen!"

Place the "Do Not Look Here!" disk in your left hand and perform the Turn/No-Turn move showing only the blank side. Tell the story of Mary Magdalene's encounter with the 2 angels outside of Christ's tomb. Reveal the "Do Not Look Here!" side of the disk and hand it out for inspection.

Retrieve the handkerchief and remaining disk from your pocket and lay them both on your hand making sure you don't expose the second disk. Next, take away the handkerchief and remove the first disk (the one that reads "Do Not Look Here!") and place it and the handkerchief in your pocket.

Repeat the trick with the remaining disk. Finally reveal the words "He Has Risen!"

TURN/NO-TURN

This maneuver is designed to show only one side of a coin twice so as to give the impression both sides have been shown.

Lay the disk/coin on the palm of your left hand. With the very tips of your thumb and forefinger touching the end furthest away from you, lift the coin and rest it on the extended fingertips of your right hand. In one smooth movement, allow the coin to fall back into your left palm but, before allowing it to rest there, flip over the coin with the tips of your fingers. Practice masking the second flip so that only a single face of the coin shows.

JOHN 20:10-16

Then the disciples went back home. Mary stood crying outside the tomb. While she was still crying, she bent over and looked in the tomb and saw 2 angels there dressed in white, sitting where the body of Jesus had been, one at the head and the other at the feet. "Woman, why are you crying?" they asked her. She answered, "They have taken my Lord away, and I do not know where they have put Him!" Then she turned around and saw Jesus standing there, but she did not know that it was Jesus. "Woman, why are you crying?" Jesus asked her. "Who is it that you are looking for?" She thought He was the gardener, so she said to Him, "If you took Him away, sir, tell me where you have put Him, and I will go and get Him." Jesus said to her, "Mary!" She turned toward Him and said in Hebrew, "Rabboni!" (This means "Teacher.")

ON THE THIRD DAY HE ROSE FROM THE DEAD
(638-658)

We share in Christ's resurrection.

WHAT YOU NEED:

a drinking glass full of water
a handkerchief
2 Kennedy half-dollars
model glue
invisible thread (see page 73)

WHAT THEY SEE:

The catechist drops a coin into a glass of water and then covers it with a handkerchief. He immediately removes the handkerchief to reveal the coin has disappeared.

WHAT YOU SAY:

"Every time we say the Creed, we always say, 'Christ descended into hell and on the third day He rose again.' What do you think we mean when we say this?"

(Drop the coin attached to the handkerchief into the drinking glass.)

"It means that He died for the sins of everyone who has ever lived, anytime, anyplace, everywhere. Even for those people who died before Jesus was born. He had to save them also because He loves all of us and He doesn't want to lose even one of us."

(Cover the drinking glass with the handkerchief.)

"You might ask yourself how Christ could enter Hell and then be resurrected and come back to visit His friends, the Apostles. For God, all things are possible."

"Just like this coin stuck here at the bottom of this glass of water. You can't retrieve the coin without getting wet. But let's see. Let's place this handkerchief over the glass and at the count of 3 ... as you see, the coin has disappeared ... and has reappeared here in my hand."

(Remove the handkerchief and place it and the attached coin aside. Open your hand and show that the coin has somehow appeared in your hand completely dry.)

"Nothing is impossible for God."

MATTHEW 18:12-14
What do you think a man does who has 100 sheep and one of them gets lost? He will leave the other 99 grazing on the hillside and go and look for the lost sheep. When he finds it, I tell you, he feels far happier over this one sheep than over the 99 that did not get lost. In just the same way your Father in heaven does not want any of these little ones to be lost.

MARK 16:6
"Don't be alarmed," he said. "I know you are looking for Jesus of Nazareth, Who was crucified. He is not here—He has been raised! Look, here is the place where He was placed."

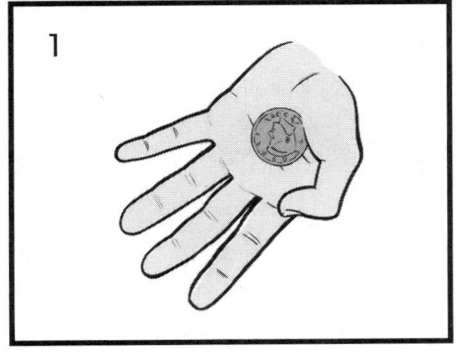
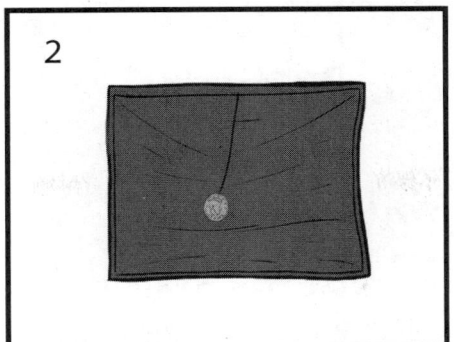
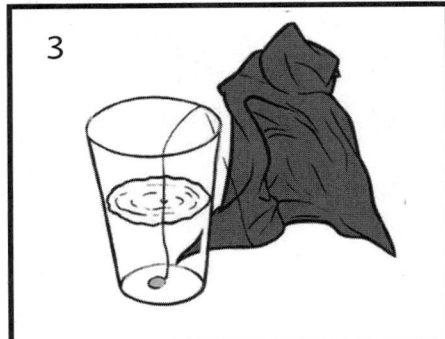
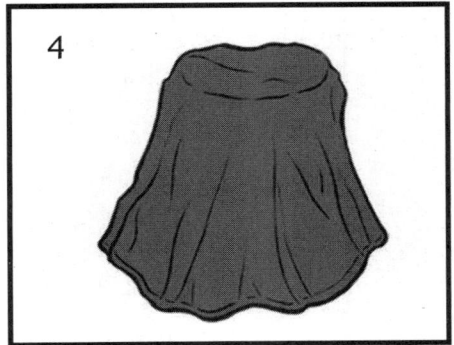
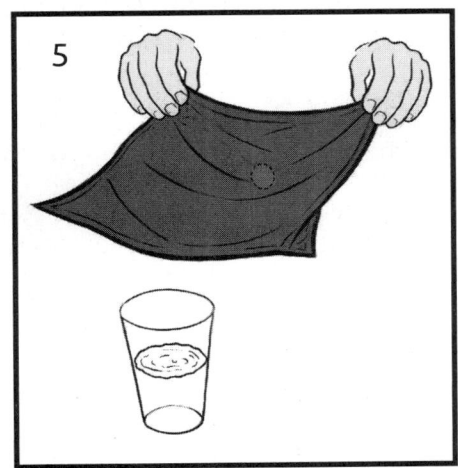
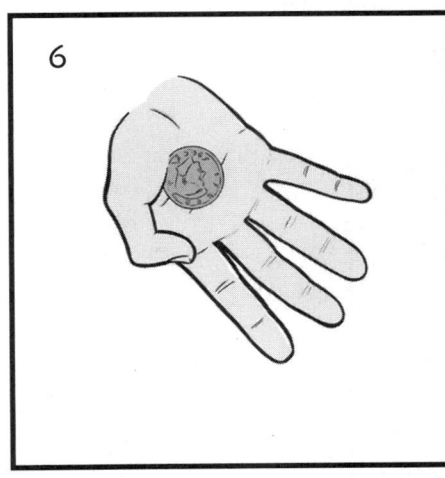

HOW YOU DO IT:

You will need a length of Invisible Thread. You can either buy a spool of wooly nylon at a crafts or fabric store or disassemble a pair of nylon stockings. You will need approximately 1 foot of thread.

Glue one end of the thread to one of the coins and the other end to the handkerchief's hem. Make sure that the length of the thread allows the coin to be hidden when the handkerchief is lifted by the top 2 corners.

Hide the other coin in your right hand. Magicians refer to this as "palming." To perform, drop the prepared coin into the glass. Drape the handkerchief across the glass and after some byplay (distracting conversation), pick up the 2 corners nearest you and lift the handkerchief off the glass. The coin will be lifted out since it is attached to the handkerchief. Dispose of the prepared coin by simply placing it in the handkerchief and putting the handkerchief in your pocket.

MAGIC TIP
Be entertaining! After all ... it's a magic show!

LUKE 15:25-32

"In the meantime the older son was out in the field. On his way back, when he came close to the house, he heard the music and dancing. So he called one of the servants and asked him, 'What's going on?' 'Your brother has come back home,' the servant answered, 'and your father has killed the prize calf, because he got him back safe and sound.' The older brother was so angry that he would not go into the house; so his father came out and begged him to come in. But he spoke back to his father, 'Look, all these years I have worked for you like a slave, and I have never disobeyed your orders. What have you given me? Not even a goat for me to have a feast with my friends! But this son of yours wasted all your property on prostitutes, and when he comes back home, you kill the prize calf for him!' 'My son,' the father answered, 'you are always here with me, and everything I have is yours. But we had to celebrate and be happy, because your brother was dead, but now he is alive; he was lost, but now he has been found.'"

HE ASCENDED INTO HEAVEN AND IS SEATED AT THE RIGHT HAND OF THE FATHER (659-667)

New life in Christ is our sure hope.

WHAT YOU NEED:

- a mylar or other non-transparent balloon
- 2 identical decks of cards
- a lighter
- an ashtray
- an envelope
- a hat pin or sharpened knitting needle

WHAT THEY SEE:

A deck of cards is shuffled. A volunteer takes the card on the top of the deck. The card is ripped up and a single corner is placed in a small pay envelope which is handed to the volunteer for safe keeping. The remainder of the card is burned in an ashtray. A blown-up balloon is introduced along with a pin. A volunteer is asked to pop the balloon. The restored selected card falls out of the popped balloon. It is missing a single corner. The volunteer checks to see if the corner she retained is a match and it is found to be so.

WHAT YOU SAY:

"What happened after Jesus died for our sins? That's right, He went into heaven and is now with His Father. What do you think it means to die and to resurrect and then to enter the Kingdom of Heaven? Let's see if we can have a demonstration."

(Force a card on your spectator using false shuffle 3 on page 109. Rip up the card.)

"If I rip up this card and burn it, it's as if it died."

(Retrieve the balloon and ask a spectator to pop it. Have the spectator check to see if the cards match.)

"Just as when the card was destroyed and then restored, we also will be restored to life after we die."

GENESIS 40:13
In 3 days the king will release you, pardon you, and restore you to your position. You will give him his cup as you did before when you were his wine steward.

2 KINGS 20:5
Go back to Hezekiah, ruler of the Lord's people, and say to him, "I, the Lord, the God of your ancestor David, have heard your prayer and seen your tears. I will heal you, and in 3 days you will go to the Temple."

ESTHER 4:16
Go and get all the Jews in Susa together; hold a fast and pray for me. Don't eat or drink anything for 3 days and nights. My servant women and I will be doing the same. After that, I will go to the king, even though it is against the law. If I must die for doing it, I will die.

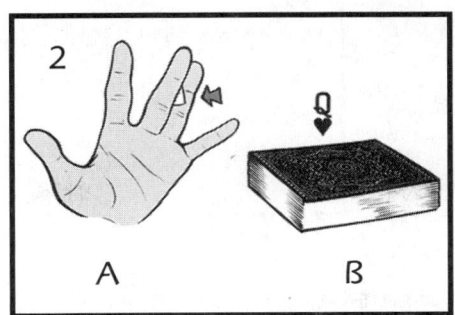
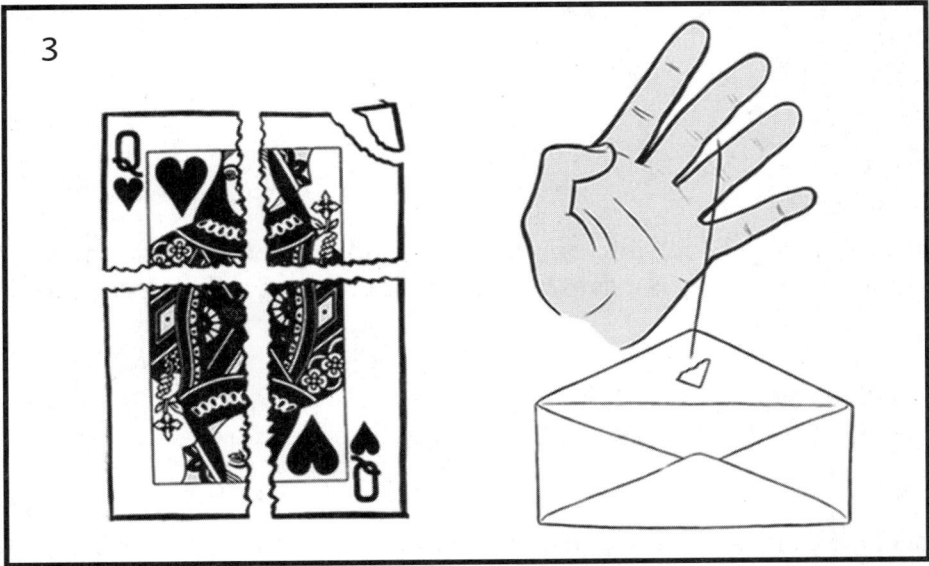
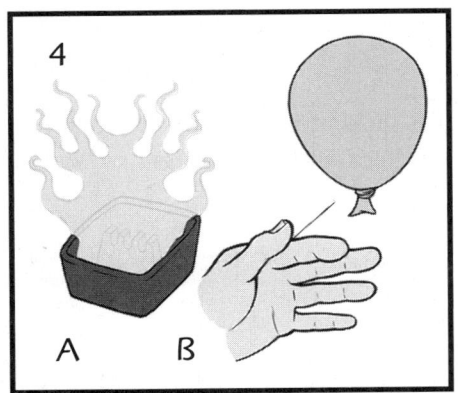
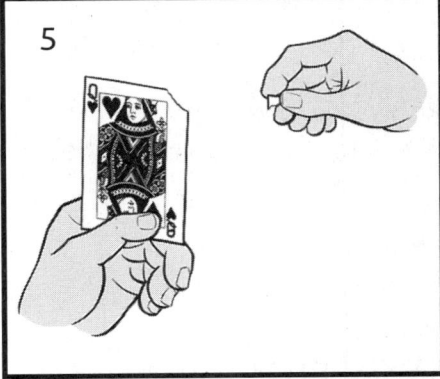

HOW YOU DO IT:

This trick requires a sleight-of-hand maneuver, a false shuffle, a force, and a bit of misdirection. A "force" is a means by which you can manipulate a volunteer to take a certain card without her knowing it.

Before your performance, rip off the upper right-hand corner of one of 2 duplicate Queen of Hearts cards and lay the torn corner aside. Roll up the card with the missing corner, insert it into a latex balloon and then inflate the balloon. I prefer to use Mylar balloons as they are opaque and can be bought at most party shops. You can also inflate balloons with helium; just remember to insert the card into the balloon before filling it.

Hide the torn corner piece between your fingers or under your watchband. Place the intact Queen of Hearts on the top of the deck. False shuffle the deck using method 3 described on page 109. Direct the volunteer to card that you planted.

Once the card is "selected" have everyone remember the card and rip it up, carefully saving a single corner. Take this corner and covertly switch it for the torn corner you have hidden between your fingers. Place this new corner in a pay envelope and hand it to the volunteer for safe keeping.

Next, burn the remainder of the pieces of the torn-up card in an ashtray. Once they've been completely destroyed, introduce your prepared balloon and a pin. I prefer to use an ornate hat pin for theatrical effect.

Once the balloon is popped, have your volunteer retrieve the card and compare it to the torn corner in the pay envelope which has been in her possession since the beginning of the trick. It will match exactly.

MATTHEW 12:40
In the same way that Jonah spent 3 days and nights in the big fish, so will the Son of Man spend 3 days and nights in the depths of the earth.

JOSHUA 1:11
Go through the camp and say to the people, "Get some food ready, because in 3 days you are going to cross the Jordan River to occupy the land that the Lord your God is giving you."

FROM THENCE WILL HE COME AGAIN TO JUDGE THE LIVING AND THE DEAD (668-686)

God is our loving Judge.

WHAT YOU NEED:

a deck of cards
5 opaque envelopes

WHAT THEY SEE:

The magician places 4 number cards and a single court card (king, queen, or jack) into separate envelopes and seals them. The envelopes are mixed and, after examining each envelope, the magician is able to locate the single court card.

WHAT YOU SAY:

"At the end of time, when we all are with God, He will look into our hearts and judge all of the good and bad that we've done. How can God see all that we've done in our lives? How can he look into us? Let's have a demonstration."

(Ask a spectator to examine 5 cards, one court card and 4 number cards. Make sure she understands the difference. Place each card into an envelope making sure the court card is placed vertically and hand them to the spectator to be sealed.)

"As you see, no one can see into the envelopes. No one knows which card is which. No on can tell which card is a court card and which one is a number card. But this is not a problem for God."

(Pretend to deliberate over each envelope and finally hand the correct one to your spectator.)

"God knows what's in our hearts and knows we love Him. God can see what is hidden to us. God looks lovingly into our souls. He is there now if we are quiet and listen. The Holy Spirit is eager to teach us how we are to live."

GOSPEL MAGIC HISTORY

St. Nicholas Owen was a congenital dwarf who had many other disabling, medical problems. He suffered perpetually from a hernia and his stomach had to be held together by a metal plate. In 1599, after a horse fell on him, his body was crushed. He had to walk with a limp for the rest of his life. It was a common idea at the time that a twisted body was a symbol of a twisted soul and therefore he was subjected to a great deal of prejudice.

Antonia Fraser, St. Nicholas Owen's hagiographer, describes him in her book **Faith and Treason: The Story of the Gunpowder Plot,** as having a "great soul and measureless courage" and as offering "the strongest possible refutation of the contemporary prejudice."

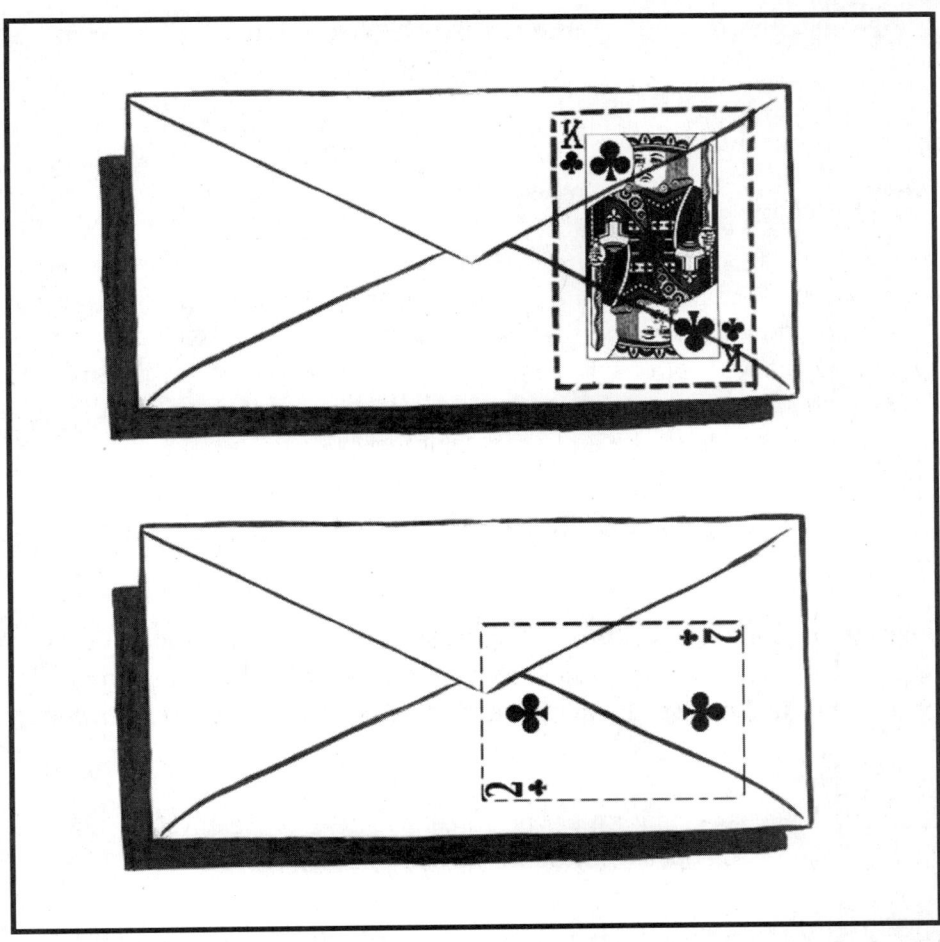

MAGIC TIPS

Be humorous as you perform. Laughter goes a long way to make sure your audience is having an enjoyable time. Furthermore, by not acting serious, your audience, especially the children, will understand that magic performances are for entertainment and education purposes only.

Decorate your props in an appropriate and interesting manner.

Don't tell secrets no matter how much they beg!

Even though everyone says they want to know how you did a trick, it's best to keep professional secrets to ourselves.

If children insist on being told how a particular trick works, recommend they go to the public library to pick up a book on stage magic.

Practice! Practice again! Practice your tricks until you are perfect! And then, practice again!

HOW YOU DO IT:

The secret to knowing which envelope contains the court card is to position the card so that it is lying vertically in the envelope. The 4 number cards should be placed in their respective envelopes horizontally. By feeling for the single upright card, you'll be able to identify the court card.

MATTHEW 7:1-2
Do not judge others, so that God will not judge you, for God will judge you in the same way you judge others, and He will apply to you the same rules you apply to others.

MATTHEW 12:37
Your words will be used to judge you—to declare you either innocent or guilty.

MARK 4:24
He also said to them, "Pay attention to what you hear! The same rules you use to judge others will be used by God to judge you—but with even greater severity.

LUKE 6:37
Do not judge others, and God will not judge you; do not condemn others, and God will not condemn you; forgive others, and God will forgive you.

LUKE 18:8
I tell you, He will judge in their favor and do it quickly. But will the Son of Man find faith on earth when He comes?

THE JOINT MISSION OF THE SON AND THE HOLY SPIRIT
(689-690)

The actions of the Holy Spirit are apparent in our lives.

WHAT YOU NEED:

the cutout on page 231
an envelope
a pair of scissors
a soft lead pencil
a ruler

WHAT THEY SEE:

A folded piece of paper with a prediction from the magician is given to a volunteer to hide on her person. Next, an envelope is displayed and the volunteer is asked to consider where she would want the catechist to cut it. After the envelope is cut, the cleaved image is examined to find that it matches the prediction given to the volunteer prior to the trick.

WHAT YOU SAY:

"In prayer, we hope to enter spiritual union with God. Imagine what that must mean. Do you have a friend who is very close to you? Have you ever said the same thing at the very same time? When you are thinking about him or her, he or she calls you on the phone. Let's see if we can recreate that situation now between 2 people with a magic trick.

(Hand a volunteer your prediction and have her hide it on her person. Have her cut the envelope any place she wishes. Maneuver the 2 cut pieces to appear as though the circle has been cut.)

"This is just an example of 2 people concentrating on the same job. Sometimes we can think and plan alike. With God, it's more powerful. When we sit in prayer with Him, He can teach us and we can love Him back."

PSALMS 51:11
Do not banish me from your presence; do not take your Holy Spirit away from me.

MATTHEW 1:18
This was how the birth of Jesus Christ took place. His mother Mary was engaged to Joseph, but before they were married, she found out that she was going to have a baby by the Holy Spirit.

MATTHEW 1:20
While he was thinking about this, an angel of the Lord appeared to him in a dream and said, "Joseph, descendant of David, do not be afraid to take Mary to be your wife. For it is by the Holy Spirit that she has conceived."

MATTHEW 3:11
I baptize you with water to show that you have repented, but the One who will come after me will baptize you with the Holy Spirit and fire. He is much greater than I am; and I am not good enough even to carry His sandals.

MARK 13:11
And when you are arrested and taken to court, do not worry ahead of time about what you are going to say; when the time comes, say whatever is then given to you. For the words you speak will not be yours; they will come from the Holy Spirit.

HOW YOU DO IT:

There is no skullduggery involved in where you cut the envelope. Cut it exactly where the volunteer asks. The secret is how you handle the envelope after its cut. You will need to use a bit of time misdirection to perform this trick successfully.

Photocopy page 231 and cut out the circle image. You will need it to hand to your volunteer before starting the trick to serve as a prediction. Next, cut out the strip of Rhine symbols so that it fits into a standard A4 envelope as described in the accompanying diagram. Mark the envelope with light pencil marks so as to separate the symbols. You'll note that the circle image is split into 2 halves. When you cut the envelope where the volunteer wishes, the only symbol that will seemingly be cut in half will be the circle, leaving the others completely intact. The prediction will always match.

Before sealing the envelope, wrap a plain sheet of opaque paper around the printed strip so that the images can't be seen through the envelope. During your performance, once the envelope is cut, absentmindedly orient the 2 halves so that the cut ends both face the same way. When you pull out both halves of the symbol strip, the circle will seem as if it was cut straight through. Ask your volunteer to check the prediction you gave her before the trick began.

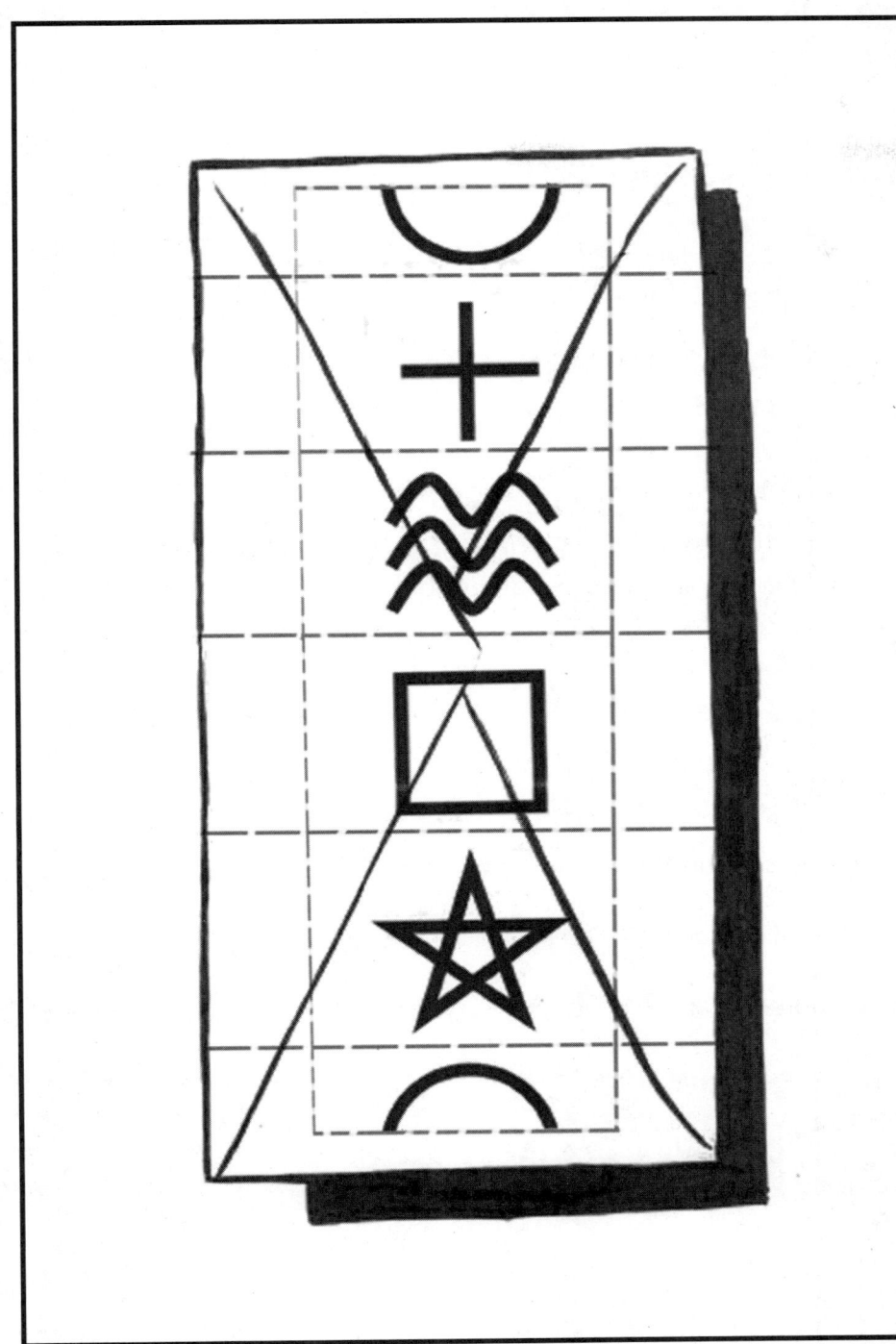

MATTHEW 28:19
Go, then, to all peoples everywhere and make them My disciples: baptize them in the name of the Father, the Son, and the Holy Spirit.

LUKE 3:22
And the Holy Spirit came down upon Him in bodily form like a dove. And a voice came from heaven, "You are My own dear Son. I am pleased with You."

THE MYSTERY OF THE CHURCH (770-690)

The Word was made flesh and dwelt among us.

WHAT YOU NEED:

2 sheets of heavy paper
a pair of scissors
a picture of Jesus

WHAT THEY SEE:

A small piece of paper is shown to be completely blank. It is folded and then immediately unfolded to find a picture of Jesus has appeared.

WHAT YOU SAY:

"In Paul's letter to the Colossians, he teaches that Christ is the visible likeness of the invisible God. He is the first-born Son, superior to all created things. That sounds complex but it's not really hard to understand."

(Show the square piece of paper.)

"As you see, we can't see anything in this paper.

(Fold the paper into a small packet.)

"We can't see God the Father but we can come to an understanding of Who the Father is by loving the Son."

(Nonchalantly, flip the packet over and open it again to reveal Christ's image.)

"When we look at Jesus and come to accept His love and sacrifice for us, we can see what God must be like."

ROMANS 1:20
Ever since God created the world, His invisible qualities, both His eternal power and His divine nature, have been clearly seen; they are perceived in the things that God has made. So those people have no excuse at all!

COLOSSIANS 1:15
Christ is the visible likeness of the invisible God. He is the first-born Son, superior to all created things.

1 TIMOTHY 1:17
To the eternal King, immortal and invisible, the only God—
to Him be honor and glory forever and ever! Amen.

HEBREWS 11:27
It was faith that made Moses leave Egypt without being afraid of the king's anger. As though he saw the invisible God, he refused to turn back.

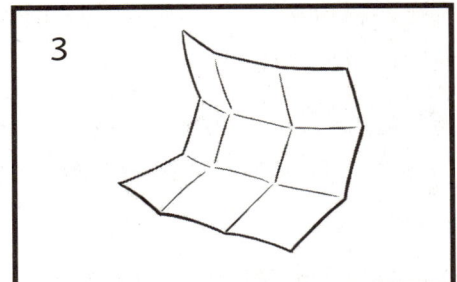
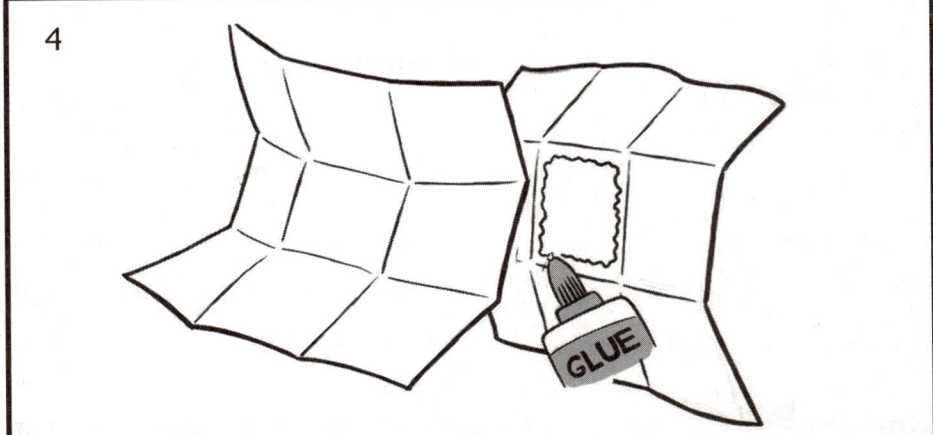

HOW YOU DO IT:

Procure 2 thick, 1-foot square sheets of paper (I prefer to use thick drawing or watercolor paper). Fold them like in the diagram so as to create 9 squares. Glue the 2 sheets back-to-back along the edges of the center square. Once dried, lay the paper flat and place a small saint card or printed icon of Jesus on the center square. Refold both sides to form a compact packet.

Unfold the empty side of the double packet and show it to be empty but keep the attached package hidden from view. Refold it and, while using the patter described opposite, flip the entire package over in your hand without bringing undue attention to what you are doing. Open the packet once again to reveal Christ's image.

MAGIC TIP
Read other magic books in addition to this one as you prepare for your performance.

MAGIC TIP
The expression hocus-pocus is a corruption of the Latin prayer "Hoc ist corpus," (lit. this is my body); the words used at the consecration during the Roman Catholic Mass. "Hocus-Pocus" originated as a derogatory term, poking fun at this transformation. Many Catholic magicians avoid the use of the word because of its original meaning.

GOSPEL MAGIC HISTORY
Fr. Henry Garnet, Superior of the English Jesuits, employed St. Nicholas Owen to construct hiding places and escape routes in the homes of Catholics throughout England. Some of these spaces were large enough to hold clandestine services.

THE CHURCH IS THE TEMPLE OF THE HOLY SPIRIT
(797-801)

The Church is directed by the Holy Spirit.

WHAT YOU NEED:

the cutout on page 233
an envelope
a photocopier
a laminator

WHAT THEY SEE:

A piece of paper (the magician's prediction) is placed on the table in plain view. 4 volunteers are asked to silently select any graphic image in a series of 16 images and then freely choose to move in different directions on the chart according to the magicians directions. The volunteers all end up on the same symbol. Volunteers are asked to concentrate on the symbol they have landed upon. The catechist then directs everyone's attention to a prediction on the table. It matches the volunteers' selection exactly.

WHAT YOU SAY:

"What does it mean when we talk about the mystery of the Church? I think it means that the Church, us ... the Children of God, are being directed, molded, and guided by the Holy Spirit. What is it like to be directed as a community to the same goal? Let's try this experiment.

1. Choose any of the 4-sided images.
2. Now move left or right to the nearest round image.
3. Now move up or down to the nearest 4-sided image.
4. Now move diagonally to the nearest round image.
5. Now move right or down to the nearest square image.

"Now ... everyone concentrate on the symbol you landed upon. Think about the shape. Think about how you were guided to it. You are all thinking about the cross. That's the symbol you landed upon. All of us were directed to the same cross. In this same way, the Holy Spirit directs us to Christ's cross. The Holy Spirit is always active in our lives. By praying, we come to a better understanding of how the Spirit moves in our lives."

MATTHEW 26:26; MARK 14:22; LUKE 22:19
While they were eating, Jesus took a piece of bread, gave a prayer of thanks, broke it, and gave it to His disciples. "Take and eat it," He said; "This is My body."

JOHN 15:1-5
I am the real vine, and My Father is the gardener. He breaks off every branch in Me that does not bear fruit, and He prunes every branch that does bear fruit, so that it will be clean and bear more fruit. You have been made clean already by the teaching I have given you. Remain united to Me, and I will remain united to you. A branch cannot bear fruit by itself; it can do so only if it remains in the vine. In the same way you cannot bear fruit unless you remain in Me. "I am the vine, and you are the branches. Those who remain in Me, and I in them, will bear much fruit; for you can do nothing without Me."

EPHESIANS 1:23
The Church is Christ's body, the completion of Him Who Himself completes all things everywhere.

ROMANS 7:4
That is how it is with you, my friends. As far as the Law is concerned, you also have died because you are part of the body of Christ; and now you belong to Him Who was raised from death in order that we might be useful in the service of God.

ROMANS 12:5
In the same way, though we are many, we are one body in union with Christ, and we are all joined to each other as different parts of one body.

1 CORINTHIANS 1:10
By the authority of our Lord Jesus Christ I appeal to all of you, my friends, to agree in what you say, so that there will be no divisions among you. Be completely united, with only one thought and one purpose.

1 CORINTHIANS 6:15
You know that your bodies are parts of the body of Christ. Shall I take a part of Christ's body and make it part of the body of a prostitute? Impossible!

1 CORINTHIANS 10:16
The cup we use in the Lord's Supper and for which we give thanks to God: when we drink from it, we are sharing in the blood of Christ. And the bread we break: when we eat it, we are sharing in the body of Christ.

1 CORINTHIANS 12:12
Christ is like a single body, which has many parts; it is still one body, even though it is made up of different parts.

COLOSSIANS 1:24
And now I am happy about my sufferings for you, for by means of my physical sufferings I am helping to complete what still remains of Christ's sufferings on behalf of His body, the Church.

COLOSSIANS 2:19
Under Christ's control the whole body is nourished and held together by its joints and ligaments, and it grows as God wants it to grow.

HOW YOU DO IT:

Place a photocopy of the cross icon in a sealed envelope and place it on the table on which you're performing. Photocopy the entire chart of icons onto an 8 1/2 by 11-inch sheet of paper and laminate it. No matter where the volunteer begins his journey around the board, he will always land on the cross symbol. Simply follow the directions on the opposite page.

MAGIC TIP

Watch your angles. Magicians should always be aware of the placement of their audiences and volunteers. If necessary, don't be shy about asking your spectators to reposition themselves to your advantage. If they won't or can't move, go on to the next trick.

THE CHURCH IS ONE (813-822)

We are all part of God's plan.

WHAT YOU NEED:

paper and pens for all participants
a calculator (if necessary)

WHAT THEY SEE:

A volunteer is led through several mathematical calculations and is asked to concentrate on his final result. The catechist then reveals the volunteer's thoughts.

WHAT YOU SAY:

"There is only one Church created and instituted by Christ. All Christians are united in Christ. Our unity comes from our common baptism with water and in the name of the Father, the Son and the Holy Spirit. At root, all Christians desire the unity that comes from membership in Christ's Mystical Body.

"Let's have an experiment. Let's see what it would be like if we all could have the same idea in mind. Let's see what it would be like if we were really united.

1. Think of a number
2. Double it
3. Add 10
4. Divide by 2
5. Add 5
6. Subtract original number
7. Subtract 6

"Now ... on the count of 3, I want you to tell me the number you came up with."

   (Say the number 4 at the same time as the volunteer.)

"As you see, even though you chose any number you wanted in the beginning of the trick, I still figured out what number you came up with. For this one moment, we are united. We can say we were of one mind. Just like the Church, we are united by our love for Christ and by His love for us.

MATTHEW 26:26-29

While they were eating, Jesus took a piece of bread, gave a prayer of thanks, broke it, and gave it to his disciples. 'Take and eat it,' He said; 'this is My body.' Then He took a cup, gave thanks to God, and gave it to them. 'Drink it, all of you,' He said; "this is My blood, which seals God's covenant, My blood poured out for many for the forgiveness of sins. I tell you, I will never again drink this wine until the day I drink the new wine with you in My Father's Kingdom.

JOHN 15:1
I am the real vine, and My Father is the gardener.

JOHN 15:5
I am the vine, and you are the branches. Those who remain in Me, and I in them, will bear much fruit; for you can do nothing without Me.

1 CORINTHIANS 12:12-31
Christ is like a single body, which has many parts; it is still one body, even though it is made up of different parts. In the same way, all of us, whether Jews or Gentiles, whether slaves or free, have been baptized into the one body by the same Spirit, and we have all been given the one Spirit to drink. For the body itself is not made up of only one part, but of many parts. If the foot were to say, "Because I am not a hand, I don't belong to the body," that would not keep it from being a part of the body. And if the ear were to say, "Because I am not an eye, I don't belong to the body," that would not keep it from being a part of the body. If the whole body were just an eye, how could it hear? And if it were only an ear, how could it smell? As it is, however, God put every different part in the body just as He wanted it to be. There would not be a body if it were all only one part! As it is, there are many parts but one body. So then, the eye cannot say to the hand, "I don't need you!" Nor can the head say to the feet, "Well, I don't need you!" On the contrary, we cannot do without the parts of the body that seem to be weaker; and those parts that we think aren't worth very much are the ones which we treat with greater care; while the parts of the body which don't look very nice are treated with special modesty, which the more beautiful parts do not need. God Himself has put the body together in such a way as to give greater honor to those parts that need it. And so there is no division in the body, but all its different parts have the same concern for one another. If one part of the body suffers, all the other parts suffer with it; if one part is praised, all the other parts share its happiness. All of you are Christ's body, and each one is a part of it. In the Church God has put all in place: in the first place apostles, in the second place prophets, and in the third place teachers; then those who perform miracles, followed by those who are given the power to heal or to help others or to direct them or to speak in strange tongues. They are not all apostles or prophets or teachers. Not everyone has the power to work miracles or to heal diseases or to speak in strange tongues or to explain what is said. Set your hearts, then, on the more important gifts. Best of all, however, is the following way.

HOW YOU DO IT:

This is a fun idea that conveys the idea that we are all the Church. Simply follow the instructions listed on the opposite page and everyone will naturally wind up at the same number: 4.

TEACHING TIPS

The best tool in a teacher's bag of tricks is empathy. Remember what it was like when you were a child and proceed accordingly.

Treat your catechism class as if they are intelligent and they will not disappoint you.

Remember: as a Gospel Magician, you are a catechist. As a catechist, you are a teacher. This is your ministry.

Give yourself plenty of time to set up for your performance. It can take as much time to prepare for your performance in situ as the actual performance.

THE HIERARCHICAL CONSTITUTION OF THE CHURCH
(874-896)

The Church guides and teaches.

WHAT YOU NEED:

a deck of cards
transparent tape
20 pennies
2 large handkerchiefs of the same color
confetti
a small desk cross

WHAT THEY SEE:

Cards are randomly tossed onto a tabletop and a handkerchief is laid over the pile. Suddenly, the magician grabs the center of the handkerchief and whisks it away. Inexplicably, a house of cards is immediately constructed exactly where the cards were piled haphazardly. Atop the house of cards is a cross.

WHAT YOU SAY:

"The Faithful are the Church. We are the Body of Christ, Like every group, we need leaders. Does anyone know who is the Church's hierarchy? Our immediate spiritual leaders are deacons and priests. But they have leaders also. They are bishops. There is one bishop in charge of every community of believers. And the Pope is the leader of all the Bishops and all Christians."

(Whisk away the handkerchiefs and produce the card tower.)

"But all of us, including the Pope has only One Leader: Christ."

(Remove the desk cross from your pocket and place it on top of the card tower. Point to the bottom of the pyramid.)

"Here we have deacons."

(Point to the second level of the pyramid.)

"Here we have the Church's priests."

(Point to the third level of the pyramid.)

"Here we have bishops."

(Point to the top level of the pyramid.)

"And here is the pope, Christ's vicar."

(Point to the cross.)

"And Christ Himself to Whom the Church belongs."

ST. JOHN OF THE CROSS
If a man wishes to be sure of the road he treads on, he must close his eyes and walk in the dark.

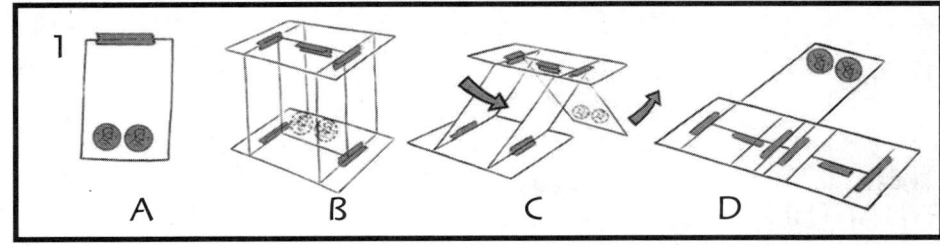
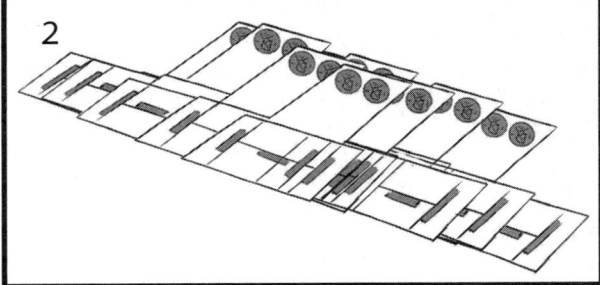
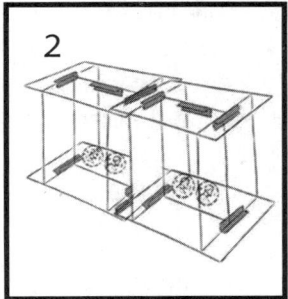
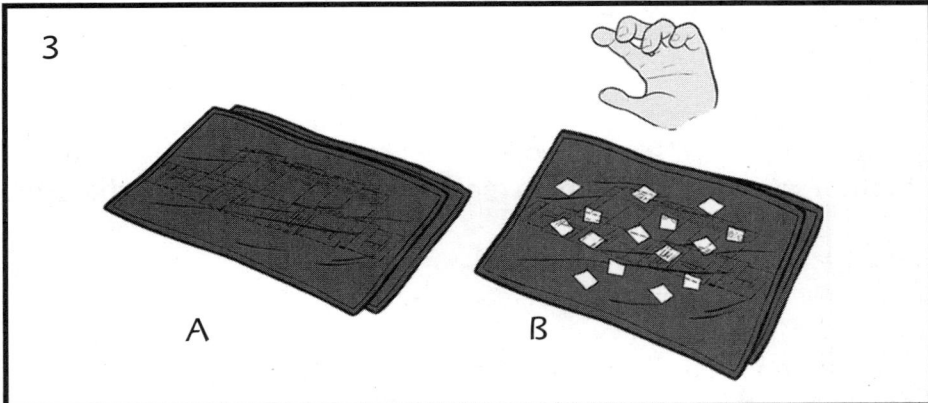

HOW YOU DO IT:

Tape 2 pennies to the bottom of ten cards as described in the diagram. Form a box from 4 other cards (without pennies). Use the diagrams to guide you. The gray lines depicted are the places where you should create a tape hinge to allow the structure to fold. Next, hang the card with the penny weights so that, once down, it will hold the entire box structure upright. If swung out, the little box will collapse. Make 10 such boxes and stack them together as per the illustration. You will notice that if you were to allow all of the weighted cards to swing out in one direction, the entire house of cards would collapse (see diagram). Place this flattened assemblage on a tray on the table at which you will perform and cover it with a handkerchief. Sprinkle confetti over this handkerchief.

When you're ready to perform, casually drop playing cards on the tray but avoid placing them in the center of the handkerchief. Place the duplicate handkerchief on top of the handkerchief that is already there and immediately grab the top card of the flattened house of cards through both handkerchiefs and pull upwards quickly. Once the house assembles itself, whisk away the handkerchiefs. No one will notice that you have 2 handkerchiefs in your hands when the confetti is sent flying.

COLOSSIANS 3:15
The peace that Christ gives is to guide you in the decisions you make; for it is to this peace that God has called you together in the one body. And be thankful.

REVELATIONS 7:17
Because the Lamb, Who is in the center of the throne, will be their Shepherd, and He will guide them to springs of life-giving water. And God will wipe away every tear from their eyes.

MAGIC TIP
Be prepared. Things can go wrong. Have extra pencils, papers or whatever else you might need for your performance.

COMMUNION IN SPIRITUAL GOODS (949-953)

God shares his blessings with us constantly.

WHAT YOU NEED:

a plastic cylindrical wastepaper basket
cardboard or foam board
a large sheet of flexible cardboard
a paper-cutter
flat black paint
various colored paints
duct tape

WHAT THEY SEE:

A square box without a top or bottom is displayed, examined, and assembled on a table. A cylinder inside the box is taken out and shown to be completely empty. When the empty cylinder is placed back in the box a plethora of objects are pulled out of what seemed an empty space.

WHAT YOU SAY:

"When you are alone, how much can you do? Let's say with homework or a school project? You probably can do a lot. But, if you partnered with someone else, you can accomplish more. There are many things that you can only do if you have help."

(Pick up the box and show your audience that it is empty, then replace it.)

"The things that you can do together would be impossible if you were alone. It's like that with the Church also."

(Pick up the cylinder and show your audience that it is empty, then replace it.)

"We are all here to worship God and to help bring about His Kingdom on Earth. As individuals, we can't bring good into this world on our own. It is only with God's help, that we are able to do good. Just like this box and this cylinder. Both are empty. You can't do a great deal of good with empty things like this. But with God, because He loves us and because He wants us all to be with Him, He willingly gives us all the blessings we need."

(Start removing the production items from the hidden basket.)

"All of creation is given freely to us as long as we keep Christ in our hearts."

JOHN 1:1-5
In the beginning the Word already existed; the Word was with God, and the Word was God. From the very beginning the Word was with God. Through Him God made all things; not one thing in all creation was made without Him. The Word was the Source of life, and this life brought light to people. The Light shines in the darkness, and the darkness has never put it out.

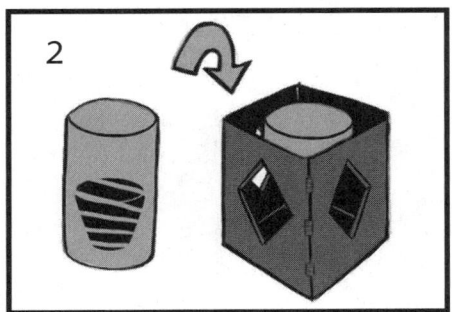

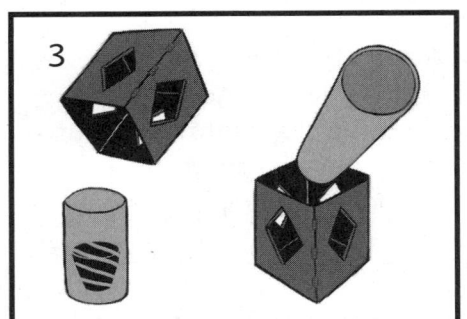

HOW YOU DO IT:

This is a very old magic trick called the "Square Circle." It is a means by which a tremendous amount of objects can appear from a seemingly empty space.

A Square Circle is easily constructed. Attach 4 pieces of cardboard together with tape to form a box (with an open top and bottom) around the wastepaper basket. You can also make a wooden version with hinges to join the sides. Cut diamond-shaped holes out of the box to waylay suspicion. Create a cylinder by rolling the sheet of flexible cardboard up on itself. Tape it so that it is big enough to conceal the wastepaper basket but still fits inside the cardboard box. It should be a bit taller than the square panels.. You can paint the outside of the box any color. Decorate it as you wish but the inside of the box should be flat black. The wastebasket must also be flat black. This is to camouflage the load basket.

Prior to performing, place as many production items as can fit in the wastepaper basket. I might suggest candy and religious gifts such as rosaries, saint cards, medals and the like. I also would include any item that packs small but opens to reveal a much larger object. I've used Chinese paper umbrellas, feather boas, a bowling ball, a fishbowl (with goldfish), rubber balls, martial arts compressible practice swords, paper streamer rolls, strings of Christmas lights, and a TV.

Place the loaded basket into the cardboard cylinder. Place this assemblage into the box. When you are ready to perform, pick up the box without disturbing the cylinder or the hidden wastepaper basket. Show both sides and return it to its original position. Next, remove the cylinder and allow everyone to look through it. Return it to its original position and then start removing the production items from the hidden wastebasket.

"THE PULLEY" by George Herbert
When God at first made man,
Having a glass of blessings standing by,
Let Us (said He) pour on him all we can:
Let the world's riches, which dispersed lie,
Contract into a span.
So strength first made a way;
Then beauty flow'd, then wisdom, honor, pleasure:
When almost all was out, God made a stay.
Perceiving that alone of all His treasures,
Rest in the bottom lay.
For if I should (said He)
Bestow this jewel also on My creature,
He would adore My gifts instead of Me,
And rest in Nature, not the God of Nature:
So both should losers be.
Yet let him keep the rest,
But keep them with repining restlessness;
Let him be rich and weary, that at least,
If goodness lead him not, yet weariness
May toss him to My breast.

MARY – MOTHER OF CHRIST, MOTHER OF THE CHURCH
(963-975)

Mary is the mother of us all.

WHAT YOU NEED:

a jacket
a 2-foot by 2-foot piece of lining material that matches the lining of performance jacket
a 3-foot by 3-foot opaque piece of cloth
an image of Mary (cutout page 235)
Topit pattern (cutout page 237)
a needle and thread or sewing machine

WHAT THEY SEE:

A large piece of cloth (known by magicians as a foulard) is shown on both sides. The catechist drapes it across his arm and then whisks it away to reveal an icon of Mary.

WHAT YOU SAY:

"Who can tell me who Mary is and why she is so important? The best way to describe Mary is as 'the perfect Christian.' If a Christian is required to bring Christ into this world, then Mary did it first and most perfectly. When she agreed to God's request, as relayed by the Archangel Gabriel, and become pregnant with Jesus, she set in motion the means by which Christ could save us. Without her humble 'yes,' we would still be lost. But because of her bravery, her love of God and her deep humility, she set the stage for Christ's triumph over death and our eternal life."

(Show both sides of the foulard and secretly grab the image from your topit. Position it in front of your chest.)

"Mary is not Christ but she is owed our gratitude and love nonetheless."

(Whisk away the foulard to reveal the image.)

"For this, as she prophesized, 'All generations will call me blessed.' Mary is the Mother of the Church; she is the mother of us all."

LUKE 1:26-55

In the Sixth month of Elizabeth's pregnancy God sent the angel Gabriel to a town in Galilee named Nazareth. He had a message for a young woman promised in marriage to a man named Joseph, who was a descendant of King David. Her name was Mary. The angel came to her and said, 'Peace be with you! The Lord is with you and has greatly blessed you!' Mary was deeply troubled by the angel's message, and she wondered what his words meant. The angel said to her, 'Don't be afraid, Mary; God has been gracious to you. You will become pregnant and give birth to a son, and you will name him Jesus. He will be great and will be called the Son of the Most High God. The Lord God will make him a king, as His ancestor David was, and He will be the king of the descendants of Jacob forever; His kingdom will never end!' Mary said to the angel, 'I am a virgin. How, then, can this be?' The angel answered, 'The Holy Spirit will come on you, and God's power will rest upon you. For this reason the holy child will be called the Son of God. Remember your relative Elizabeth. It is said that she cannot have children, but she herself is now 6 months pregnant, even though she is very old. For there is nothing that God cannot do.' 'I am the Lord's servant,' said Mary; 'may it happen to me as you

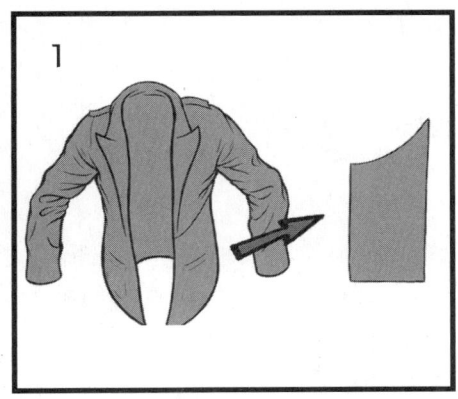

HOW YOU DO IT:

A Topit is an extra pocket sewn over the inner lining of a jacket. There are many styles of Topits. Most Topits make objects disappear. In this case, we're using one to make something appear.

Enlarge the topit pattern on page 237 at a photocopying shop to fit your jacket. The dimensions will be different for each person but, in general, the front corner of the pocket should be at about elbow height (when the arm is relaxed down) and start at the buttoning edge of the jacket, the back corner of the pocket should be as high as the armpit. The bottom should align with the hem of the jacket. This pocket should be hemmed and sewn onto the lining of the jacket.

Place an icon of Mary in the Topit prior to performing. Show both sides of the foulard by holding it in front of you. When you show the back side, cross your arms in front of you, grab a corner of the icon hidden in your topit with your inside arm (inside arm should be the right one if topit is on left side) and pull it out under cover of the cloth as you uncross your arms. When you've positioned it in front of your chest, whisk the foulard away to reveal the icon.

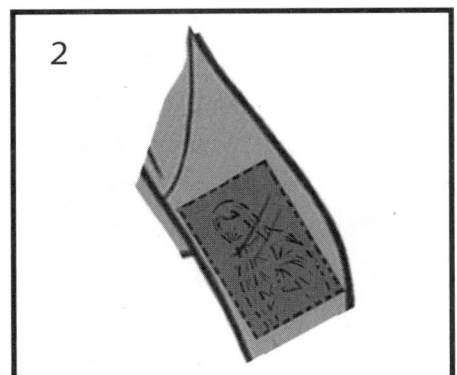

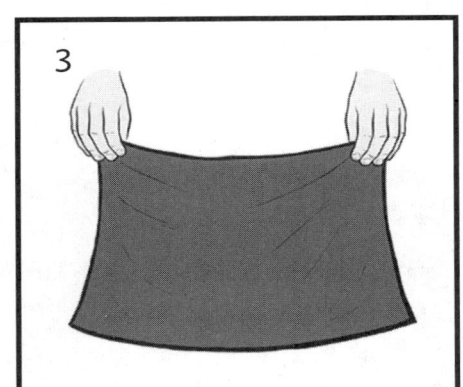

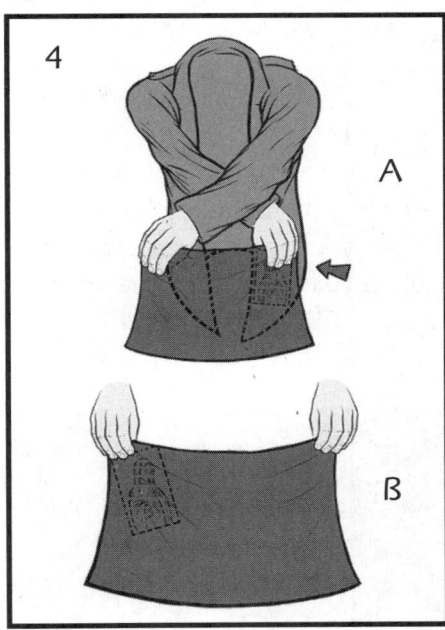

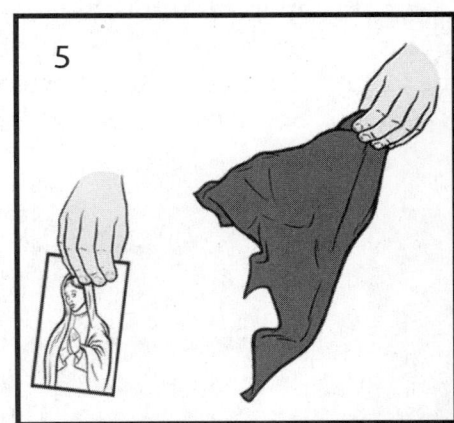

(LUKE 1:26-55 continued)
have said.' And the angel left her. Soon afterward Mary got ready and hurried off to a town in the hill country of Judea. She went into Zechariah's house and greeted Elizabeth. When Elizabeth heard Mary's greeting, the baby moved within her. Elizabeth was filled with the Holy Spirit and said in a loud voice, 'You are the most blessed of all women, and blessed is the child you will bear! Why should this great thing happen to me, that my Lord's mother comes to visit me? For as soon as I heard your greeting, the baby within me jumped with gladness. How happy you are to believe that the Lord's message to you will come true!' Mary said, 'My heart praises the Lord; my soul is glad because of God my Savior, for He has remembered me, His lowly servant! From now on all people will call me happy, because of the great things the Mighty God has done for me. His name is holy; from one generation to another He shows mercy to those who honor Him. He has stretched out His mighty arm and scattered the proud with all their plans. He has brought down mighty kings from their thrones, and lifted up the lowly. He has filled the hungry with good things, and sent the rich away with empty hands. He has kept the promise He made to our ancestors, and has come to the help of His servant Israel. He has remembered to show mercy to Abraham and to all His descendants forever!'

THE POWER OF THE KEYS (981-983)

The authority of the Church is a sign of God's love and grace.

WHAT YOU NEED:

an old-fashioned key approximately 4-inches long

WHAT THEY SEE:

An old-fashioned key is displayed and placed across the catechist's palm. Without moving his hand, the key mysteriously starts to tremble and then turns of its own accord.

WHAT YOU SAY:

"Peter's job was so important that Christ gave him 'the keys of the Kingdom of heaven.' The Power of the Keys refers to the function of the Church and her representatives to forgive sins in Christ's Name. Has anyone ever given you the keys to their house or car? If they did, they must have trusted you a great deal. It's an awesome responsibility. It's very powerful because keys are very powerful. Let me show you how powerful keys can be."

(Perform the trick as described in the How You Do It section.)

"Keys are important symbols. If your parents give you a key to your house, that means they trust you a lot. Jesus trusted Peter with the keys to the Kingdom of heaven. Jesus didn't really give Peter some keys in his hand but He trusted and respected Peter to be in charge of the Church until He returned. This key is a symbol of God's love for us and for the authority of the Church."

MARK 2-1:12

A few days later Jesus went back to Capernaum, and the news spread that he was at home. So many people came together that there was no room left, not even out in front of the door. Jesus was preaching the message to them when 4 men arrived, carrying a paralyzed man to Jesus. Because of the crowd, however, they could not get the man to Him. So they made a hole in the roof right above the place where Jesus was. When they had made an opening, they let the man down, lying on his mat. Seeing how much faith they had, Jesus said to the paralyzed man, "My son, your sins are forgiven." Some teachers of the Law who were sitting there thought to themselves, "How does He dare talk like this? This is blasphemy! God is the only One Who can forgive sins!" At once Jesus knew what they were thinking, so He said to them, "Why do you think such things? Is it easier to say to this paralyzed man, 'Your sins are forgiven,' or to say, 'Get up, pick up your mat, and walk'? I will prove to you, then, that the Son of Man has authority on earth to forgive sins." So He said to the paralyzed man, "I tell you, get up, pick up your mat, and go home!" While they all watched, the man got up, picked up his mat, and hurried away. They were all completely amazed and praised God, saying, "We have never seen anything like this!"

MARK 4:12

They may look and look, yet not see; they may listen and listen, yet not understand. For if they did, they would turn to God, and He would forgive them.

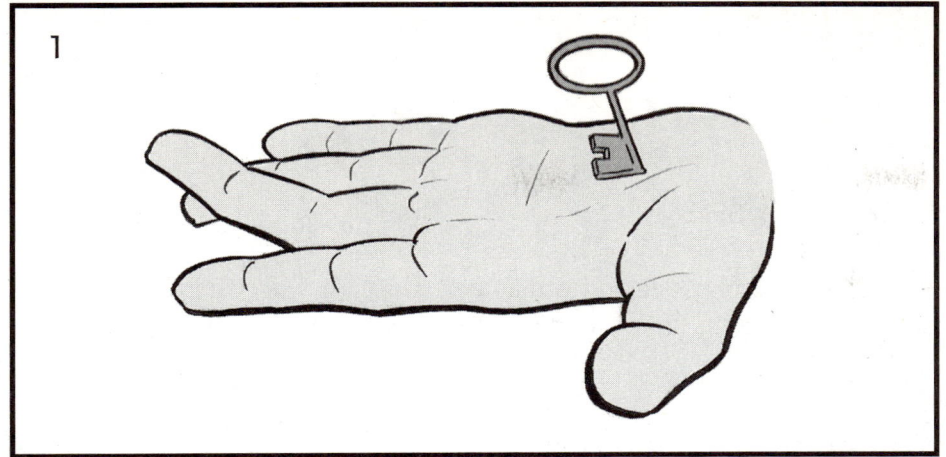

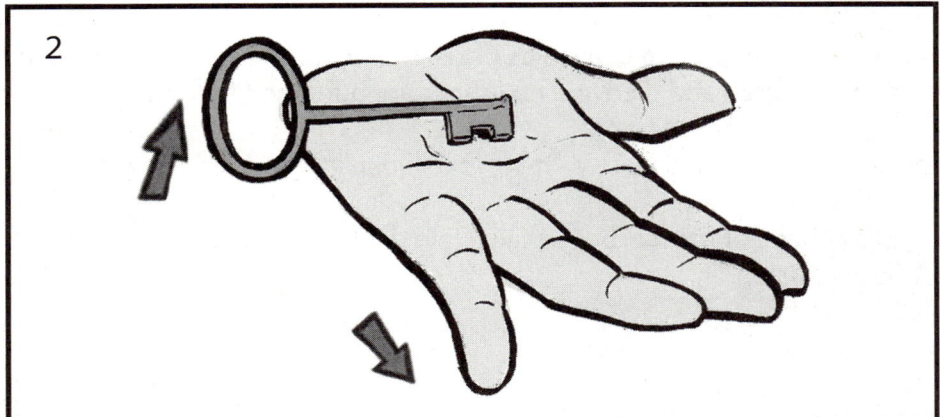

HOW YOU DO IT:

This is an extremely easy magic trick to perform. The only difficulty is finding a suitable key. You will probably have to go through quite a few until you find a perfectly balanced key. Most established hardware stores have such keys. The longer the shank, the better the trick. A heavier key will function better than a lighter one. If necessary, a gimmicked key can be found at most magic stores very cheaply that functions as described above.

Lay the key across your left palm making sure that the key's handle is off the palm so that its turning is unobstructed. By carefully and imperceptibly moving your little finger downwards, the key will turn over. The trick is quite startling and inexplicable.

MATTHEW 16:15-19
"What about you?" He asked them. "Who do you say I am?" Simon Peter answered, "You are the Messiah, the Son of the living God." "Good for you, Simon son of John!" answered Jesus. "For this truth did not come to you from any human being, but it was given to you directly by My Father in heaven. And so I tell you, Peter: you are a rock, and on this rock foundation I will build my church, and not even death will ever be able to overcome it. I will give you the keys of the Kingdom of heaven; what you prohibit on earth will be prohibited in heaven, and what you permit on earth will be permitted in heaven."

MATTHEW 6:14-15
If you forgive others the wrongs they have done to you, your Father in heaven will also forgive you. But if you do not forgive others, then your Father will not forgive the wrongs you have done.

EPHESIANS 4:32
Instead, be kind and tender-hearted to one another, and forgive one another, as God has forgiven you through Christ.

I BELIEVE IN THE RESURRECTION OF THE BODY
(988-1019)

We share in Christ's resurrection.

WHAT YOU NEED:

a deck of cards
an additional copy of one card
a pen

WHAT THEY SEE:

A card is randomly selected from a deck. The card is ripped into 4 quarters. The pieces are pressed together and instantly reassembled.

WHAT YOU SAY:

"What do we mean when we say Jesus was resurrected? We believe as Christians that Jesus died for our sins and, after 3 days, came back to life. When He suffered and died, we no longer are burdened by Original Sin."

(Force duplicate card on volunteer. Retrieve card and place palmed, folded duplicate behind it.)

"We're still required to be ethical and kind to others, of course, but because He died for us we don't have to be scared of death. It's meaningless to us. It is an illusion."

(Rip up the selected card.)

"If I rip up this card and show you all of the pieces it will seem as if its existence as a card is over."

(Dump the 4 ripped-up pieces into your pocket under the pretense of retrieving the pen. Wave the pen over the folded card in your hand and open it.)

"But, as you see ... it's an illusion. Death is an illusion also. Only Christ gives us Truth and Life and Hope."

LUKE 9:22
He also told them, "The Son of Man must suffer much and be rejected by the elders, the chief priests, and the teachers of the Law. He will be put to death, but 3 days later He will be raised to life."

1 PETER 1:3
Let us give thanks to the God and Father of our Lord Jesus Christ! Because of His great mercy He gave us new life by raising Jesus Christ from death. This fills us with a living hope.

REVELATIONS 1:18
I am the Living One! I was dead, but now I am alive forever and ever. I have authority over death and the world of the dead.

1 CORINTHIANS 11:26
This means that every time you eat this bread and drink from this cup you proclaim the Lord's death until He comes.

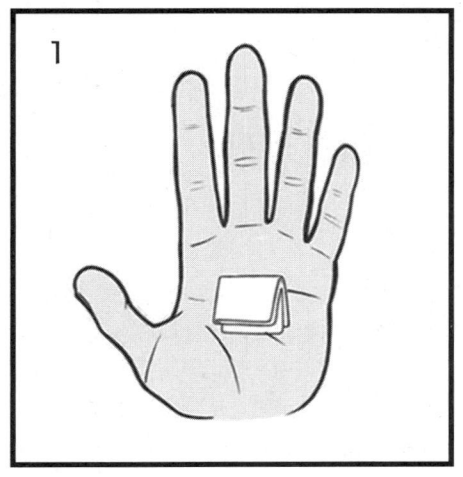
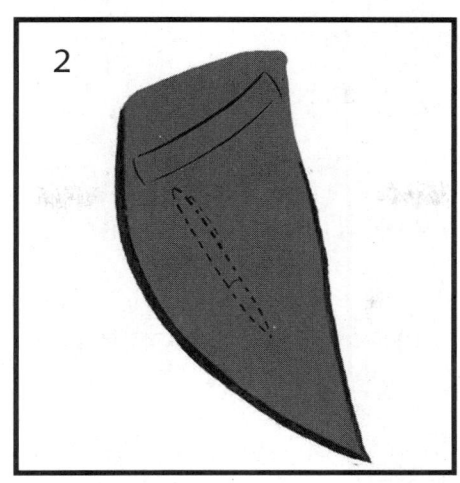
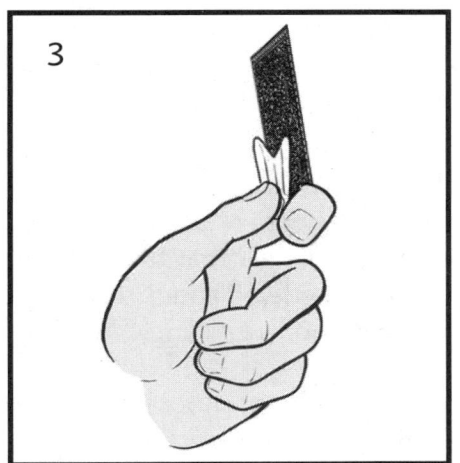
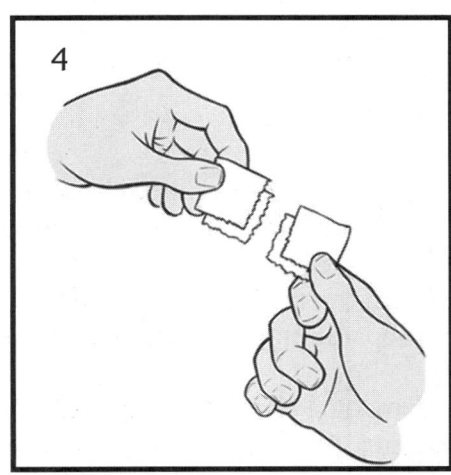
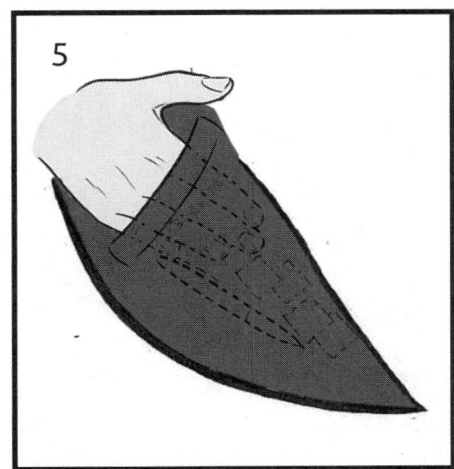
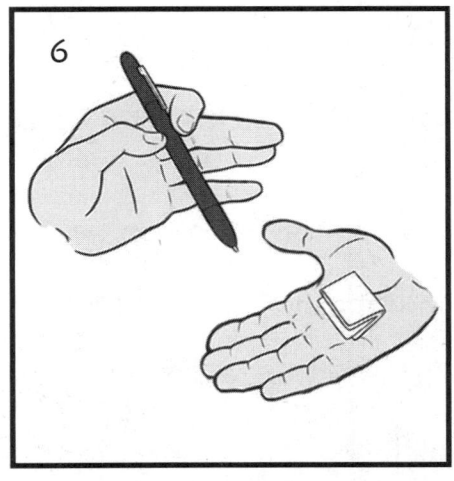

HOW YOU DO IT:

Fold the duplicate card into quarters and palm it in your right hand. For instructions on palming, refer to page 195. Place the pen in your pocket.

Stack the deck of cards with the unfolded duplicate card at the very top of the deck. You will need to force this card. Use False Shuffle Force 1, 2, or 3 on page 109.

As soon as you take the selected card back from your volunteer hold it up and place the palmed folded card behind it, hidden from the audience's view. Rip the selected card in half and then those 2 halves again into quarters. You will find that the folded, intact, duplicate card will not be difficult to conceal since it is the same size as the smallest ripped section of its duplicate.

Take the entire packet of ripped-up pieces and the intact folded card between your right thumb and forefinger and show that you have nothing else in your hands. Turn the packet over in your hand and openly place the intact folded card into your left hand while retaining the ripped up pieces in your right hand.

With your right hand, dispose of the ripped-up pieces as you retrieve the pen from your pocket. Using the pen as a magic wand, wave it over the folded card and slowly open it to reveal the now restored card.

COLOSSIANS 1:18
He is the head of His body, the Church; He is the source of the body's life. He is the first-born Son, Who was raised from death, in order that He alone might have the first place in all things.

HEBREWS 10:19
We have, then, my friends, complete freedom to go into the Most Holy Place by means of the death of Jesus.

THE FINAL PURIFICATION, OR PURGATORY (1030-1032)

We must be prepared before we can stand before God.

WHAT YOU NEED:

a wide-mouthed glass
a dental dam
latex balloon or a square of latex taken from a surgical glove
a penny and a quarter
a marker
a rubber band

WHAT THEY SEE:

A wide-mouthed glass is introduced to the audience. Across its mouth is a small sheet of latex. Resting on the latex sheet are 2 coins. The catechist gives a volunteer a choice of either coin. A coin is removed and the volunteer is invited to push on the remaining coin. Inexplicably, the coin is visibly pushed though the latex and into the glass. Everything can be examined immediately afterwards.

WHAT YOU SAY:

"Purgatory means 'the place where we are cleaned.' We believe in this kind of existence because we understand that no one is pure enough to stand before God and that we are completely dependent upon God's grace for our salvation. No one knows if Purgatory is a place or a state of being but it's clear that there is a distinction between when a person dies and the Final Judgment. The Church had wondered about this in between time. We consider it a time of preparation, purification, and anticipation of God's Coming Glory."

"Imagine the latex sheet is Purgatory and imagine also these coins represent Believers. Please choose one. Now, imagine that the inside of this jar is Heaven ... God's presence. And, here we are, waiting just outside of it."

> (Ask a volunteer to choose one of the coins. If she chooses the penny, remove the quarter and place it aside. If she chooses the quarter, remove it.)

"And when we are pure enough ... when God's grace works upon our souls and purifies us ... watch what happens."

> (Have the volunteer push on the penny until it pops into the glass.)

"As you see, God's love and grace is sufficient to heal and purify us before He welcomes us into Heaven."

PSALMS 15:1-5
Lord, who may enter Your Temple? Who may worship on Zion, Your sacred hill? Those who obey God in everything and always do what is right, whose words are true and sincere, and who do not slander others. They do no wrong to their friends nor spread rumors about their neighbors. They despise those whom God rejects, but honor those who obey the Lord. They always do what they promise, no matter how much it may cost. They make loans without charging interest and cannot be bribed to testify against the innocent. Whoever does these things will always be secure.

PSALMS 5:4
You are not a God who is pleased with wrongdoing; you allow no evil in Your presence.

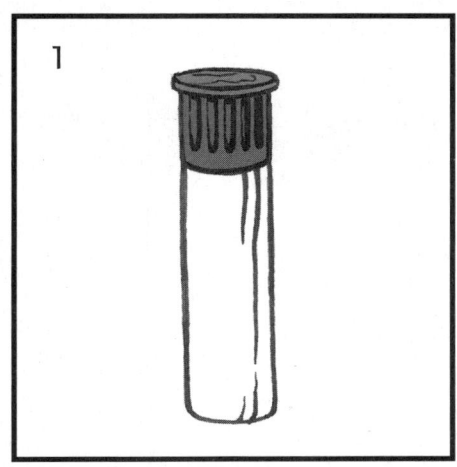

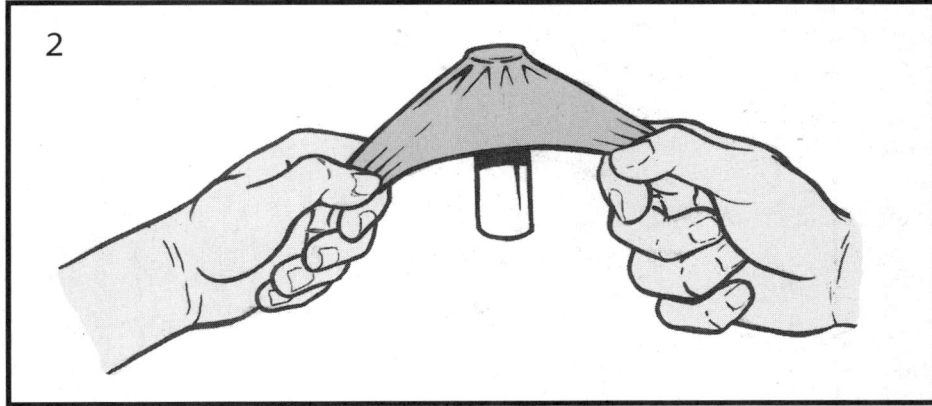

HOW YOU DO IT:

Ideally, this trick is performed with dental dams which can be bought at any medical or dental supply store. Without access to such a store, you can use a latex balloon or surgical glove for this trick. Remove the cap of a marker and stand the cap on its end. Place a penny on top of the cap. Stretch the latex as much as possible and center it over the penny. Pull down on the latex and allow it to stretch over the penny thus "grabbing" it. When you relax your grip on the latex sheet, you will find that the latex on top of the penny is nearly invisible, but behind the penny it has recoiled to its normal density. The penny although wrapped up by the latex sheet will seem to be resting on top of it. Place this assemblage onto the top of the glass (see diagram) and put a rubber band around the rim of the glass to secure the dam to the glass.

This trick utilizes a force called "Magician's Choice." No matter which coin the volunteer chooses, inevitably the prepared penny will remain. If she chooses the penny, simply remove the quarter and proceed with the trick as described. If she chooses the quarter say, "OK ... we'll remove the quarter." As you see, either way, the volunteer is stuck with the prepared penny.

MAGIC TIP
Dress well.
Shine the shoes.
Look sharp.
Smell nice.
Be an artist.

I believe in Purgatory ... the saved soul, at the very foot of the throne, begs to be taken away and cleansed. It cannot bear for a moment longer "With its darkness to affront that light." Religion has reclaimed Purgatory. Our souls demand Purgatory, don't they? Would it not break the heart if God said to us, "It is true ... that your breath smells and your rags drip with mud and slime, but we are charitable here and no one will upbraid you with these things, nor draw away from you. Enter into the joy"? Should we not reply, "With submission, Sir, and if there is no objection, I'd rather be cleaned first." – "It may hurt, you know." – "Even so, Sir." — CS Lewis

THE LAST JUDGMENT (1038-1041)

We stand before God's throne.

WHAT YOU NEED:

2 identical decks of cards

WHAT THEY SEE:

A deck of cards is inspected and randomly shuffled by several audience members. The catechist retrieves the cards and immediately separates them into 2 piles. He turns them over to show that the cards have somehow mysteriously separated into reds and blacks.

WHAT YOU SAY:

"We hear a lot about how Jesus will judge the living and the dead and separate the good from the wicked, the sheep from the goats. Imagine these cards are people.

"Would you like to see a trick?

(Place the deck in the same pocket as the prepared, duplicate deck.)

"You've just been "tricked!" I'm just joking ..."

(Retrieve the prepared deck and perform a false shuffle.)

"Some people will be good ..."

(Break the deck to expose a red card.)

"... and some will be bad ..."

(Break the deck to expose a black card.)

"Of course, we're not allowed to judge others so we really don't know who is good or bad in the depths of his or her heart. But God can read our hearts very easily. We belong to Him."

(Separate the deck into 2 piles and offer a choice of either pile. Direct her to spread out her pile faceup as you do the same.)

"As you can see, God knows which side we belong on. Just as these cards are separated into piles of black and red cards, so too will Jesus separate us when he judges us. By accepting Jesus as Savior, we allow the Holy Spirit into our lives."

> **REVELATIONS 20:4**
> Then I saw thrones, and those who sat on them were given the power to judge. I also saw the souls of those who had been executed because they had proclaimed the truth that Jesus revealed and the word of God. They had not worshiped the beast or its image, nor had they received the mark of the beast on their foreheads or their hands. They came to life and ruled as kings with Christ for a thousand years.

FALSE SHUFFLE FORCE 1
(Keeps the top card in place.)
Riffle shuffle the cards by dovetailing them into each other. Be careful to keep the top card in place. Offer the volunteer the top card.

FALSE SHUFFLE FORCE 2
(Maintains the order of the whole deck.)
Holding the deck in your left hand, remove a third of the cards from the bottom of the deck and place them squarely on the tabletop in front of you. Take the bottom half of the cards in your hands and place them on top of the cards you just laid down. Place the remainder of the cards in your left hand on top of the pile on the table. This may seem simplistic but if done immediately after the false shuffle described above and the top part is placed down quickly, casually and absent-mindedly, everyone will be convinced. Offer the volunteer the top card.

FALSE SHUFFLE FORCE 3
(Directs volunteer to selecting a planted card.)
Plant a card on top of a deck of cards. Have your volunteer cut the deck and place the portion of the deck that she cut on the table. Immediately, take the remainder of the cards and place it on top of volunteer's pile at right angles to it. At this point, magicians would use a thing called "time misdirection." You need to give the volunteer some time to forget how she just handled the deck in order to direct her to choose the wrong pile.

You can review the events that led up to this point. Mention the fact that she cut the deck anywhere she wanted and that there was no way that you could have influenced her to cut at that specific point. Take time to make sure she understands all of the steps and ask her if she agrees that it would be impossible to know which card she cut to. Once she agrees, remove the top pile from the deck and motion to the top card of the lower section. This will be the card that you planted on the top of the deck. She will think that this is the card she cut to randomly when, in reality, the card that she cut to is on top of the other pile.

HOW YOU DO IT:
This is accomplished with a sleight-of-hand maneuver called a "Deck Switch." Prepare a deck of cards so that all of the red cards are on the top of the deck. Place this deck in your jacket pocket, preferably in your breast pocket.

Give your volunteer a deck of cards and ask her to shuffle it. Retrieve it and ask her if she would like to see a trick. When she assents, simply nod and place the deck in the same pocket as the prepared, duplicate deck. Announce that you have now "tricked" your volunteer. Apologize for the pun and retrieve the prepared deck leaving your volunteer's deck in your pocket. Your audience will not suspect you are now using a different deck of cards.

Perform false shuffle 1 or 2. Cut the deck in the middle of the red half to expose a red card and then in the middle of the black half to expose a black card. Put the cards back together in their previous order, fan them face toward you, and separate the 2 colors of the deck into 2 piles. Ask your volunteer which pile she would prefer and hand that pile to her. Have her spread her pile at the same time as you do. One half will be all red, one half will be all black.

MAGIC TIP
While adults might not say anything if you make a mistake during your performance, children have no such self-restrictions. Don't let it bother you; the lesson is more important than the magic. Simply use this experience to make sure you practice more before attempting the trick again.

Part 2:
THE CELEBRATION OF THE CHRISTIAN MYSTERY

You were told (at your baptism): Don't believe only in what you see. You might say, is that all this great mystery is about? The mystery that "eye has not seen and ear has not heard, and that has not entered the human heart"? I see water like this every day! Is it able to cleanse me, though I have often gone into it without being cleansed? Learn from this that water without the Spirit does not cleanse. That is why, too, you have read that in baptism there are "Three that testify, the water, the blood and the Spirit," If you leave one of them out, the sacrament of baptism no longer occurs. For what is water without the cross of Christ? An ordinary element without sacramental significance. In the same way, without water there is no mystery of new birth: "No one can enter the kingdom of God without being born of water and Spirit."

—St. Ambrose (c.340-397), **The Mysteries,** 16-21

THE LITURGY – WORK OF THE HOLY TRINITY (1077-1112)

God heals and restores us.

WHAT YOU NEED:

a large handkerchief
2 matches
a magic marker
a secret confederate

WHAT THEY SEE:

A wooden match is marked with a pen and snapped in half. The pieces are placed under a handkerchief and several volunteers are asked to feel under the cloth to make sure the match pieces are still there. Then, seemingly without any subterfuge, the cloth is shaken and the match is restored.

WHAT YOU SAY:

"Like all of the sacraments, the Eucharistic liturgy is central to our faith and to our community. The word "Eucharist" comes from the Greek verb ευχαριστω (eucharisto), meaning 'to give thanks' or 'to rejoice.' We call it this because we are thankful to come together to share this beautiful meal.

"Why do we need to share this meal so often? It's so that we can be healed. Did you know that we call God, 'The Great Physician?' It's because He knows how to heal us. If we allow Him, His grace will make us whole. Imagine that this match is us."

(Mark the match with a magic marker and then break the match.)

"Now, imagine this handkerchief is God's grace."

(Cover the match with the handkerchief.)

"He covers us with His love."

(Ask several volunteers to reach under the handkerchief to examine the match. Once the match is switched using whichever method you prefer, whisk away the handkerchief.)

"Only God's loving grace can heal and restore us. Just as this match was broken and then restored, so too are we brought to new life in Christ."

IGNATIUS OF ANTIOCH, LETTER TO THE SMYRNEANS 8:2 [A.D. 110]
Let no one do anything of concern to the Church without the bishop. Let that be considered a valid Eucharist which is celebrated by the bishop or by one whom he ordains [i.e., a presbyter]. Wherever the bishop appears, let the people be there; just as wherever Jesus Christ is, there is the Catholic Church.

ST. GERARD MAJELLA
The Most Blessed Sacrament is Christ made visible. The poor sick person is Christ again made visible.

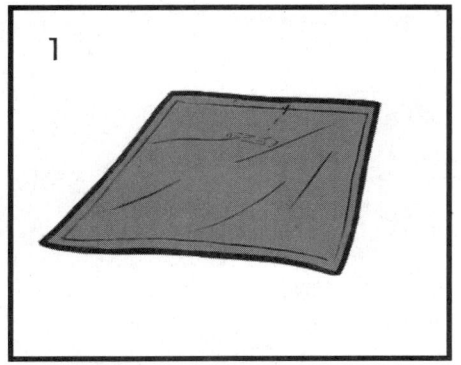
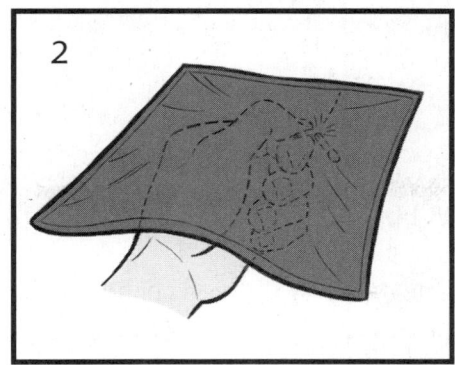
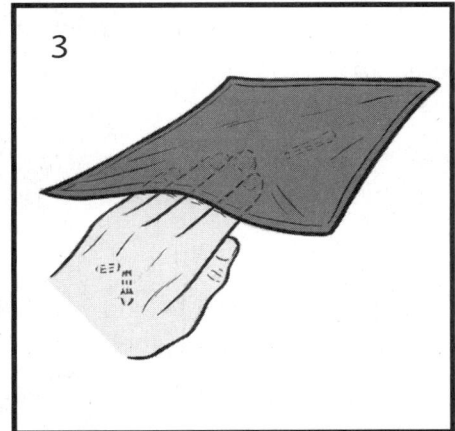
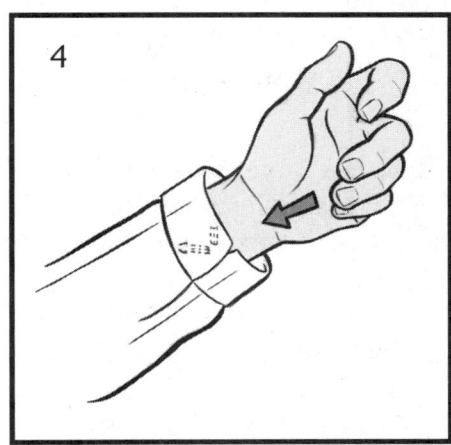

HOW YOU DO IT:

This is a twist on an old trick. The last volunteer to reach under the handkerchief is your confederate. When he reaches under the handkerchief, he steals the match pieces and replaces them with an intact and similarly marked match. While his hand is under the handkerchief, he simply takes the match pieces and drops them into the sleeve of the same hand.

The same trick can be accomplished without a confederate. Before performing this trick, insert a marked, intact wooden match into a hole in the hem of a handkerchief. Snap the other match in half as above, and allow people to feel the pieces under the handkerchief. Then hide them in sleeve and remove the intact match from hem.

1 KINGS 17:12
She answered, "By the living Lord your God I swear that I don't have any bread. All I have is a handful of flour in a bowl and a bit of olive oil in a jar. I came here to gather some firewood to take back home and prepare what little I have for my son and me. That will be our last meal, and then we will starve to death."

MATTHEW 18:20
For where 2 or 3 come together in My name, I am there with them.

LUKE 9:2
Then He sent them out to preach the Kingdom of God and to heal the sick.

LUKE 10:9
Heal the sick in that town, and say to the people there, 'The Kingdom of God has come near you.'

JOHN 6:51
I am the Living Bread that came down from heaven. If you eat this bread, you will live forever. The bread that I will give you is My flesh, which I give so that the world may live.

1 CORINTHIANS 11:24-25
[He] gave thanks to God, broke it, and said, "This is My body, which is for you. Do this in memory of Me." In the same way, after the supper He took the cup and said, "This cup is God's new covenant, sealed with My blood. Whenever you drink it, do so in memory of Me."

THE PASCHAL MYSTERY IN THE CHURCH'S SACRAMENTS (1113-1134)

We are invited to experience God.

WHAT YOU NEED:

monofilament or fishing line
model glue
20 fifty-cent pieces, quarters or similar size coins
a champagne or ice bucket

WHAT YOU SAY:

WHAT THEY SEE:

The catechist shows a champagne bucket to be empty. Immediately, he pulls a coin out of a volunteer's ear and drops into the bucket. He pulls another one out of thin air and adds it to the bucket. Other coins appear from a variety of other places. Each coin is thrown into bucket with a loud clink. When all of the available coins are exhausted, the catechist empties his bucket to show a plethora of coins.

"The sacraments are ways in which we Believers can experience God directly. They were instituted, or started, by Jesus during His ministry on Earth. The reason Jesus gave us these wonderful symbols is to draw us away from sin and closer to Him. Without them, we are eternally tied to sin."

(Pretend to pull a coin out of a child's ear and, instead of dropping it into the bucket, hide it behind your hand. At the same time allow one of the coins hidden in your other hand to drop noisily into the bucket. Pretend to find more coins in other places. Each time pretend to throw the coin in the bucket and each time allow a coin from the other hand to fall into the bucket in its place.)

"Because we are weak and sinful, we can't do this for ourselves. That's why we rely upon the blessing God gives us freely and liberally in the sacraments. All we need do is ask Him.

(Repeat the trick a few more times.)

"God loves us so much that He gave us these sacraments as a means by which we may meet Him. We can't help ourselves but, with the grace that comes from the sacraments, we can come to love God more and more."

MATTHEW 5:3-12

Happy are those who know they are spiritually poor; the Kingdom of heaven belongs to them!
Happy are those who mourn; God will comfort them!
Happy are those who are humble; they will receive what God has promised!
Happy are those whose greatest desire is to do what God requires; God will satisfy them fully!
Happy are those who are merciful to others; God will be merciful to them!
Happy are the pure in heart; they will see God!
Happy are those who work for peace; God will call them His children!
Happy are those who are persecuted because they do what God requires; the Kingdom of heaven belongs to them!
Happy are you when people insult you and persecute you and tell all kinds of evil lies against you because you are My followers.
Be happy and glad, for a great reward is kept for you in heaven. This is how the prophets who lived before you were persecuted.

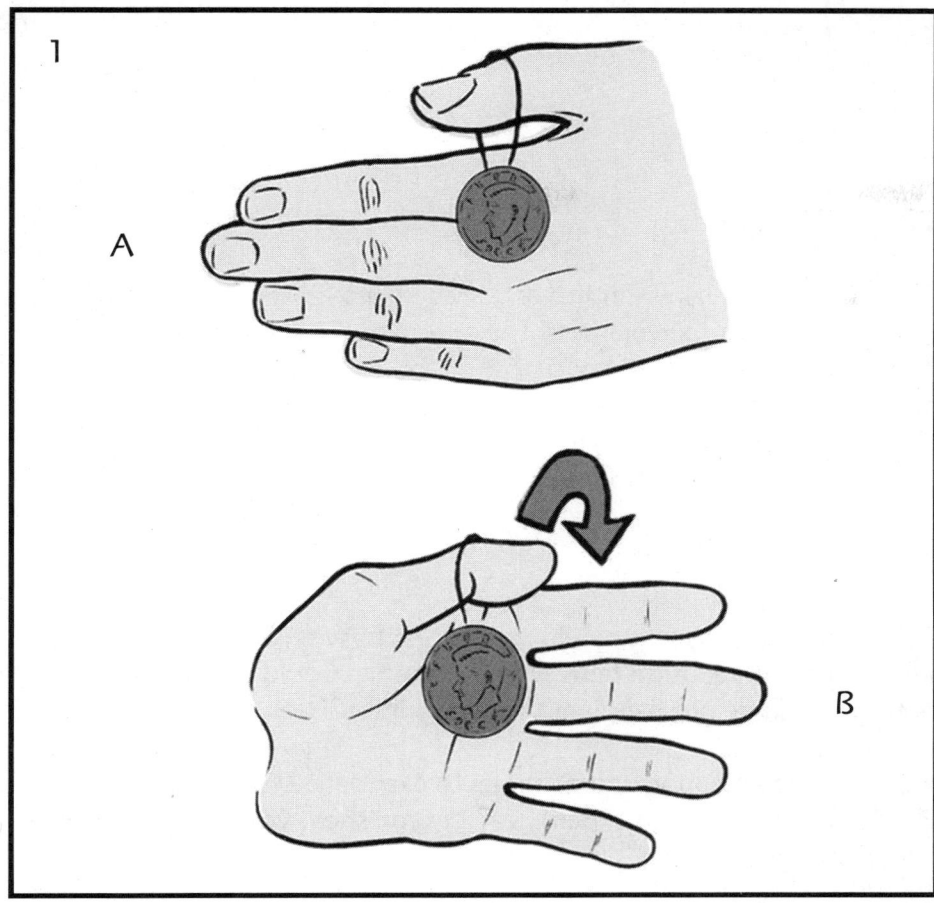

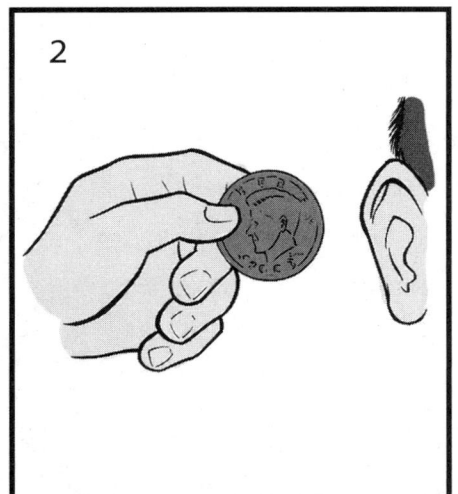

HOW YOU DO IT:

The Miser's Dream is a very old magic trick. It's also one of the most beautiful. The coins that are pulled out of children' ears aren't "actually" pulled out of their ears. In reality, the same coin is used over and over again. This is accomplished with the help of a small loop of monofilament glued to a fifty-cent piece. The filament should be long enough so that the coin rests exactly in the middle of your palm when the loop is around your thumb.

Magicians would be more likely to use a special type of wax known as "Magicians' Wax" to glue the monofilament to the coin, but if you don't wish to invest in this, experiment with different adhesives to find one you prefer. Affix the monofilament to the coin and hang the coin on your thumb. To make a coin appear in thin air or behind someone's ear, all you need do is maneuver the coin sufficiently to make it swing to your fingertips.

The coins make a sound and accumulate in the bucket because you are holding approximately twenty coins in the hand with which you are holding the bucket. When you are ready to place the coin into the bucket, simply drop one of the coins hidden by your left hand and hide the fact that the gimmicked coin has swung behind your right palm.

1 CORINTHIANS 11:22
Don't you have your own homes in which to eat and drink? Or would you rather despise the Church of God and put to shame the people who are in need? What do you expect me to say to you about this? Shall I praise you? Of course I don't!

CELEBRATING THE CHURCH'S LITURGY (1136-1199)

We come together in our love for God.

WHAT YOU NEED:

a deck of cards

WHAT THEY SEE:

A deck of cards is fairly shuffled and divided into 2 halves; one for the catechist and one for the volunteer. The catechist asks the volunteer to do as he does. They both randomly choose a card and then lose it in the middle of their respective halves. The 2 parts of the deck are traded and both the catechist and the volunteer are able to find the other's cards.

WHAT YOU SAY:

"Why do we go to Church on Sundays and other holy days? It would be a very empty feeling for us as Christians if we all stayed home and didn't share our beautiful faith with each other. Could you imagine what it would be like if we had no place to go to share our happiness or our sadness?"

"The liturgies in which we participate and share are all opportunities for us to experience God as community. What do you think it would be like if 2 people could share an experience? Let me show you what it would be like for both of us to have a common experience between us."

(Perform the trick as described in the How You Do It section.)

"The only thing better than having a happy and wonderful experience is sharing it with other people who want us to be happy. In this trick, 2 people with 2 separate experiences were brought together. The Church's liturgies work in the same way. We are many individuals but, by God's grace, we are brought together in worshiping Him."

MATTHEW 26:26-30; MARK 14:22-26; LUKE 22:14-20
While they were eating, Jesus took a piece of bread, gave a prayer of thanks, broke it, and gave it to His disciples. "Take and eat it," He said; "this is My body." Then He took a cup, gave thanks to God, and gave it to them. "Drink it, all of you," he said; "This is My blood, which seals God's covenant, My blood poured out for many for the forgiveness of sins. I tell you, I will never again drink this wine until the day I drink the new wine with you in My Father's Kingdom." Then they sang a hymn and went out to the Mount of Olives.

ACTS 20:7
On Saturday evening we gathered together for the fellowship meal. Paul spoke to the people and kept on speaking until midnight, since he was going to leave the next day.

1 CORINTHIANS 11:24
He gave thanks to God, broke it [the bread], and said, "This is My body, which is for you. Do this in memory of Me."

GOSPEL MAGIC HISTORY

St. Nicholas Owen, one of the Forty Martyrs of England and Wales, went by several nicknames, including John Owen, Little John, Little Michael, Andrewes, and Draper. St. Nicholas Owen successfully arranged Fr. John Gerard's escape from the Tower of London.

In November 1605, Guy Fawkes and the Gunpowder Plot were uncovered. This led to a crackdown on Catholics and St. Nicholas Owen's arrest in early 1606. At that point, St. Nicholas had been secreted in one of his hiding places for 2 weeks, while priest-hunters, or poursuivants, searched the house. He was captured when he attempted to escape. He claimed to be a priest in order to throw the hunters off the trail of the real priests who remained hidden nearby.

St. Nicholas Owen completed many dozens of hiding places through Britain. Some were so clever that they defied detection even until the present time.

Fr. John Gerard wrote about St. Nicholas Owen, "I verily think that no man can be said to have done more good for all those who laboured in the English vineyard. For, first, he was the immediate occasion of saving the lives of many hundreds of persons, both ecclesiastical and secular, and of the estates also of these seculars, which had been lost and forfeited many times over if the priests had been taken in their houses."

Because of St. Nicholas Owen's unique ministry at a time of great misfortune for the Catholic Church, he is credited for saving many lives and keeping the Faith alive in Great Britain.

HOW YOU DO IT:

Shuffle a deck of cards and offer your volunteer half of the deck. As you hand it to her, note the bottom card of her half of the deck. Ask her to copy all of your actions. Tell her to randomly select a card from the middle of the deck, note it, and place it on the top of her pile. You should do the same. Both of you should now cut your respective piles and complete the cut, placing the bottom half on top of the top half. This will effectively lose your cards in the middle of the piles but since you've spied the bottom card of your volunteer's deck, you can use it as a "key card" to locate her selection.

Next, exchange halves of the deck with the volunteer. Have your volunteer fan the cards with their faces towards her and ask her to remove the card you picked from the center of the fan and place it on the table. While she is doing that, look through the cards in your hand and remove the card beneath the key card you memorized in your volunteer's deck. Place it face down on the table. This is the card she selected earlier.

Ask the volunteer to turn over the card she placed on the table. As soon as she does, tell her that she found your card; whether it is your card or not is unimportant. Immediately, ask her to name her card. When she does, turn over the card you placed on the table in front of you. She will verify that it is, in fact, her selected card.

LITURGICAL DIVERSITY & THE UNITY OF THE MYSTERY
(1200-1209)

Many voices unite to worship God.

WHAT YOU NEED:

2 decks of cards
a Change Bag
a small stapler
twenty handkerchiefs

WHAT THEY SEE:

The catechist allows a volunteer to choose any card she wishes. She is then asked to lose her card in the deck and to place it into a cloth bag followed by a stapler and 7 small handkerchiefs. Immediately, the magician puts his hand into the bag and pulls out a string of knotted handkerchiefs with the volunteer's selected card stapled neatly in the middle of the line of handkerchiefs.

WHAT YOU SAY:

"To Catholics in the Western World, sometimes we get the idea that the Church here is just like the Church in all parts of the world. The truth is that there are 22 rites in the Catholic Church. Here in America, most Catholics belong to the Latin Rite. Each of these rites is an expression of historical or cultural differences that have existed for many, many centuries. But even though we are very different, we are all Catholic and all have the Pope as our spiritual leader."

"Let's have an experiment. I want you to select a card."

(Direct your volunteer to place her selection and a stapler into the Change Bag.)

"These handkerchiefs represent the many rites we have in the Catholic Church. Even though they look different, they are actually all the same."

(Direct your volunteer to place the handkerchiefs into the Change Bag. Immediately pull out the string of handkerchiefs from the secret compartment.)

"We are all united in our love of God and our Catholic faith."

LUKE 24:45-47
Then He opened their minds to understand the Scriptures, and said to them, "This is what is written: the Messiah must suffer and must rise from death 3 days later, and in His name the message about repentance and the forgiveness of sins must be preached to all nations, beginning in Jerusalem.

ISAIAH 2:4
He will settle disputes among great nations. They will hammer their swords into plows and their spears into pruning knives. Nations will never again go to war, never prepare for battle again.

ROMANS 16:26
Now, however, that truth has been brought out into the open through the writings of the prophets; and by the command of the eternal God it is made known to all nations, so that all may believe and obey.

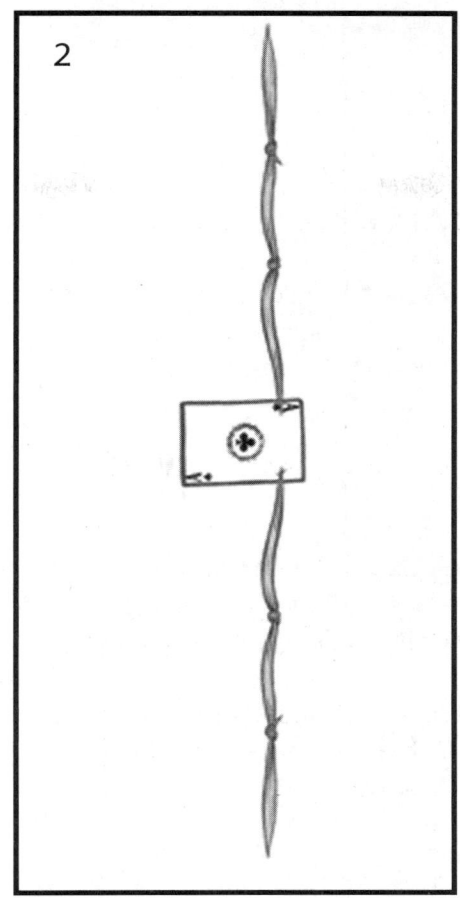

HOW YOU DO IT:

Prepare 5 small handkerchiefs by tying opposite corners to create a long chain. Next staple a copy of your force card to the end of this string of handkerchiefs. Tie 5 more handkerchiefs together and staple one end to the other edge of the card. Place this assemblage into one of the pockets of your Change Bag. For instructions on how to make a Change Bag, see page 59. When you are ready to perform this trick, force a copy of the card you've stapled on the handkerchiefs on your volunteer. Use False Shuffle Force 1, 2, or 3 on page 109.

Have your volunteer return the card to the deck and to place it along with a small stapler and ten small, separate handkerchiefs into the empty pocket of the Change Bag. To reveal the selected card, simply pull the string of handkerchiefs out of the extra pocket.

THE SACRAMENT OF BAPTISM (1213-1284)

We are reborn in Christ.

WHAT YOU NEED:

a Change Bag
a black handkerchief
a white handkerchief

WHAT THEY SEE:

A black handkerchief is examined and placed into an empty bag. Immediately, a white handkerchief is withdrawn from the same bag. The bag is shown to be empty afterwards.

WHAT YOU SAY:

"Did you ever try to be very, very, very good? Maybe your mom or dad told you that you couldn't expect any Christmas presents unless you improved your behavior. Having that threat held over your head, you realized that you had best change your behavior immediately or you could kiss your presents good-bye."

"How long did it last? Probably not very long, I guess. No one can be perfectly good. It's impossible. Why? It's because humans are sinful. We can't help ourselves out of the mess we've put ourselves in. It's called 'Original Sin' and none of us can stop it on our own."

"Imagine this black handkerchief is our sinfulness."

(Place the black handkerchief into the empty side of the Change Bag.)

"That's why Jesus Christ came to save us. It is only through belief in Him that we can be become holy Children of God. Accepting God's Will in our lives, receiving baptism and the other sacraments and committing our lives to God cleans us from Original Sin and helps to orient us towards God."

(Remove the while handkerchief from the Change Bag.)

"The black handkerchief, the one representing our sins, has become white. In the same way, our sins are wiped clean by God when we are baptized."

ROMANS 5:15
But the 2 are not the same, because God's free gift is not like Adam's sin. It is true that many people died because of the sin of that one man. But God's grace is much greater, and so is His free gift to so many people through the grace of the one man, Jesus Christ.

ROMANS 5:17
It is true that through the sin of one man death began to rule because of that one man. But how much greater is the result of what was done by the one man, Jesus Christ! All who receive God's abundant grace and are freely put right with Him will rule in life through Christ.

ROMANS 5:20
Law was introduced in order to increase wrongdoing; but where sin increased, God's grace increased much more.

HOW YOU DO IT:

Use the Change Bag described on page 59. Prior to starting the performance, load the white handkerchief into one of the pockets. When performing this trick, show the empty pocket to be empty. Have the volunteer place the black handkerchief into that pocket. Immediately, pull out a small corner of the handkerchief out so that it protrudes slightly from the bag. Then, push that corner back into the bag while simultaneously pulling out the white handkerchief. Again, have the empty pocket examined.

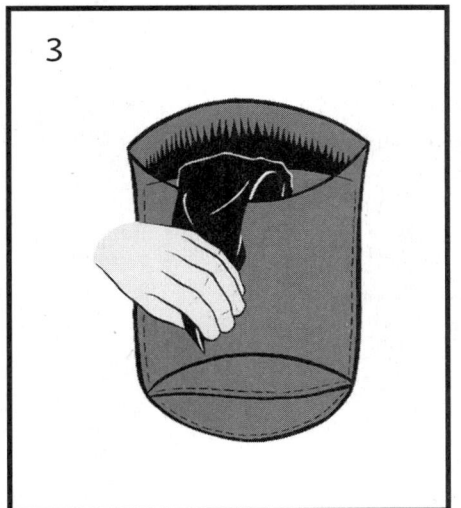
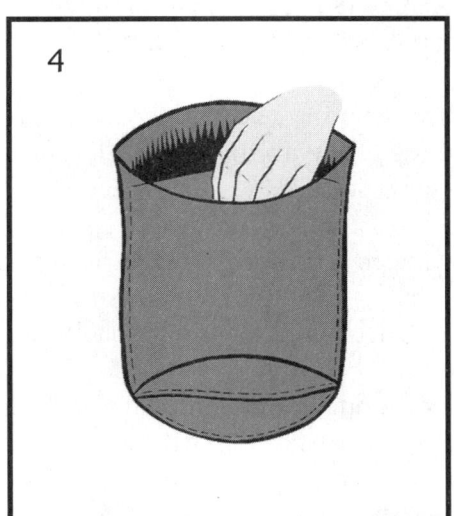

MAGIC TIP

Abracadabra – a "magic" word used by modern stage magicians as a means by which to build suspense or pretend to "cause" a magic effect. In reality, it is derived from ancient pagan and Gnostic prayers. The word was originally believed to cure disease.

MATTHEW 3:13-17

At that time Jesus arrived from Galilee and came to John at the Jordan to be baptized by him. But John tried to make Him change His mind. "I ought to be baptized by You," John said, "and yet You have come to me!" But Jesus answered him, "Let it be so for now. For in this way we shall do all that God requires." So John agreed. As soon as Jesus was baptized, He came up out of the water. Then heaven was opened to Him, and He saw the Spirit of God coming down like a dove and lighting on Him. Then a voice said from heaven, "This is My own dear Son, with Whom I am pleased."

ROMANS 5:2

He has brought us by faith into this experience of God's grace, in which we now live. And so we boast of the hope we have of sharing God's glory!

THE SACRAMENT OF CONFIRMATION (1285-1321)

We are sealed with the Holy Spirit.

WHAT YOU NEED:

invisible thread 18 inches long (see page 73)
a deck of cards
a drinking glass wide enough to accommodate a deck of cards
a dab of Blue Tac

WHAT THEY SEE:

The catechist gives a volunteer a free choice in selecting a card. The card is shuffled back into the deck and the deck is placed upright into a clear drinking glass on the table. Mysteriously, the volunteer's selected card rises from the glass. The card is picked up and handed out for examination.

WHAT YOU SAY:

"Clearly, humans can not on our own raise ourselves to meet God. We are sinful and full of pride. These are the main obstacles to developing a deep relationship with Him."

(Have a volunteer select a card. Return the card to the deck and maneuver it to the top of the deck (see description). Affix the string to the card with the dab of Blue Tac. Move back and manipulate the card to rise, using tension on the invisible string.)

"Confirmation gives us the gifts that we need to meet God. We rise to accept God in our lives."

(Detach the card from the string and show the card openly in your hand.)

"It looks as if this card has done amazing things but we know it's just a trick. In the sacrament of Confirmation, God blesses us with many spiritual gifts. These gifts raise us up and renew us; they remake us as disciples of Christ."

LUKE 3:21-22
After all the people had been baptized, Jesus also was baptized. While He was praying, heaven was opened, and the Holy Spirit came down upon Him in bodily form like a dove. And a voice came from heaven, "You are My own dear Son. I am pleased with You."

LUKE 12:12
For the Holy Spirit will teach you at that time what you should say.

JOHN 20:22
Then He breathed on them and said, "Receive the Holy Spirit."

JOHN 1:33
I still did not know that He was the one, but God, Who sent me to baptize with water, had said to me, "You will see the Spirit come down and stay on a man; He is the One Who baptizes with the Holy Spirit."

MANEUVERING A CARD TO THE TOP OF THE DECK

This sleight-of-hand maneuver is designed to surreptitiously move a selected card from the middle of the deck to the top. While your spectator is looking at her freely selected card, cut the remainder of the deck in your hand into 2 halves. Offer the bottom half of the deck in your left hand to your spectator and ask her to place her selected card on top of this pile. Without hesitating, drop the top half of the deck in your right hand on top of her selected card but do so in such a way as to keep a small overhang of cards on top of the spectator's selected card. By lifting this little "ledge" of cards to shuffle them into the remainder of the deck, you will thus bring the spectator's selected card to the top of the deck.

GOSPEL MAGIC HISTORY

An excellent hagiography of St. Nicholas Owen's life is Margaret Waugh's 1959 book, **Blessed Nicholas Owen: Jesuit Brother and Maker of Hiding Holes**. St. Nicholas is also a character in Antonia Fraser's book **Faith and Treason: The Story of the Gunpowder Plot**. David Herber's **The Gunpowder Plot Society** also depicts St. Nicholas' contribution to the Catholic Church.

HOW YOU DO IT:

The card rises from the deck with the assistance of a strand of invisible thread. In lieu of this, a single strand of black thread will suffice. Magicians would normally use a substance called "magician's wax" when performing this trick but Blue Tac will do. The advantage of magician's wax is that it leaves no telltale trace on the card when handed out for inspection. Affix one end of the thread to a shirt or jacket button and roll the other end into a small dab of Blue Tac. Stick the Blue Tac to the card. By holding your hands out in front of you dramatically, you can manipulate this thread. Keep your hands completely still, and lean back or turn your torso to manipulate the string. Watch the card rather than the string; this will be a less suspicious way of affecting the card.

LUKE 10:21
At that time Jesus was filled with joy by the Holy Spirit and said, "Father, Lord of heaven and earth! I thank You because You have shown to the unlearned what You have hidden from the wise and learned. Yes, Father, this was how You were pleased to have it happen."

LUKE 11:13
As bad as you are, you know how to give good things to your children. How much more, then, will the Father in heaven give the Holy Spirit to those who ask Him!

THE SACRAMENT OF THE EUCHARIST (1322-1419)

We commune with Christ and with each other.

WHAT YOU NEED:

12 poker chips
a magic marker

WHAT THEY SEE:

Twelve poker chips are placed on the table and a folded piece of paper (the magician's prediction) is placed in plain sight. Three volunteers are led through a series of instructions and come to rest on a single chip. The 3 announce where they landed and are surprised to find it's the same spot. The prediction is checked and is found to match exactly.

WHAT YOU SAY:

"During the Last Supper, Jesus instituted the sacrament of the Eucharist. When He shared His Body and Blood with His friends, He wanted us to always remember Him and the sacrifice that He made for us."

(Lay out the poker chips, making sure you keep the one marked with a cross facedown at the 6 o'clock position.)

"Let me show what I mean about coming together as a community in Christ.

(Referring to the poker chips.)

1. Please choose a number between 5 and 10.
2. Place your finger on the first chip.
3. Count your number aloud and place your finger on each as you progress around the circle and rest your finger where you land.
4. Now count the same number backwards around the circle of chips.
5. Point to the chip you've landed upon.

"If you check the prediction, you'll see that it matches the same spot you stopped on."

(Turn over all of the other chips.)

"You'll also note that none of the other poker chips have any symbols on them at all. Now, turn over the chip all of you chose. As you see, God is involved in all of our decisions."

(Hold up the chip with the cross.)

"Every Sunday, we come together as a community to worship Him and thank Him for what He did for us and what He continues to do for us. When we are together, we become one mind. We all come together, we are there for Christ."

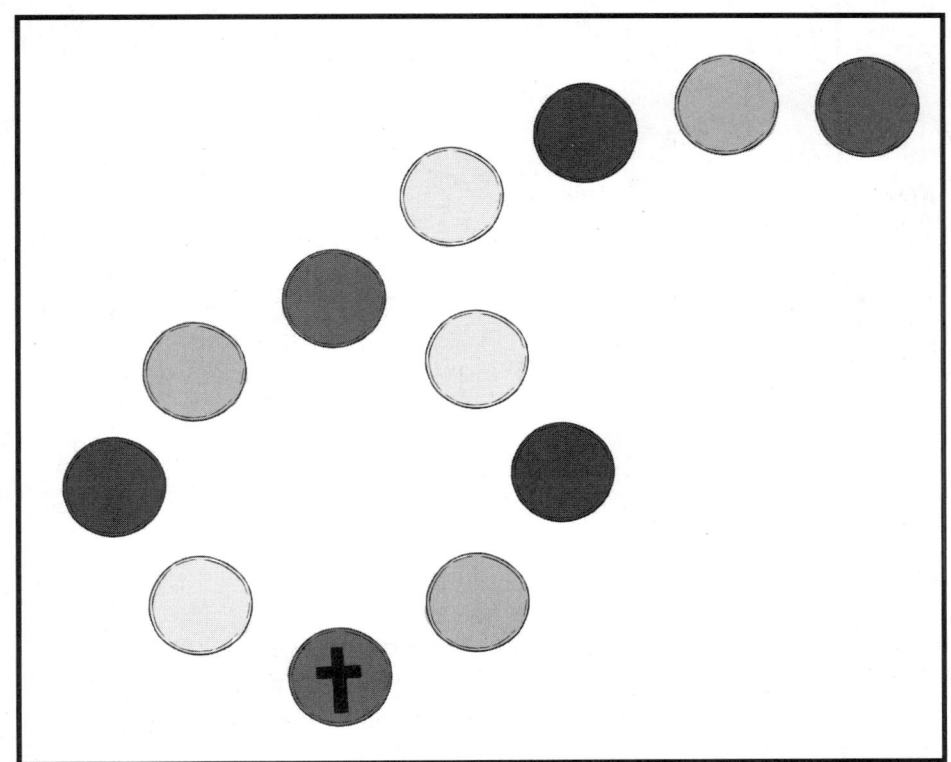

HOW YOU DO IT:

Mark one of the poker chips with a cross and place it facedown at the 6 o'clock position as in the diagram. On a separate piece of paper, draw a cross. This will be the spot upon which all volunteers will stop. Have the volunteers start on the first chip (the dark gray chip all the way to the right in the diagram.) By following the instructions listed opposite, the volunteers will always wind up on the cross chip.

CATECHETICAL TIP
Pray about your performance, asking the Spirit to guide you as you teach your class.

MATTHEW 26:17-29
On the first day of the Festival of Unleavened Bread the disciples came to Jesus and asked Him, "Where do You want us to get the Passover meal ready for You?" "Go to a certain man in the city," He said to them, "and tell Him: 'The Teacher says, My hour has come; My disciples and I will celebrate the Passover at your house.' " The disciples did as Jesus had told them and prepared the Passover meal. When it was evening, Jesus and the twelve disciples sat down to eat. During the meal Jesus said, "I tell you, one of you will betray Me." The disciples were very upset and began to ask Him, one after the other, "Surely, Lord, You don't mean me?" Jesus answered, "One who dips his bread in the dish with Me will betray me. The Son of Man will die as the Scriptures say he will, but how terrible for that man who will betray the Son of Man! It would have been better for that man if he had never been born!" Judas, the traitor, spoke up. "Surely, Teacher, You don't mean me?" he asked. Jesus answered, "So you say." While they were eating, Jesus took a piece of bread, gave a prayer of thanks, broke it, and gave it to His disciples. "Take and eat it," He said; "this is My body." Then He took a cup, gave thanks to God, and gave it to them. "Drink it, all of you," He said; "this is My blood, which seals God's covenant, My blood poured out for many for the forgiveness of sins. I tell you, I will never again drink this wine until the day I drink the new wine with you in My Father's Kingdom.

1 CORINTHIANS 11:23-29
For I received from the Lord the teaching that I passed on to you: that the Lord Jesus, on the night He was betrayed, took a piece of bread, gave thanks to God, broke it, and said, "This is My body, which is for you. Do this in memory of Me." In the same way, after the supper He took the cup and said, "This cup is God's new covenant, sealed with My blood. Whenever you drink it, do so in memory of Me." This means that every time you eat this bread and drink from this cup you proclaim the Lord's death until He comes. It follows that if one of you eats the Lord's bread or drinks from His cup in a way that dishonors Him, you are guilty of sin against the Lord's body and blood. So then, you should each examine yourself first, and then eat the bread and drink from the cup. For if you do not recognize the meaning of the Lord's body when you eat the bread and drink from the cup, you bring judgment on yourself as you eat and drink.

THE SACRAMENT OF PENANCE AND RECONCILIATION
(1422-1498)

We find healing in Christ's love and forgiveness.

WHAT YOU NEED:

a handkerchief
a small swatch of cloth exactly matching the handkerchief you are using
a pair of scissors

WHAT THEY SEE:

A handkerchief is inspected and handed back to the catechist. Using a pair of scissors, the catechist cuts a hole in the center of the handkerchief. The handkerchief is then handed out for inspection once again but no sign of the damage can be found.

WHAT YOU SAY:

"Reconciliation is a sacrament of healing. How do you think we need to be healed? Do we receive the sacrament when we have a cold or a bruise? Of course not ... it's not that kind of healing we need. But it's a similar feeling. When you are sick, what are you feeling? Now, when you've done something wrong, how do you feel?"

(Pick up the handkerchief and push it upwards into your fist. Allow the small swatch to push through. To the audience, it will appear as if it was the same handkerchief.)

"Imagine this handkerchief is us, and the sins that we commit are like the damage that you see done to this handkerchief."

(Snip off pieces of the small swatch in your hand.)

"Sins hurt us more than we might think. They make us less whole. They make us less perfect. They make us less like God."

(Dispose of the cut pieces of cloth, ball up the handkerchief, have someone blow on it, and then open it to show that it is completely intact.)

"God's love and forgiveness can heal us ... just like this handkerchief."

DANIEL 9:24
Seven times seventy years is the length of time God has set for freeing your people and your holy city from sin and evil. Sin will be forgiven and eternal justice established, so that the vision and the prophecy will come true, and the holy Temple will be rededicated.

MATTHEW 6:14
If you forgive others the wrongs they have done to you, your Father in heaven will also forgive you. But if you do not forgive others, then your Father will not forgive the wrongs you have done.

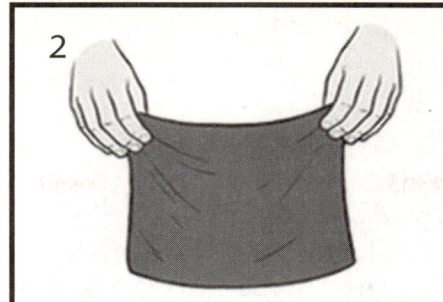
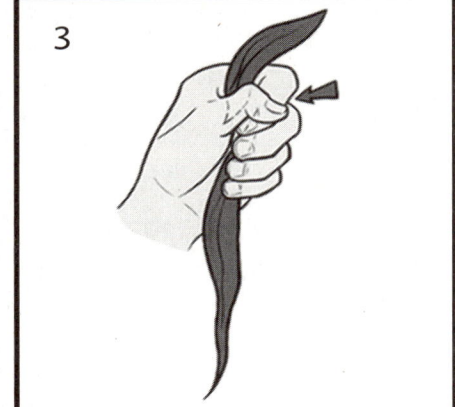

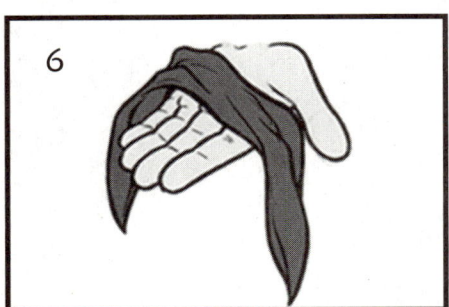
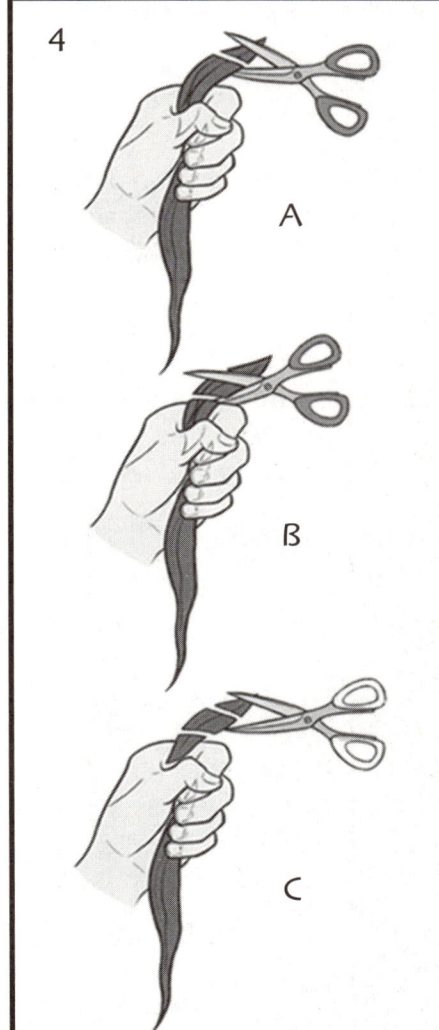

HOW YOU DO IT:

Palm the extra swatch of cloth in your right hand before starting the performance. Have a volunteer inspect the handkerchief. Take it back from her and pretend to push it through your fist, allowing its center to poke upwards. Don't actually push the center of the handkerchief through your fist; instead push the extra swatch of cloth through. Pick up the scissors and cut the very tip off. It will seem as though you are cutting the handkerchief, but actually you will only be cutting the extra swatch.

Make a second cut about halfway down the swatch peak. Pretend to make the third cut but, instead, allow the remainder of the swatch to simply fall to the table. Pick up the pieces that you've cut off and place them under the handkerchief. While your hand is hidden, push the pieces into your sleeve or under your watchband. This will let you end clean; you will only have the unmarred cloth in your hand. Ball up the handkerchief and have your volunteer blow across your closed fist. At that, open your hand and reveal the intact handkerchief.

> It is in pardoning that
> we are pardoned.
> — St. Francis of Assisi

MARK 2:8-12
At once Jesus knew what they were thinking, so He said to them, "Why do you think such things? Is it easier to say to this paralyzed man, 'Your sins are forgiven,' or to say, 'Get up, pick up your mat, and walk'? I will prove to you, then, that the Son of Man has authority on earth to forgive sins." So He said to the paralyzed man, "I tell you, get up, pick up your mat, and go home!" While they all watched, the man got up, picked up his mat, and hurried away. They were all completely amazed and praised God, saying, "We have never seen anything like this!"

THE ANOINTING OF THE SICK (1499-1532)

We are truly healed in Christ.

WHAT YOU NEED:

2 lengths of thread approximately 18 inches long
a pair of scissors

WHAT THEY SEE:

The catechist shows a piece of thread and cuts it into little pieces. He rolls the little pieces into a small ball and then unravels it. To the surprise of the audience, the string is restored.

WHAT YOU SAY:

"Many Catholics and non-Catholics believe that the Anointing of the Sick is "Last Rites." This might have been true especially at a time when severe illness inevitably meant death but the truth is that the Anointing of the Sick is simply offered when someone is sick. Let me show you what I mean."

(Perform the trick as described in the How You Do It section.)

"We, as a believing community, accept the healing power of prayer, whether that healing is physical or spiritual. The truth is, the Anointing of the Sick doesn't release the soul. Instead, it releases sin's grasp on our souls. It heals us; it restores us to God just like this string is healed and restored."

MATTHEW 9:28
When Jesus had gone indoors, the 2 blind men came to Him, and He asked them, "Do you believe that I can heal you?" "Yes, Sir!" they answered.

MATTHEW 10:1
Jesus called His twelve disciples together and gave them authority to drive out evil spirits and to heal every disease and every sickness.

MATTHEW 10:8
Heal the sick, bring the dead back to life, heal those who suffer from dreaded skin diseases, and drive out demons. You have received without paying, so give without being paid.

MATTHEW 12:9-13
Jesus left that place and went to a synagogue, where there was a man who had a paralyzed hand. Some people were there who wanted to accuse Jesus of doing wrong, so they asked him, "Is it against our Law to heal on the Sabbath?" Jesus answered, "What if one of you has a sheep and it falls into a deep hole on the Sabbath? Will you not take hold of it and lift it out? And a human being is worth much more than a sheep! So then, our Law does allow us to help someone on the Sabbath." Then He said to the man with the paralyzed hand, "Stretch out your hand." He stretched it out, and it became well again, just like the other one.

MATTHEW 13:15
Because their minds are dull, and they have stopped up their ears and have closed their eyes. Otherwise, their eyes would see, their ears would hear, their minds would understand, and they would turn to me, says God, and I would heal them.

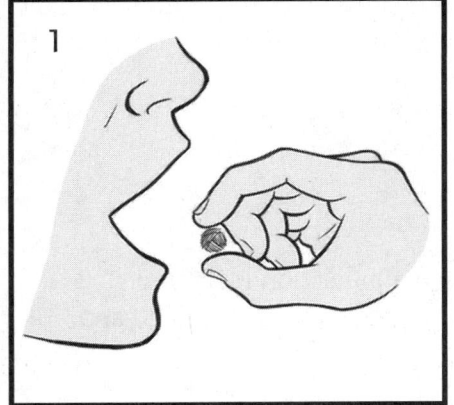
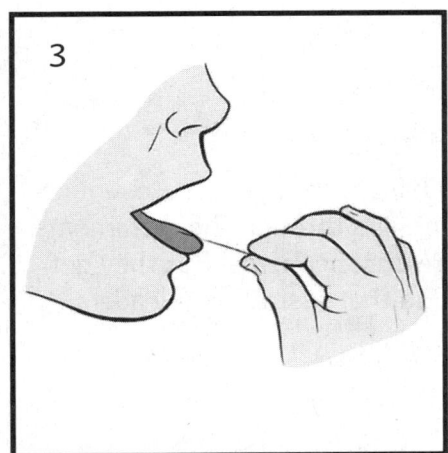
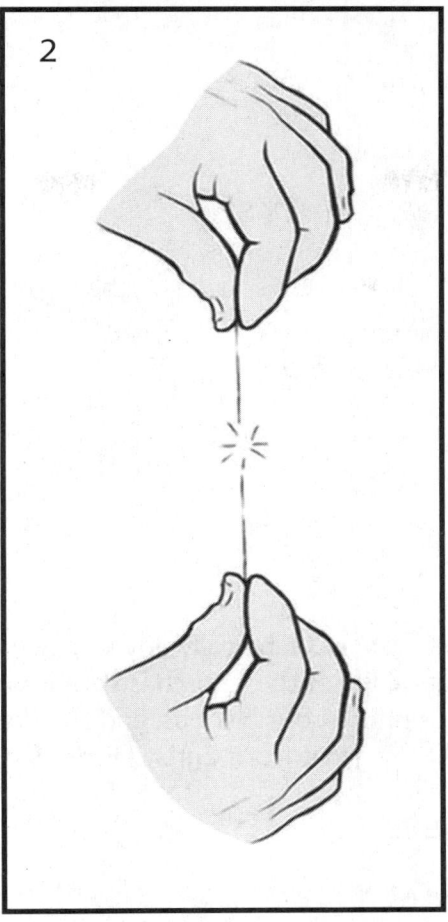

HOW YOU DO IT:

This is an old trick referred to as "The Gypsy's Thread." Roll up one of the strings and place it in your mouth prior to the performace. When you perform the trick, either break the other thread into little pieces or use a pair of scissors. Collect the pieces together and pretend to lick your fingers as if gathering saliva to "glue" the strings together. Use one lick to put the small ball of many little pieces into your mouth and another to take the intact string out.

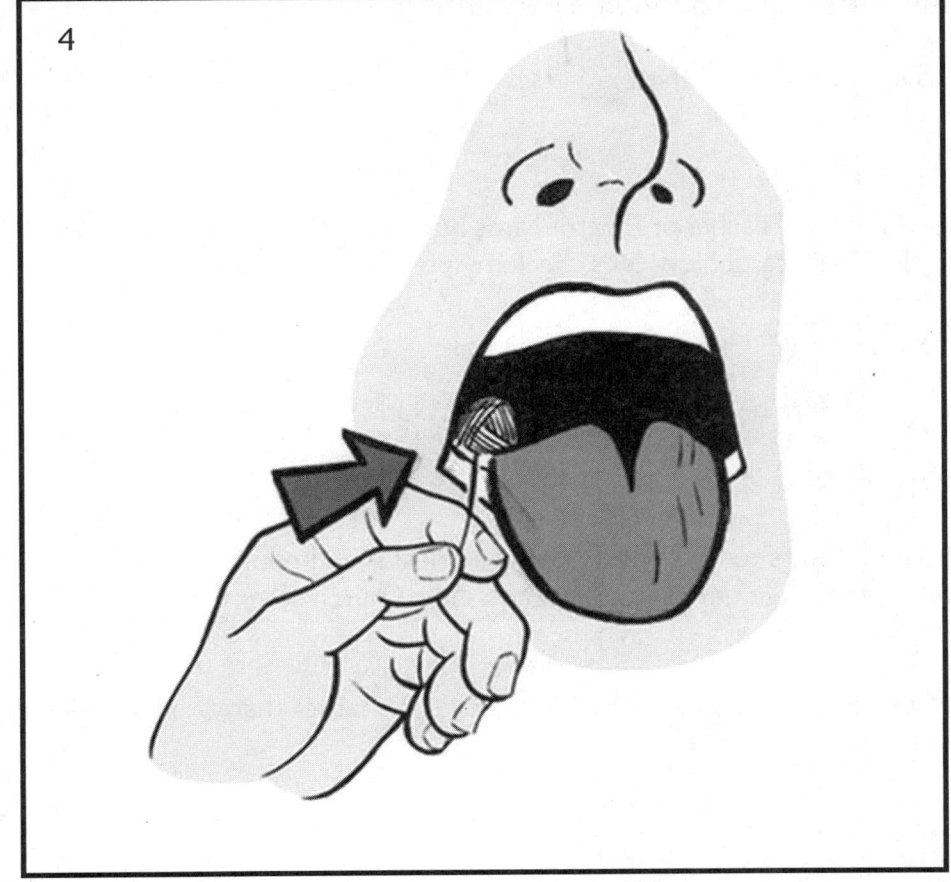

TEACHING TIPS

You can maintain discipline best by clearly demarcating a point past which your class should not encroach. This will help you maintain order and keep prying eyes away from your magic equipment.

The best tool in a teacher's bag of tricks is empathy. Remember what it was like when you were a child and proceed accordingly.

Give yourself plenty of time to set up for your performance. On-site preparation can take as long as the actual performance.

THE SACRAMENT OF HOLY ORDERS (1536-1600)

We are invited to serve the community of believers.

WHAT YOU NEED:

profession cards (cutout page 239)
an envelope
a black magic marker
an old 8-inch by 10-inch photo
   of a boy with priest image
   glued on back

WHAT THEY SEE:

Six cards are displayed on the tabletop and a prediction is set aside. A volunteer is asked to choose a card. The prediction is examined and found to be an exact match.

WHAT YOU SAY:

"Who dispenses most sacraments? It's true that technically any Christian can baptize, but priests are required for the other sacraments. The sacramental life of the Church is very important. It is through the sacraments that we principally experience God. Our priests, our bishops, and the Pope are our shepherds. But they get their authority from the Apostles and they got it from Christ Himself. It is God that sustains our leaders."

    (Motion to the cards on the table before you.)

"Please choose a number between 1 and 6."

    (Whatever number the volunteer chooses, direct her to the Priest card.)

"You chose the Priest card. You could have chosen any of these others ..."

    (Turn over the remaining cards.)

"You could have chosen the Chef, Artist, Fireman, Teacher or Doctor cards but, instead, you chose the Priest card. I knew you were going to choose the Priest card. Now, let's check my prediction."

    (Open the prediction envelope and show the infant's photo.)

"As you see ... this is a photo of a priest long before he was ordained ... what? Don't you believe me?"

    (Turn the photo around to show priest image.)

"Does anyone here know a priest? Who here wants to be a priest? Being a priest is an important job in the Church. Without them, we wouldn't be able to experience the sacraments. The Church community needs priests. Always keep priests in your prayers."

TIP: When looking for a volunteer for this trick, it's best to ask a boy to assist you rather than a girl as only males are allowed to become priests in the Catholic Church.

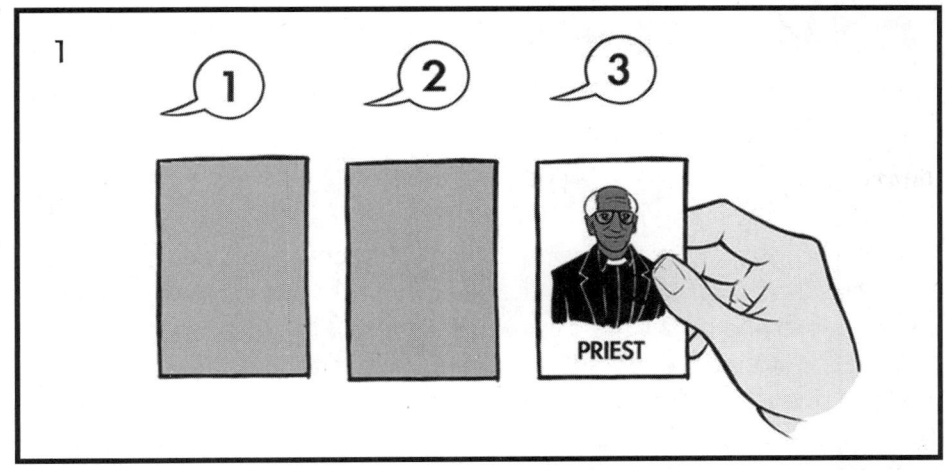

HOW YOU DO IT:

The Priest card should be third card from the left. The other cards do not need a specific positioning. This trick is another example of a "force." No matter what the volunteer chooses, he will always be directed to the Priest card.

When a volunteer is asked to choose between 1 and 6, the volunteer will generally choose 3. In this case, simply count to the third card and turn it over. The second most popular choice will be 4. In this case, simply start counting from the right-hand side and turn over the Priest card. If the volunteer choose 1, 2 or 6, spell out the number starting from the left-hand side. This will inevitably make the volunteer land on the Priest card. If the volunteer chooses 5, spell out the word "f-i-v-e" starting from the right-hand side.

> "The Catholic faith never changes. But the language and mode of manifesting this one faith can change according to peoples, times and places." —Cardinal Francis Arinzet

131

THE SACRAMENT OF MATRIMONY (1601-1666)

God's love is abundant and without limit.

WHAT YOU NEED:

clear adhesive tape
a deck of cards
a pair of scissors

WHAT THEY SEE:

The catechist shows 5 playing cards. He counts them aloud and then discards 3 of them, dropping them to the floor. He recounts the cards in his hand but is surprised to find he still has 5 cards. He discards 3 more and then recounts what he has in his hands; he still has 5 cards. The catechist continues in this way and always has 5 cards in his hands despite the fact that he is discarding cards. Finally, he discards all of the cards in his hands as he stands in a pile of cards on the floor around him.

WHAT YOU SAY:

"Does anyone here want to get married? Is anyone here already married? Later on, as you get older, you might find a person you will want to marry. You will want to live with this person and start your own family. How do you think this happens? What makes you want to live and spend time together? That's right! It's love. When you love someone, it doesn't matter how much you give to the person, you will always have enough."

(Count 5 cards and then discard 3 of them.)

"The more you give, the more you have. This is impossible for anything else on Earth."

(Count 5 cards and then discard 3 of them.)

"Nothing that a human being can do can last forever, but with God's help, anything is possible."

(Count 5 cards and then discard 3 of them.)

"It's like these cards. If I love someone, I can give them a bunch of my cards. But, if I give them to the person I love, I still have more."

(Count 5 cards and then discard 3 of them.)

"Love can't be depleted. It can't run out. It's always there, if it's true love."

(Count 5 cards and then discard 3 of them.)

"The more you give, the more you have. Again and again. Love overflows."

(Count 5 cards and then discard 3 of them.)

"Love is patient and kind. It is not jealous or conceited or proud. Love is not ill-mannered or selfish or irritable. Love does not keep a record of wrongs. Love is not happy with evil, but is happy with the truth. Love never gives up, and its faith, hope, and patience never fail. Love is eternal."

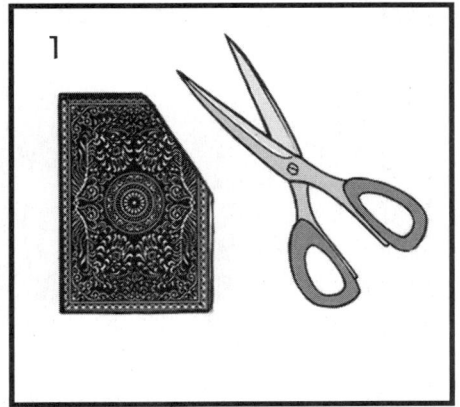

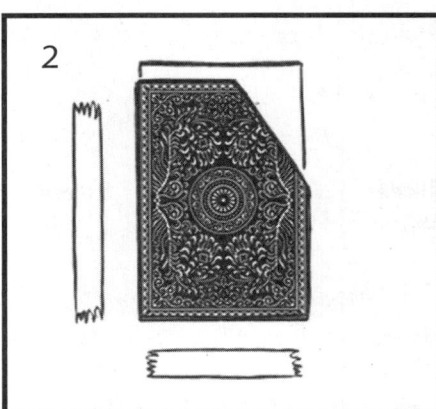

HOW YOU DO IT:

This trick is made possible with the help of several gimmicked cards. A gimmicked card is a folder made of 2 cards that are taped together. The gimmicked card can hide more cards within it while still handling like a single card. To make a gimmicked card, take 5 cards and cut off a corner of each as described in the diagram. Next, take a card with the corner cut off and tape it to the back of a card with the corner intact along the bottom and left side so that the design on the back matches perfectly and the 2 cards appear to be one. Repeat this with all of the other 4 sets of cards. Load 3 extra cards into each of these gimmicked cards.

To perform this trick, handle and count the packaged cards as if they were individual cards. When you count the 3 cards to discard them, you're actually only removing 3 of the cards stuffed inside the "packet" of cards. Once a packet is empty, simply discard it into the growing pile of cards at your feet. If you would prefer, you can use a top hat or a small, decorated box to collect the discarded cards.

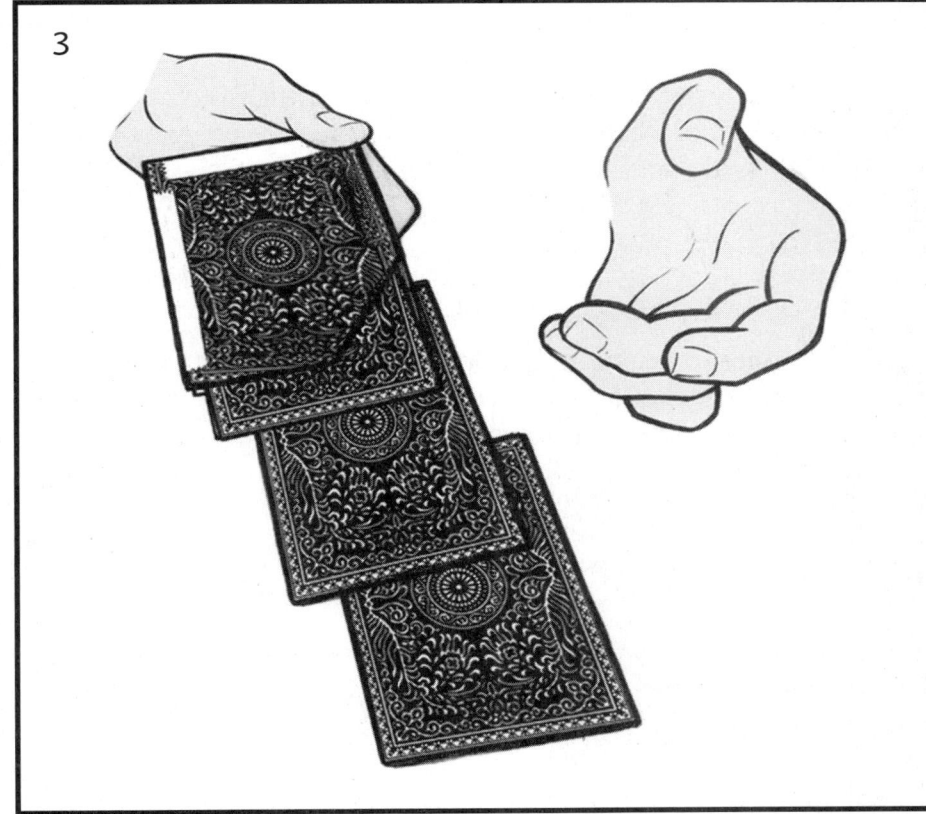

1 CORINTHIANS 13:1-10

I may be able to speak the languages of human beings and even of angels, but if I have no love, my speech is no more than a noisy gong or a clanging bell. I may have the gift of inspired preaching; I may have all knowledge and understand all secrets; I may have all the faith needed to move mountains—but if I have no love, I am nothing. I may give away everything I have, and even give up my body to be burned—but if I have no love, this does me no good. Love is patient and kind; it is not jealous or conceited or proud; love is not ill-mannered or selfish or irritable; love does not keep a record of wrongs; love is not happy with evil, but is happy with the truth. Love never gives up; and its faith, hope, and patience never fail. Love is eternal. There are inspired messages, but they are temporary; there are gifts of speaking in strange tongues, but they will cease; there is knowledge, but it will pass. For our gifts of knowledge and of inspired messages are only partial; but when what is perfect comes, then what is partial will disappear.

SACRAMENTALS (1667-1679)

God invites us to experience His love in our lives.

WHAT YOU NEED:

corrugated cardboard or 1/2 inch ply or solid wood
duct tape or nails
fabric and glue, or paint to decorate the inside of the box
possible production items: goldfish bowl, flowers, fake rocks (made of foam rubber), a rabbit, folding umbrellas, books, handkerchiefs streamers, balls, candy →

WHAT THEY SEE:

A box is shown to be completely empty and then closed. Immediately, the box is opened once again and a seemingly endless supply of objects is pulled out.

You're limited only by your imagination and the dimensions of the box. I would definitely not recommend using sacramentals as production items as it would be sacrilegious to make light of them.

WHAT YOU SAY:

"Being Catholic means living a life of prayer and service to help us orient our lives towards God. One of the magnificent aspects of being Catholic is our constant daily reminders including what we call 'sacramentals.' Sacramentals include: rosaries, holy water, icons, relics, scapulars, statues, medals, saint cards, crucifixes and blessed candles. Many of us already have these things in our homes. When we see, touch or use them in our daily devotions we are preparing a place for God in our lives."

(Show the box to be empty by opening the front door.)

"Sacramentals serve as focuses and reminders. When we keep them in our lives and use them appropriately, we will receive many, many blessings. The blessings we receive are a flood. God never stops the flow of these beautiful and wondrous things in our lives."

(Close front lid and then open top to beginning pulling out production items.)

MARK 9:29
"Only prayer can drive this kind (of demon) out," answered Jesus; "nothing else can."

ROMANS 5:21
So then, just as sin ruled by means of death, so also God's grace rules by means of righteousness, leading us to eternal life through Jesus Christ our Lord.

ROMANS 6:1
What shall we say, then? Should we continue to live in sin so that God's grace will increase?

ROMANS 6:14
Sin must not be your master; for you do not live under law but under God's grace. What, then? Shall we sin, because we are not under law but under God's grace? By no means!

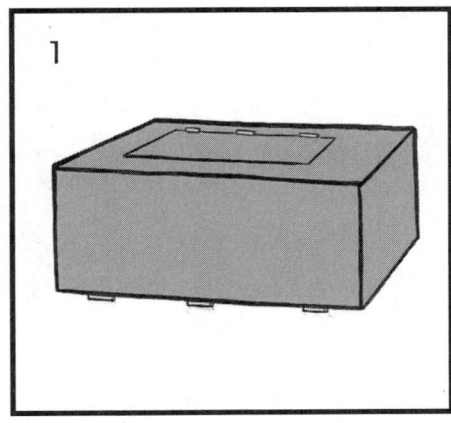

HOW YOU DO IT:

Assemble a box approximately the size of a shoe box. A box with a length of 18 inches, a height of 12 inches, and a depth of 12 inches requires a mirror that is 16.9 inches by 18 inches. For those who are not inclined to cabinetry, you can make such a box from corrugated cardboard. A mirror should be glued or taped in place, at a 45-degree angle to the bottom of the box. The mirror's top edge should be flush and slightly inset from the top, front edge of the box. The mirror's bottom should be affixed to the back bottom edge of the inside of the box. This positions the mirror at a proper angle to create the illusion of empty space. Though it is common to use a striped pattern in the interior of the box to give the illusion of empty space, it is not absolutely necessary.

The box should have 2 hinged openings; one at the top (cut into the middle of the top's surface) to allow access to objects and one in the front to demonstrate the box's "innocence." The front hinged opening is actually the whole front side of the box. To perform this illusion, first open the front door. There's no real need to point out that the box is empty as it only raises suspicions when one does so. Close the front lid and then open the top to access the stored items.

If you choose to produce a live animal, you will need to include a few breathing holes. Make sure that you inconvenience and stress the animal as little as possible by not keeping it in the box for too long.

You may adjust the dimensions of the box to fit your needs. The Pythagorean theorem dictates that in a right triangle the square of the hypotenuse, (in this case the height of the mirror) is equal to the sum of the squares of the other 2 sides (the height and depth of the box). Thus, determining the height of the mirror held at a 45-degree angle will determine the depth and height of the box.

CHRISTIAN FUNERALS (1680-1690)

Death is not the end.

WHAT YOU NEED:

7 blocks of wood
  each drilled with 2 holes
2 pieces of clothesline rope
a pair of scissors
friction tape

WHAT THEY SEE:

Seven wooden blocks, each with 2 holes are strung together with 2 ropes. A volunteer selects one of the ropes and the other is wrapped around all of the blocks and then tied with a simple knot. The catechist and the volunteer hold the ropes while the catechist cuts the selected rope. After that, the catechist pulls out a completely restored rope.

WHAT YOU SAY:

"It's always sad when we lose someone. But we Christians understand death as an opportunity for perfect peace and rest in God. We are not bodies that have souls. We are souls that temporarily have bodies. We are immortal. We can't really die. Despite our sad feelings, we know that those who have died are now with their Creator. Nothing in the world could be better than this."

(Allow the blocks to rest lengthwise on the table. Lift the entire assemblage into the air and, when returning them to the table, turn the first and last blocks so that the ropes are twisted.)

"The dead are truly happy. We should celebrate and not be sad. Imagine that these ropes are our lives. It seems that our lives can end ... just like a rope being cut."

(Tie one of the ropes around all the blocks of wood as in diagram. Take the scissors and cut the remaining rope. Then remove the rope from the assemblage and show that the rope is still intact.)

"But it's only an illusion. An illusion is something that seems real, but isn't. We Christians know that death is meaningless to us. Though a life looks cut short ... our souls live on forever. Christian funerals are not an acknowledgment of death but a celebration of life and of eternal life yet to come."

PSALM 23:1-6

The Lord is my shepherd; I have everything I need. He lets me rest in fields of green grass and leads me to quiet pools of fresh water. He gives me new strength. He guides me in the right paths, as He has promised. Even if I go through the deepest darkness, I will not be afraid, Lord, for You are with me. Your shepherd's rod and staff protect me. You prepare a banquet for me, where all my enemies can see me; You welcome me as an honored guest and fill my cup to the brim. I know that Your goodness and love will be with me all my life; and Your house will be my home as long as I live.

MATTHEW 27:57-60

When it was evening, a rich man from Arimathea arrived; his name was Joseph, and he also was a disciple of Jesus. He went into the presence of Pilate and asked for the body of Jesus. Pilate gave orders for the body to be given to Joseph. So Joseph took it, wrapped it in a new linen sheet, and placed it in his own tomb, which he had just recently dug out of solid rock. Then he rolled a large stone across the entrance to the tomb and went away.

Ave Maria, gratia plena, Dominus tecum, benedicta tu in mulieribus, et benedictus fructus ventris tui, Jesus. Sancta Maria, Mater Dei, ora pro nobis peccatoribus, nunc et in hora mortis nostrae. Amen

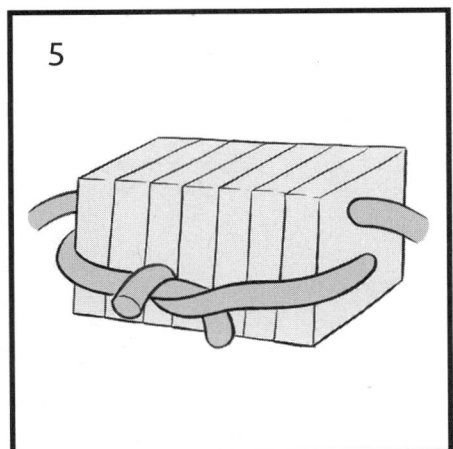

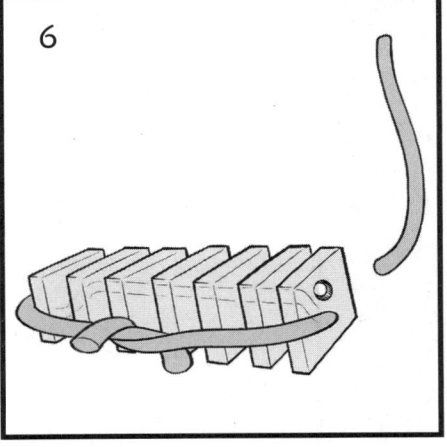

HOW YOU DO IT:

Cut 7 pieces out of a 1/2-inch thick sheet of solid wood. The dimensions should be 6-inches by 3-inches by 1/2 inch. Drill 2 holes. To soften clothesline rope, simply remove the center strands of string and then wash the ropes in a washing machine. Pass the clothesline through the holes as shown in the diagram. When flexible, cover the ends of the rope with friction tape.

When performing, allow the blocks to rest lengthwise on the table. Lift the entire assemblage into the air and, when returning it to the table, twist the first and last blocks. This will twist the ropes between the end pieces and the rest of the blocks, allowing you to cut what appears to be one rope but will actually be the other.

HAIL MARY

Hail Mary, full of grace. Our Lord is with you. Blessed are you among women, and blessed is the fruit of your womb, Jesus. Holy Mary, Mother of God, pray for us sinners, now and at the hour of our death. Amen.

PRAYERS OF COMMENDATION

Go forth, Christian soul, from this world in the name of God the Almighty Father, Who created you, in the name of Jesus Christ, Son of the Living God, Who suffered for you, in the name of the Holy Spirit, Who was poured out upon you. May you live in peace this day, may your home be with God in Zion, with Mary, the Virgin Mother of God, with Joseph and all the angels and saints.

Part 3:
LIFE IN CHRIST

What the Lord has commanded us: "Whoever wishes to come after Me must deny himself" seems hard and difficult. Yet it isn't either hard or difficult because the One Who commands it is the One Who helps us to fulfill what He commands. For if the psalm is true, that: "according to the words of Your lips I have pursued difficult paths", so also are true the words of Jesus: "My yoke is easy and My burden light." For anything hard in the command, love turns to sweetness. We know well what marvels love can accomplish, (though there are also times when love is of doubtful worth and is depraved). Yet how many difficulties will not men endure, what humiliating and unendurable treatment will they not suffer if only they might attain to what they love!

— St. Augustine, "Sermon 96"

MAN: THE IMAGE OF GOD (1701-1715)

We are reflections of God's love.

WHAT YOU NEED:

2 tablespoons
a large handkerchief

WHAT THEY SEE:

The catechist displays a common household spoon and places it under a handkerchief. He takes another spoon and hands it out for inspection. He retrieves it and immediately drops it onto the table. It is shown to be bent at a severe angle. When the other spoon is examined, it is shown to be similarly bent.

WHAT YOU SAY:

"We are always hearing about how we humans are made in God's image. What does that mean? Does it mean that God has 2 arms, 2 legs and 2 eyes? Of course not. When we say that we are made in His image, it means that we are made in His image of love. We would be very unfortunate creatures if we were made incapable of love. But because we can love each other and return God's love, we say that we are made in His image."

"Let's see what it would be like to share in God's image of love. God already loved you even before you were born. As we grow and live, we come to an understanding of how we are to love God. Love affects both people in a relationship. The longer is lasts, the stronger and deeper it becomes, the more necessary and indispensable it becomes."

"Let's say that love affects this spoon."

> (Show a spoon and place it under the handkerchief on the table. Secretly bend the spoon to a 90-degree angle under the cover of the handkerchief as you place it down.)

"When you meet people who have experienced love, they are noticeably different. The same is also true of the spoon. As you see, it's different now. It's been changed."

> (Show that the spoon has been bent.)

"Let's see what's happened to its partner."

> (Lift the handkerchief and show the spoon has also been bent.)

"As you see, it's been affected also. Love changes all ... if we allow it to enter into our souls."

GENESIS 1:26-30

Then God said, "And now We will make human beings; they will be like Us and resemble Us. They will have power over the fish, the birds, and all animals, domestic and wild, large and small." So God created human beings, making them to be like Himself. He created them male and female, blessed them, and said, "Have many children, so that your descendants will live all over the earth and bring it under their control. I am putting you in charge of the fish, the birds, and all the wild animals. I have provided all kinds of grain and all kinds of fruit for you to eat; but for all the wild animals and for all the birds I have provided grass and leafy plants for food"—and it was done.

COLOSSIANS 3:10
Put on the new self. This is the new being which God, its Creator, is constantly renewing in His own image, in order to bring you to a full knowledge of himself.

2 CORINTHIANS 3:18
All of us, then, reflect the glory of the Lord with uncovered faces; and that same glory, coming from the Lord, Who is the Spirit, transforms us into His likeness in an ever greater degree of glory.

HOW YOU DO IT:

Show one of the spoons and place it under the large handkerchief. Before retracting your arm, secretly bend the spoon to create a right angle. Make sure the spoon's lines aren't noticeable under the handkerchief.

Hold the second spoon with the thumb and forefinger of your dominant hand and demonstrate that it is, in fact, solid and largely inflexible. Rest the bottom of the spoon's handle against the base of your pinky and very lightly hold the tip of the spoon's bowl with your other hand's thumb and forefinger.

Turn your body so that your side is towards your audience. As you do so, keep the spoon's bowl perpendicular and unmoving, but push up with the base of your other palm, effectively bending the spoon. As soon as you bend it, start waving the spoon quickly so as to not allow your audience to see the spoon's bent angle.

After a few seconds, drop the spoon which is now clearly bent into the middle of the table. Next, have the volunteer pick up the handkerchief to expose the "sympathetically" bent spoon under it.

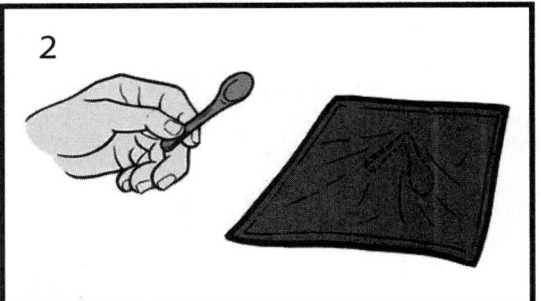
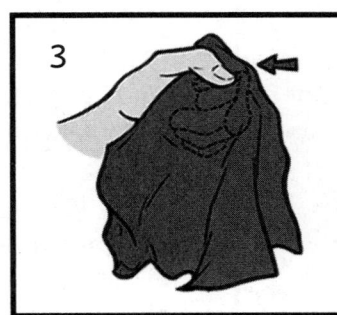

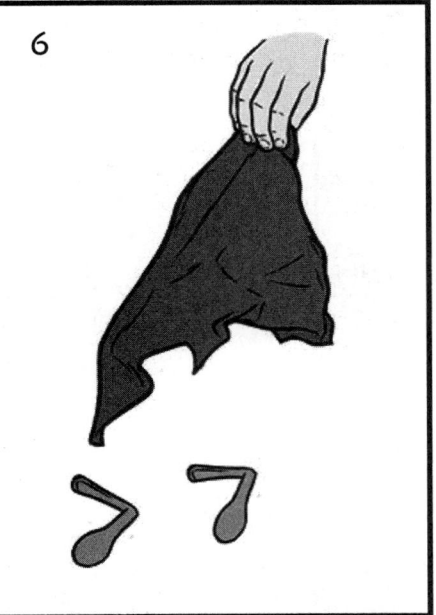
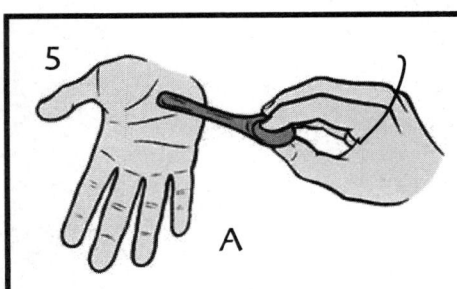
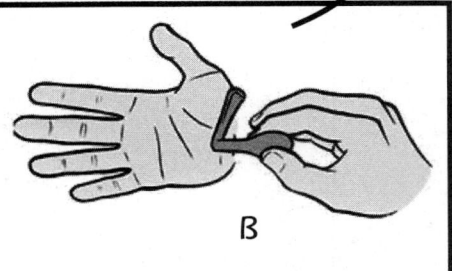

THE BEATITUDES (1716-1729)

Christ explains how we must behave towards each other.

WHAT YOU NEED:

a quarter or half-dollar
the penny is borrowed

WHAT THEY SEE:

The catechist borrows a single penny from a volunteer and rubs it against his elbow in the hope of making it disappear. He seemingly fails, but when he opens his hand the penny has mysteriously changed into a quarter.

WHAT YOU SAY:

"Jesus gave us the Beatitudes as guides of how to adjust our behavior. He wants us to be humble, reverent, merciful, resilient, pure of heart, happy, and brave peacemakers."

(Palm a quarter in your left hand. Borrow a penny from a spectator and hold it in your right hand. Bend your left arm and hold your left shoulder with your left hand. Press the penny against your left elbow and rub it. Drop the coin and pick it up with your left hand. Palm it as you pretend to transfer it to your right hand. Transfer the quarter to your right hand instead of the penny.)

"And for our efforts, He will give us great rewards in Heaven. In fact, He will give us His kingdom as our inheritance. He will comfort us and He will give us everything that God has promised us. He will be completely satisfied with us!"

(Place your left hand on your neck again and drop the penny into your collar as you continue rubbing the quarter in your right hand on your left elbow.)

"He will be merciful to us! We will see God! He will call us His children! He will make us lights to the whole world and salt of the earth! All will see us and praise our Father in Heaven!"

(After a few seconds of rubbing, expose the quarter.)

"He asks only a penny's worth of effort from us ... and for that he will give us something so much more worthwhile."

MATTHEW 5:1-16

Jesus saw the crowds and went up a hill, where he sat down. His disciples gathered around Him and He began to teach them: Happy are those who know they are spiritually poor; the Kingdom of Heaven belongs to them! Happy are those who mourn; God will comfort them! Happy are those who are humble; they will receive what God has promised! Happy are those whose greatest desire is to do what God requires; God will satisfy them fully! Happy are those who are merciful to others; God will be merciful to them! Happy are the pure in heart; they will see God! Happy are those who work for peace; God will call them His children! Happy are those who are persecuted because they do what God requires; the

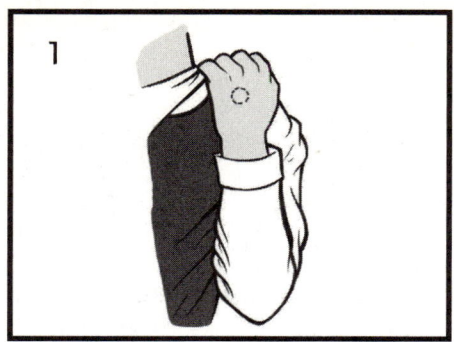

HOW YOU DO IT:

Before starting the trick, palm a quarter in your left hand. To learn how to palm a coin, see page 195.

Borrow a penny and hold it in your right hand. Announce that you will make it disappear. Bend your left arm and hold your left shoulder with your left hand. Press the penny against your left elbow and rub it vigorously as if you are hoping that it would somehow disappear. Drop the coin to the floor "accidentally." Retrieve the coin with your left hand and palm it as you pretend to transfer it to your right hand. Pass the quarter to your right hand instead. Place your left hand on your neck again. Hide the penny in your collar as you continue rubbing the quarter in your right hand on your left elbow. After a few seconds of rubbing, expose the quarter. I recommend giving the quarter to the volunteer in place of the penny; generosity will increase your popularity with your audience.

In necessasariis, unitas; In dubiis, libertas; in omnibus, caritas.

In things essential, unity; in doubtful, liberty; in all things, charity.
—Thomas à Kempis, *Imitation of Christ*

CATECHETICAL TIP
Pray about your performance, asking the Spirit to guide you as you teach your class.

MATTHEW 5:1-16 – (continued)
Kingdom of heaven belongs to them! Happy are you when people insult you and persecute you and tell all kinds of evil lies against you because you are My followers. Be happy and glad, for a great reward is kept for you in Heaven. This is how the prophets who lived before you were persecuted. You are like salt for the whole human race. But if salt loses its saltiness, there is no way to make it salty again. It has become worthless, so it is thrown out and people trample on it. You are like light for the whole world. A city built on a hill cannot be hid. No one lights a lamp and puts it under a bowl; instead it is put on the lampstand, where it gives light for everyone in the house. In the same way your light must shine before people, so that they will see the good things you do and praise your Father in Heaven.

MAN'S FREEDOM (1730-1748)

Sin binds and restricts us.

WHAT YOU NEED:

a 6-foot piece of rope

WHAT THEY SEE:

A piece of rope is held out for examination and is tied tightly around the catechist's wrists. The catechist slowly opens his hands upwards and, immediately, the rope slips off his hands without a struggle.

WHAT YOU SAY:

"Sometimes our sins weigh us down and make it impossible to love God, others and ourselves. Why? Sins make us self-centered. Pride is frequently the cause of our sins. That's what happens when we think that it is acceptable for us to do something wrong but still condemn other people for doing the same thing."

(Ask a spectator to tie your hands together as described in the How You Do It section.)

"Sins, like this rope, stop us from loving and caring. But, with God's help, with God's grace, we can escape our sins and live like authentic children of God."

(Open your hands and the rope will loosen to release your wrists. Bring fingertips together, towards your body, and down, rotating wrists in a final flourish.)

GENESIS 3:1-7

Now the snake was the most cunning animal that the Lord God had made. The snake asked the woman, "Did God really tell you not to eat fruit from any tree in the garden?" "We may eat the fruit of any tree in the garden," the woman answered, "except the tree in the middle of it. God told us not to eat the fruit of that tree or even touch it; if we do, we will die." The snake replied, "That's not true; you will not die. God said that because He knows that when you eat it, you will be like God and know what is good and what is bad." The woman saw how beautiful the tree was and how good its fruit would be to eat, and she thought how wonderful it would be to become wise. So she took some of the fruit and ate it. Then she gave some to her husband, and he also ate it. As soon as they had eaten it, they were given understanding and realized that they were naked; so they sewed fig leaves together and covered themselves.

DEUTERONOMY 30:1

I have now given you a choice between a blessing and a curse. When all these things have happened to you, and you are living among the nations where the Lord your God has scattered you, you will remember the choice I gave you.

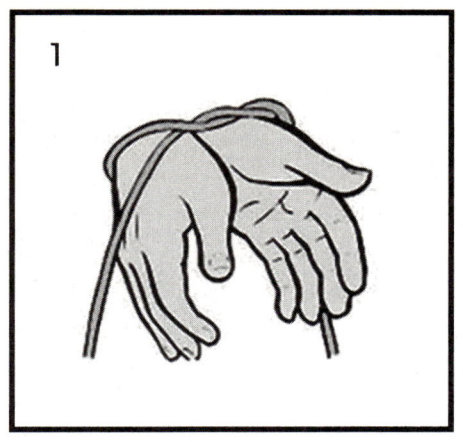 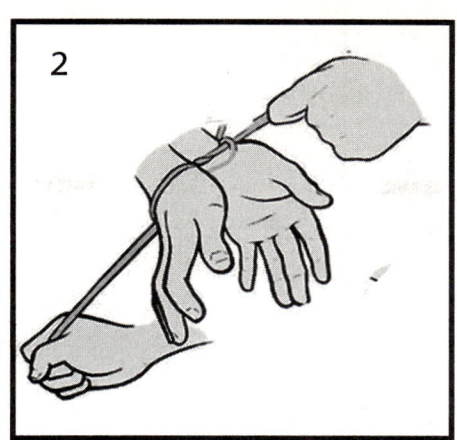
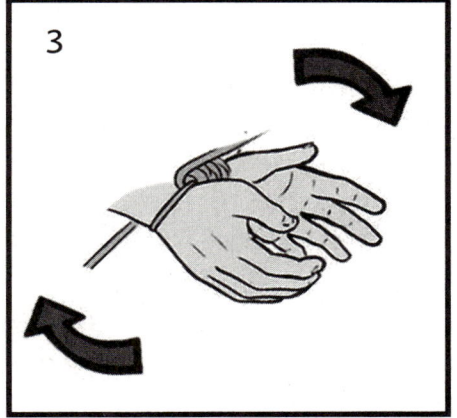 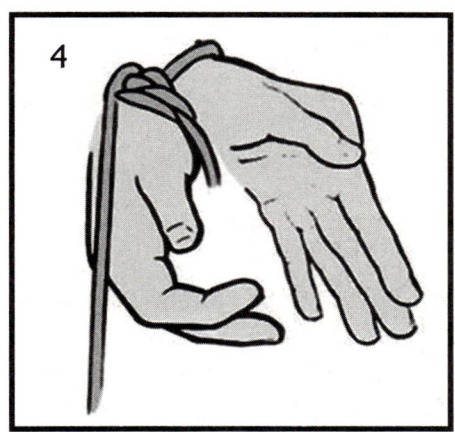
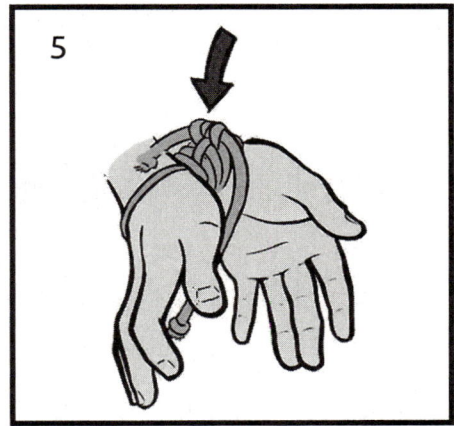 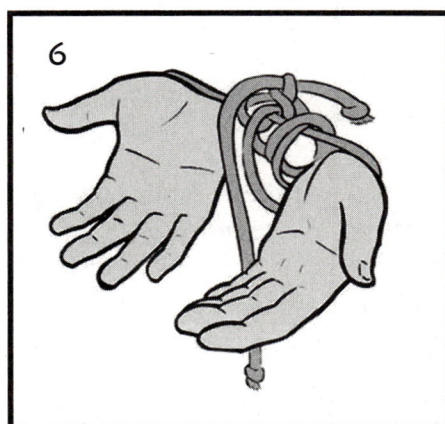
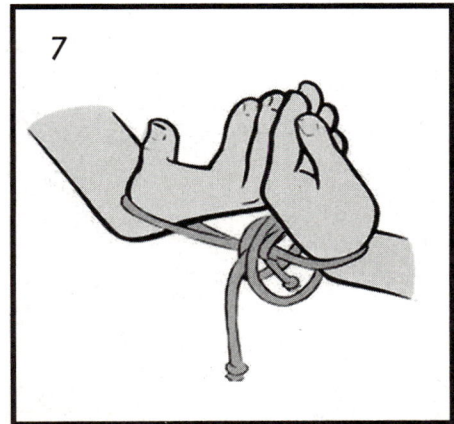 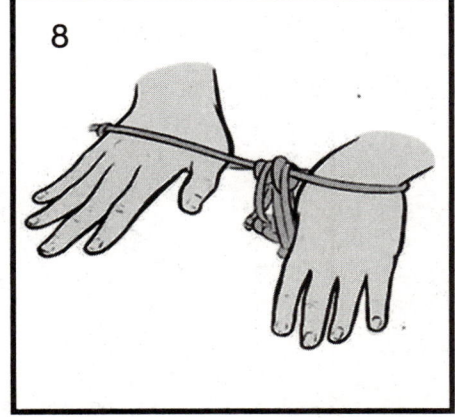

HOW YOU DO IT:

I'm unsure who invented this trick but I attribute it to the British magician, Ali Bongo, who taught it to me. Use a 4-foot piece of soft rope with the ends carefully taped up.

1. Tie a loose overhand knot in a piece of rope.
2. Place your hands into the loop.
3. Keep your wrists pressed together as tightly as possible.

If you release the pressure on your wrists you will be truly tied. You will have a great deal of difficulty releasing yourself.

4. Ask a volunteer to take both ends of the rope and pull them, tightening them against your wrists.
5. The end in his right hand goes through your arms and down and around your wrists. The other end of the rope goes in the opposite direction. He can alternate which end is used but ultimately the entire rope will need to be used up.
6. What remains of the ends are tied in at least 2 more tight, overhand knots.
7. Move the thumbs away from each other and the pinkies toward each other as if you were opening a book in your hands. This will release the tension on the ropes and allow you to escape.
8. After ropes have loosened bring fingertips together, towards your body, and down, rotating the wrists in a final flourish. You can let the ropes drop off if you wish.

This is a very visual and even graceful escape if performed correctly. Even if the ropes are tied tightly, one barely has to struggle at all; the ropes will simply fall away from your wrists as you open your palms.

THE MORALITY OF HUMAN ACTS (1749-1761)
God teaches us right and wrong in the silence of our hearts.

WHAT YOU NEED:

black thread
a black handkerchief
a white handkerchief
a large handkerchief (foulard)
a clear glass bottle
a cork
a small gouge
shellac and a small paintbrush
access to a jewelry drill
adhesive tape

WHAT THEY SEE:

A black handkerchief is shown inside a clear bottle. The bottle is corked and a foulard is used to cover it. Instantly, the catechist whisks away the foulard to find the handkerchief has turned white.

WHAT YOU SAY:

"How do we know what is good or bad? Everyone has an internal sense of what is right and wrong. Whenever we see acts of compassion or cruelty, we instantly know how we should behave. But we have to ask ourselves, how do we know these things? How is it that everyone in the world, despite culture, education, era or geography knows what is good and evil? It must be God that helps us know."

"Let's say this bottle symbolizes a person. And that the black handkerchief inside symbolizes his sin. This large cloth is God's grace that covers us.

>(Cover the bottle with the foulard.)

"It's a symbol of His incredible love for us. As you see, it takes only our acceptance of His Grace to allow Him into our lives. Ultimately, it is God who is the source of love."

>(Pull the black handkerchief out of the bottle and pull the white handkerchief out of the cork by yanking on the threads. Keep the black handkerchief hidden under the foulard as you whisk it away.)

"It is belief in Him and our reliance on Him that will allow us to reject sin and to accept love. It is He alone who can forgive us of our sins."

DEUTERONOMY 30:19
I am now giving you the choice between life and death, between God's blessing and God's curse, and I call heaven and earth to witness the choice you make. Choose life.

1 SAMUEL 9:24
So the cook brought the choice piece of the leg and placed it before Saul. Samuel said, "Look, here is the piece that was kept for you. Eat it. I saved it for you to eat at this time with the people I invited." So Saul ate with Samuel that day.

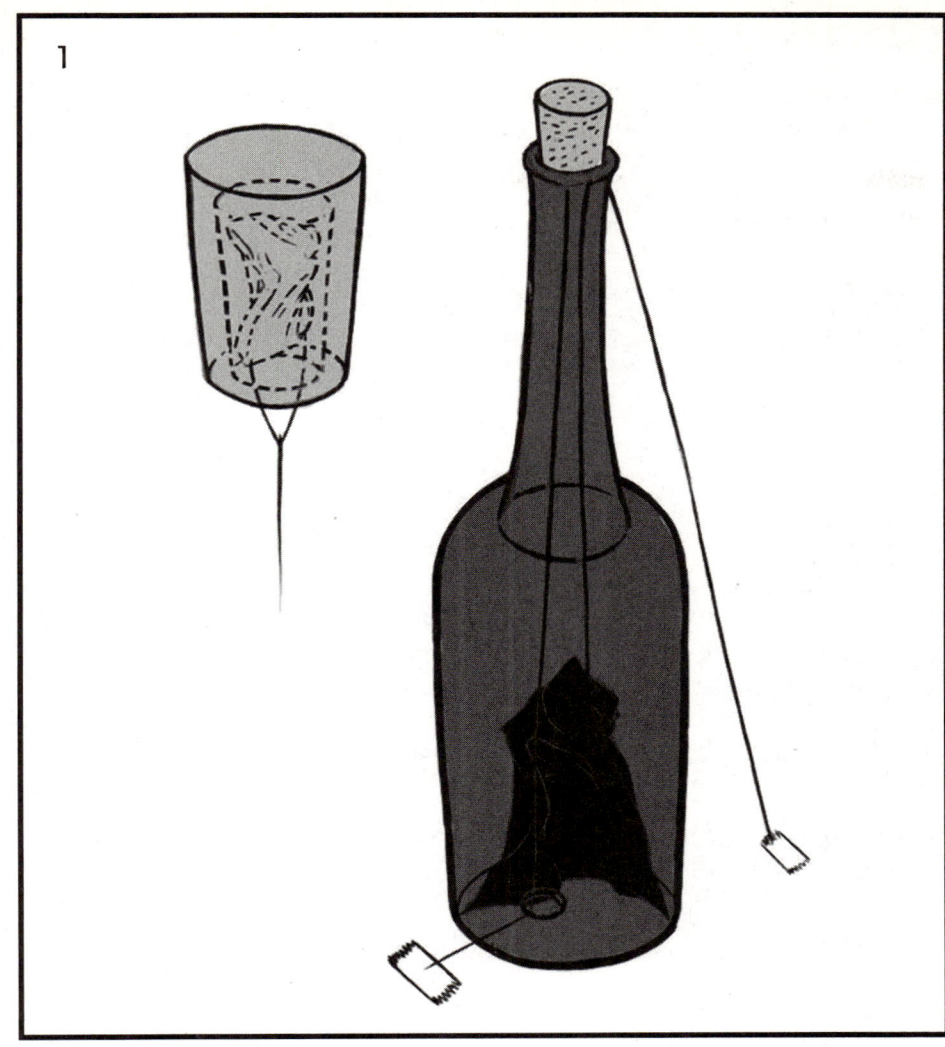

HOW YOU DO IT:

Shellac the outside of a large wine cork to strengthen its sides. Use a small gouge to hollow out a cavity into which you will stuff a white handkerchief. Tie a black thread to 2 corners of the white handkerchief. These will help maneuver the white handkerchief into the bottle.

Ask a jeweler to drill a small hole in the bottom of the bottle. Alternately, you can have the entire bottom of the bottle removed. Stuff the white handkerchief into the cork's cavity. Guide the black thread that is attached to the white handkerchief through the mouth and then out the bottom of the bottle.

Place the black handkerchief in the bottle, guiding its thread out of the mouth of the bottle. Cork the bottle lightly with the gimmicked cork. Anchor the 2 threads to your table with adhesive tape.

When performing this trick, first show the bottle with the black handkerchief in it. Then cover the bottle with a foulard. Pick up the cork slightly and yank on the thread attached to the black handkerchief to pull it out of the mouth of the bottle. Pull on the thread attached to the white handkerchief to bring it out of its hiding spot in the cork and into the bottle. Moving both handkerchiefs can be accomplished simultaneously by giving a quick tug to both black threads. Keep the black handkerchief hidden under the foulard as you whisk the foulard away.

> **JAMES 2:17**
> So it is with faith: if it is alone and includes no actions, then it is dead.

THE MORALITY OF THE PASSIONS (1762-1775)

With God's grace comes maturity and proper control of our emotions.

WHAT YOU NEED:

a balloon
a large double-pointed knitting needle
clear adhesive tape
petroleum jelly

WHAT THEY SEE:

An inflated balloon is inspected and a very long knitting needle is passed through it without puncturing it.

WHAT YOU SAY:

"Everyone has feelings. There's nothing wrong with them. They help us love others. They help us create and appreciate art. They help us feel sympathy for those who are suffering. God made us to experience these feelings. But, like all good things, sometimes we can misuse them."

(Pierce the base of the balloon with the knitting needle.)

"With control over our passions, we can live our lives safely and morally, keeping ourselves dedicated to God. As you see, needles are dangerous to balloons. I don't think that many balloons like needles."

(Pierce the top of the balloon with the knitting needle and then pull the needle through the top and out of the balloon.)

"But, with full control over our passions, we can safely live our Christ-centered lives. This balloon wasn't destroyed when a large, sharp needle passed through it. When we ask God to help us control our passionate side, He will give us the grace to do so. If we let our emotions get out of hand, they can completely destroy us."

(Pop the balloon.)

JEREMIAH 2:21
I planted you like a choice vine from the very best seed. But look what you have become! You are like a rotten, worthless vine.

JEREMIAH 21:8
Then the Lord told me to say to the people, "Listen! I, the Lord, am giving you a choice between the way that leads to life and the way that leads to death."

ROMANS 7:21
So I find that this law is at work: when I want to do what is good, what is evil is the only choice I have.

ROMANS 11:6
His choice is based on His grace, not on what they have done. For if God's choice were based on what people do, then His grace would not be real grace.

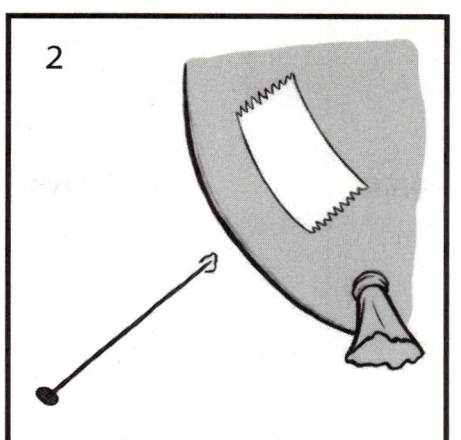
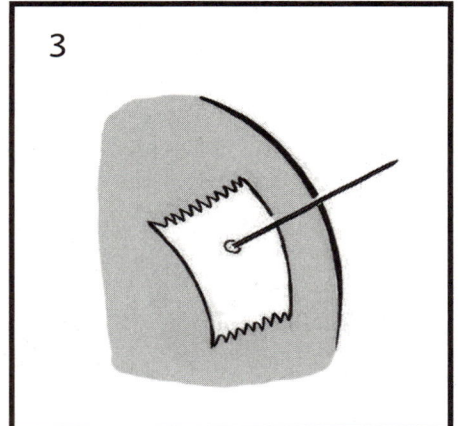

HOW YOU DO IT:

Most people don't realize that a needle can pass safely through an inflated balloon as long as it first passes the material nearest the knot. If your knitting needle is long enough, it can also pass safely through the very top of the balloon. To strengthen the material near the knot, place a piece of adhesive tape over the spot you plan to enter with your needle. Place another piece of adhesive tape at the top of the balloon so that you can pierce that spot also. Try to obtain the narrowest gauge knitting needle possible. Sharpening both ends will help the needle penetrate the balloon. Coating the needle with petroleum jelly will help seal the holes you've made in the balloon. Once you've removed the needle, pop the balloon by pricking its side so that the slow leak won't be noticeable.

MORAL CONSCIENCE (1776-1t02)

The choice between good and evil is ever before us.

WHAT YOU NEED:

a deck of cards
a piece of paper
a pen

WHAT THEY SEE:

The catechist writes a prediction on a piece of paper and sets it aside in plain view. He then lays 4 cards facedown onto the tabletop and the volunteer is given a free choice of them. Once the volunteer chooses, she is directed to examine the prediction. The prediction and the volunteer's chosen card match exactly.

WHAT YOU SAY:

"When you are about to do something good ... or bad ... how do you make a choice between the two? Who helps you make this decision? We get knowledge from the Church, from our spiritual leaders, our parents, our teachers, our consciences, and God. If we listen to these sources of information, we will not make the wrong decision."

(Introduce the prediction and set it aside. Lay out the 4 cards as described.)

"I would like you to make a choice now. You have a free choice of any card here. Now turn over the card and check the piece of paper that's been in plain view the entire time we've spoken."

(Give the volunteer an opportunity to examine the prediction.)

"As you see, you made the right decision. And all you did was listen to the little voice inside you. Similarly, our conscience leads us to make the right moral decision if we trust it. If we open ourselves to God, we will find we make good moral choices in our lives."

---

2 CHRONICLES 1:11
God replied to Solomon, "You have made the right choice. Instead of asking for wealth or treasure or fame or the death of your enemies or even for long life for yourself, you have asked for wisdom and knowledge so that you can rule my people, over whom I have made you king."

PHILIPPIANS 1:9-10
I pray that your love will keep on growing more and more, together with true knowledge and perfect judgment, so that you will be able to choose what is best. Then you will be free from all impurity and blame on the Day of Christ.

2 PETER 1:10
So then, my friends, try even harder to make God's call and His choice of you a permanent experience; if you do so, you will never abandon your faith.

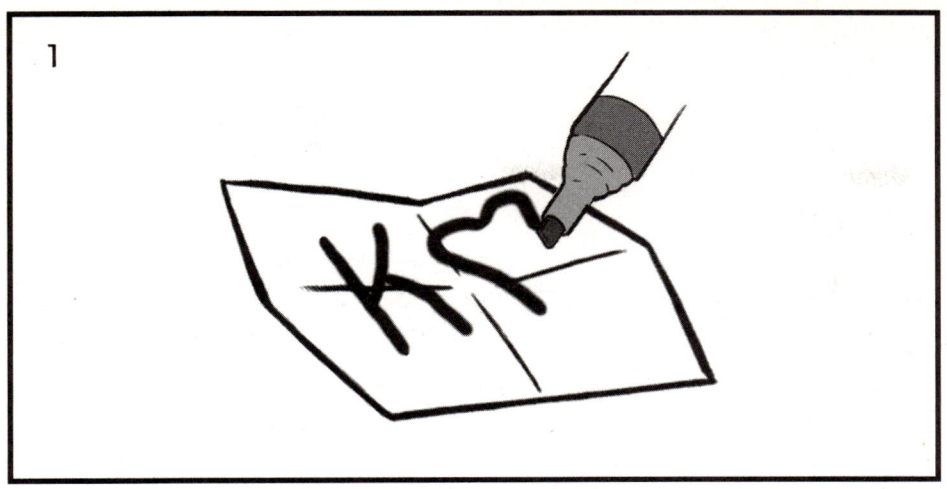

HOW YOU DO IT:

Write the words "King of Hearts" on a small square of paper, fold it, and set it aside in plain view. Place 4 kings face down on the table between you and the volunteer. It is imperative that you be on the opposite side of the table from your volunteer when performing this trick. Make sure the king of hearts is the second one from the volunteer's right.

This force is a seemingly completely free choice. When 4 identical objects are placed at a 45-degree angle away from the volunteer, most people will take the third object from their left. Remember that this force is most effective when the objects are placed between the catechist and the volunteer, and are otherwise completely identical. They should be equidistant from each other and aligned exactly. If the volunteer chooses a different one, apologize and ask her to choose 2 cards instead. If she picks the 2 that include the king of hearts keep them and remove the other 2. If she chooses the 2 that do not include the king of hearts, remove them. Then ask her to pick another card. If she chooses the king of hearts ask her to show it. If she chooses the other card remove it, leaving her the king of hearts. This force is called the Magician's Choice. For another example of Magician's Choice see the Fifth Commandment on page 172.

JEREMIAH 21:8
Then the Lord told me to say to the people, "Listen! I, the Lord, am giving you a choice between the way that leads to life and the way that leads to death."

ROMANS 2:18
You know what God wants you to do, and you have learned from the Law to choose what is right.

THE GIFTS AND FRUITS OF THE HOLY SPIRIT (1803-1832)

The Spirit bestows His gifts on us.

WHAT YOU NEED:

a clear drinking glass
12 pennies

WHAT THEY SEE:

The catechist walks over to a volunteer and holds a glass under her nose. He gives her nose a little squeeze and a torrent of pennies fills the glass.

WHAT YOU SAY:

"The gifts and fruits of the Holy Spirit complete and perfect the virtues of those who receive them. They make the faithful docile in readily obeying divine inspirations. This is a fancy way of saying that if we pray, accept, and trust Jesus in our lives, He will reward us with magnificent gifts. Not because we deserve them or earn them but because he wants to give them to us and because we accept them. These Gifts of the Holy Spirit are unexpected ... just like pennies from heaven."

(Squeeze your volunteer's nose and release the pennies underneath it, making it look as if they are falling from the nose into the glass.)

"Magnificent gifts for which we are very grateful."

1 CORINTHIANS 12:1-14

Now, concerning what you wrote about the gifts from the Holy Spirit. I want you to know the truth about them, my friends. You know that while you were still heathen, you were led astray in many ways to the worship of lifeless idols. I want you to know that no one who is led by God's Spirit can say "A curse on Jesus!" and no one can confess "Jesus is Lord," without being guided by the Holy Spirit. There are different kinds of spiritual gifts, but the same Spirit gives them. There are different ways of serving, but the same Lord is served. There are different abilities to perform service, but the same God gives ability to all for their particular service. The Spirit's presence is shown in some way in each person for the good of all. The Spirit gives one person a message full of wisdom, while to another person the same Spirit gives a message full of knowledge. One and the same Spirit gives faith to one person, while to another person he gives the power to heal. The Spirit gives one person the power to work miracles; to another, the gift of speaking God's message; and to yet another, the ability to tell the difference between gifts that come from the Spirit and those that do not. To one person He gives the ability to speak in strange tongues, and to another He gives the ability to explain what is said. But it is one and the same Spirit Who does all this; as He wishes, He gives a different gift to each person. Christ is like a single body, which has many parts; it is still one body, even though it is made up of different parts. In the same way, all of us, whether Jews or Gentiles, whether slaves or free, have been baptized into the one body by the same Spirit, and we have all been given the one Spirit to drink. For the body itself is not made up of only one part, but of many parts.

> Lord, make me an instrument of your peace; where there is hatred, let me sow love; where there is injury, pardon; where there is doubt, faith; where there is despair, hope; where there is darkness, light; and where there is sadness, joy.
>
> — St. Francis of Assisi

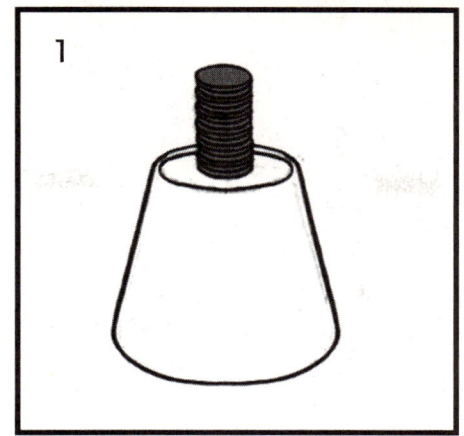

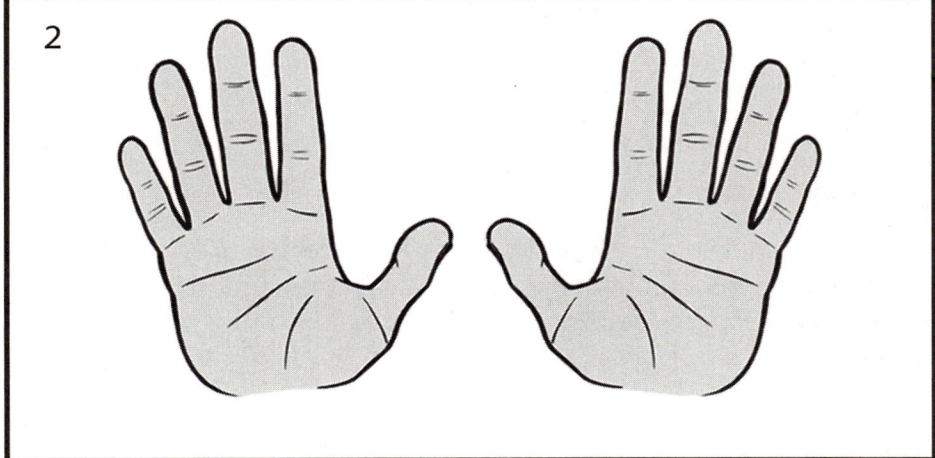

HOW YOU DO IT:

This is a remarkably easy trick to perform that requires a great deal of braggadocio and gumption. Place an empty drinking glass upside-down on your performance table. Stack the 12 pennies on top of it. Make sure you put it in such a place where people will not see it or the stack of pennies resting on top of it.

When you're ready to perform this trick, show that your hands are empty and then immediately grab the cup with your right hand in such a way that you automatically palm the coins as you pick it up. Take the glass with your left hand but retain the coins in your right hand. Hold the glass under your unsuspecting volunteer's chin. Lightly pinch your volunteer's nose with your right hand and allow the pennies to fall into the waiting glass.

I recommend giving the pennies to the volunteer as a gift; your generosity will increase your popularity with your audience.

> Where there is charity and wisdom, there is neither fear nor ignorance.
>
> — St. Francis of Assisi

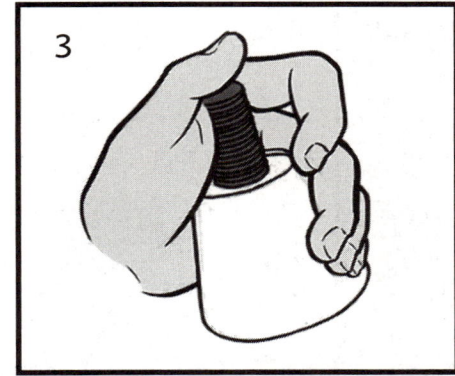

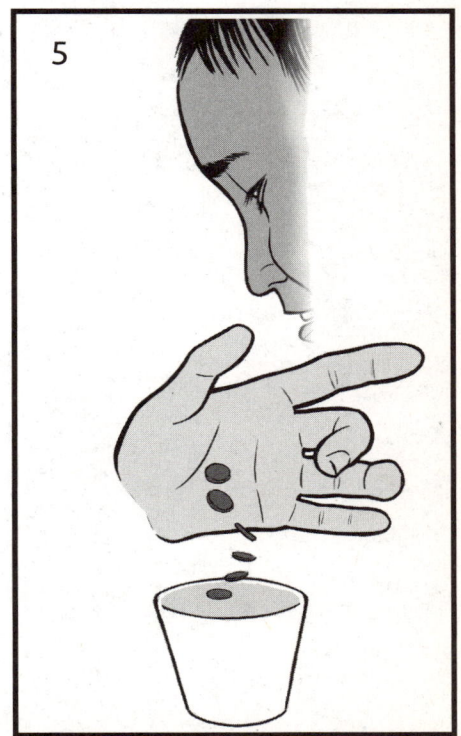

SIN (1846-1876)

Christ sacrificed Himself for us.

WHAT YOU NEED:

3 plastic swimming pool buoys
  or plastic/wooden balls
  with holes drilled through
a spool of black thread
two 6-foot lengths of rope
a red foulard
letter stickers

WHAT THEY SEE:

The catechist shows 3 swimming pool buoys strung together on 2 ropes. He places a red foulard over the assemblage and asks the 2 volunteers to pull on their ropes. Immediately, the center buoy falls off of the rope. The catechist whisks away the foulard to show that the 2 outside buoys have now met in the middle of the rope.

WHAT YOU SAY:

"Do you know what separates us from God? It's sin. We all want to love God and God will always love us even if we sin. But Christ's sacrifice on the cross brings us together with God once again. If it wasn't for Him being born, living among us, and then ultimately dying for our sins, we would never be able to know God. Let me demonstrate what that can look like."

  (Perform the trick as described.)

"Do you know what separates us from God? It's sin. We all want to love God but sin gets in our way. Because of Christ's sacrifice on the cross, sin no longer controls us. It falls out of the way, just like this buoy. Then, we are free to become reunited with God."

1 CORINTHIANS 12:9
One and the same Spirit gives faith to one person, while to another person He gives the power to heal.

1 CORINTHIANS 12:28-30
In the Church God has put all in place: in the first place apostles, in the second place prophets, and in the third place teachers; then those who perform miracles, followed by those who are given the power to heal or to help others or to direct them or to speak in strange tongues. They are not all apostles or prophets or teachers. Not everyone has the power to work miracles or to heal diseases or to speak in strange tongues or to explain what is said.

JAMES 5:15
This prayer made in faith will heal the sick; the Lord will restore them to health, and the sins they have committed will be forgiven.

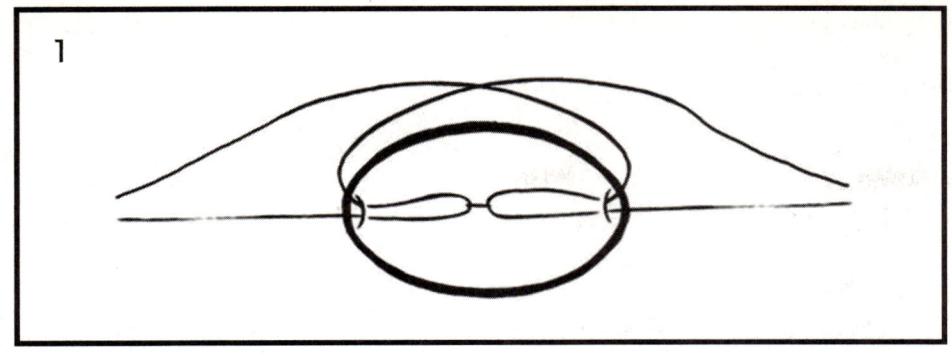

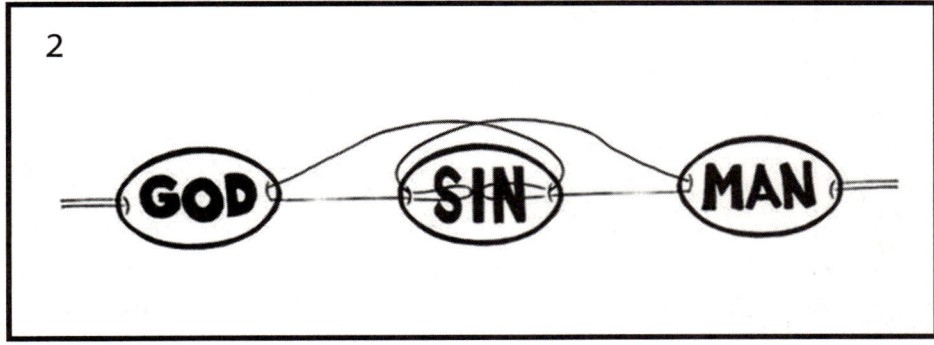

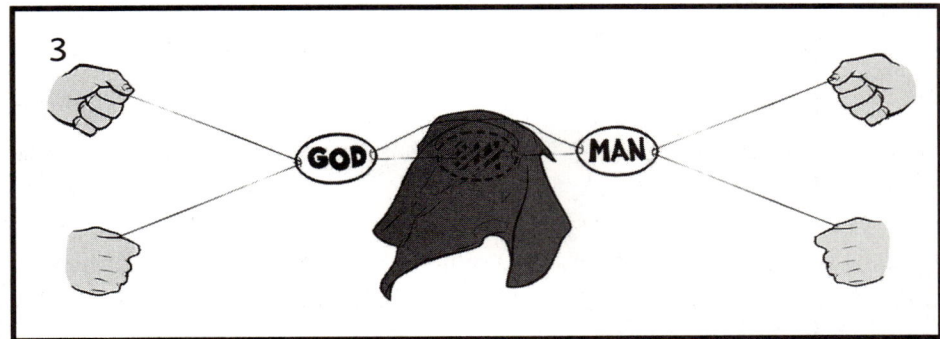

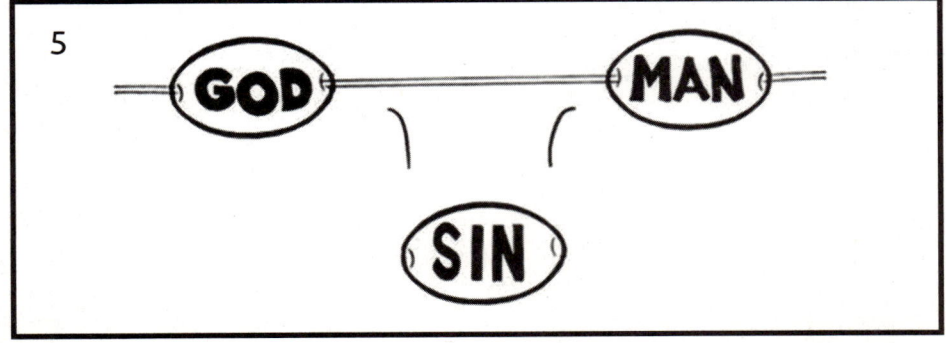

HOW YOU DO IT:

Traditionally, this trick is performed with hollow wooden or plastic balls but Fr. Jerry Jecewiz, (a.k.a. "Priesto"), a Brooklyn Diocesan priest and dedicated Gospel Magician, suggests using swimming pool buoys instead. They are light, easily portable, inexpensive, and come with a suitable hole built in. Using the letter stickers, mark the 3 buoys or balls with the following words: "GOD," "MAN," and "SIN." Alternatively, you may write the words on them with a thick, black magic marker.

Tie the middle of the 2 ropes together with a light, easily breakable string. Hide this juncture inside the middle buoy/ball labeled "SIN." Start off the presentation with the "SIN" buoy already strung on the ropes. Thread the ropes through the additional buoys, but first covertly cross the ends of 2 ropes over the back of "SIN" buoy as shown in the diagram. Ask one volunteer to hold the 2 ropes at one end of this assemblage and another volunteer to hold the 2 ropes at the other end. Drape a red foulard over the buoys, and direct your volunteers to pull on their ropes. The single thread will snap and allow the "SIN" buoy to fall out. The "GOD" and "MAN" buoys will now have nothing between them.

CATECHETICAL TIP

As a catechist, you are the hands and eyes of the Holy Spirit. You don't convert hearts and souls; instead, the Spirit does.

155

THE PERSON & SOCIETY (1878-1896)

By showing compassion towards others, we show our love for God.

WHAT YOU NEED:

a pencil
a piece of paper
a prepared page of symbols
  (cutout page 241)

WHAT THEY SEE:

A volunteer is asked to choose one of 5 symbols and to secretly draw it on a sheet of paper. After concentrating, the catechist reveals the symbol that the volunteer was thinking of.

WHAT YOU SAY:

"Other than our duty to love God, our defining aspect as humans is our ability to communicate and to feel compassion. This means that we can know each other's thoughts and feelings simply by looking into our own humanity and the humanity of those around us. Let me show you an example of what it would be like if we could know another person's heart."

  (Have the volunteer draw one of the symbols while you look away. After a few seconds of concentration, tell her which one she drew.)

"If we look into ourselves, we can see what's inside another person's heart. This is just a trick, of course, but it seemed as if I knew what shape you chose. But when you stop to think what another person is feeling when they are sad or hurt, that's not an illusion. We call it empathy or sympathy. In fact, the Golden Rule, doing to others as you would have them do to you, is an important part of knowing and understanding how to relate to one another. Simply remember that we are all human and therefore Children of God. God will give you the compassion necessary to forgive and love everyone."

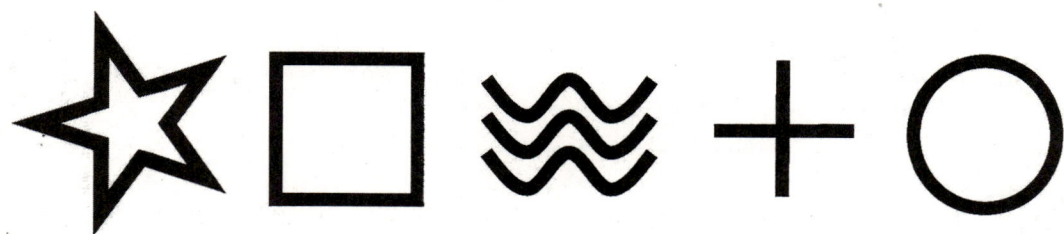

LUKE 15:11-32

Jesus went on to say, "There was once a man who had 2 sons. The younger one said to him, 'Father, give me my share of the property now.' So the man divided his property between his 2 sons. After a few days the younger son sold his part of the property and left home with the money. He went to a country far away, where he wasted his money in reckless living. He spent everything he had. Then a severe famine spread over that country, and he was left without a thing. So he went to work for one of the citizens of that country, who sent him out to his farm to take care of the pigs. He wished he could fill himself with the bean pods the pigs ate, but no one gave him anything to eat. At last he came to his senses and said, 'All my father's hired workers have more than they can eat, and here I am about to starve! I will get up and go to my father and say, "Father, I have sinned against God and against you. I am no longer fit to be called your son; treat me as one of your hired workers."' So he got up and started back to his father. He was still a long way from home when his father saw him; his heart was filled with pity, and he ran, threw his arms around his son, and kissed him. 'Father,' the son said, 'I have sinned against God and against you. I am no longer fit to be called your son.' But the father called to his servants. 'Hurry!' he said. 'Bring the best robe and put it on him. Put a ring on his finger and shoes on his feet. Then go and get the prize calf and kill it, and let us celebrate with a feast! For this son of mine was dead, but now he is alive; he was lost, but now he has been found.' And so the feasting began. In the meantime the older son was out in the field. On his way back, when he came close to the house, he heard the music and dancing. So he called one of the servants and asked him, 'What's going on?' 'Your brother has come back home,' the servant answered, 'and your father has killed the prize calf, because he got him back safe and sound.' The older brother was so angry that he would not go into the house; so his father came out and begged him to come in. But he spoke back to his father, 'Look, all these years I have worked for you like a slave, and I have never disobeyed your orders. What have you given me? Not even a goat for me to have a feast with my friends! But this son of yours wasted all your property on prostitutes, and when he comes back home, you kill the prize calf for him!' 'My son,' the father answered, 'you are always here with me, and everything I have is yours. But we had to celebrate and be happy, because your brother was dead, but now he is alive; he was lost, but now he has been found.' "

HOW YOU DO IT:

Photocopy the cutout before the performance. Place the page of symbols in front of your volunteer, and have her select any shape. Ask her to draw the symbol on a piece of paper while you look away. With your back turned and your eyes shielded, listen for the number of scratches the volunteer's pencil makes. One continuous pencil scratch means she drew a circle. Two scratches are a cross. Three separate scratches are the three wavy lines. Four clear scratches are necessary to create a square. Finally, five scratches are required to form a star. I find soft lead pencils (#2) make a louder sound than would a hard one (#3.) The alternative way to perform this trick is to simply cheat. When your volunteer is drawing the symbol, sneak a peek at what she has drawn. The least obtrusive way to do this is to hold your hand over your eyes and peek through or under your fingers.

CATECHETICAL TIP

Gospel magicians are catechists also. Like all catechists, they:

1) proclaim God's Word in their performances so that others might learn,
2) lead others in prayer and worship to honor and give glory to their Creator,
3) develop a sense of community among those they instruct so that they are unified in their love of God and
4) foster service to God and the world in order to realize social justice in our communities and throughout the world.

PARTICIPATION IN SOCIAL LIFE (1897-1927)

Man is a social creature.

WHAT YOU NEED:

5 quarters or 50-cent pieces

WHAT THEY SEE:

The catechist shows 4 coins on a tabletop. Merely by passing his hands over them, he can make them teleport mysteriously to form a small pile.

WHAT YOU SAY:

"What is Man's natural state? Certainly we want God's love and His peace. But an important part of being human is being social. We live in society not to ignore each other but to help each other. Other than Christ's admonition to love God, He also asks us to love each other and to help whenever we see that our neighbors, our brothers and sisters, are in need of our help."

"It's natural to be a part of society ... to be a part of our families, our communities, our schools, and our friends. These small objects represent us. Sometimes we live far away from each other."

(Perform the trick as described.)

"As you see, God puts a natural desire to be with each other in our hearts. Our compassion is like a magnet. We seek out the company of others. We feel the pain of others and want to help them. We can't turn others away without risking the loss of our humanity. As you see, we all seek the society of others and just like these coins, we want to be together."

MATTHEW 12:47-50; LUKE 8:20-21

So one of the people there said to Him, "Look, your mother and brothers are standing outside, and they want to speak with You. Jesus answered, "Who is My mother? Who are My brothers?" Then He pointed to His disciples and said, "Look! Here are My mother and My brothers! Whoever does what My Father in heaven wants is My brother, My sister, and My mother."

MARK 10:29-30

"Yes," Jesus said to them, "and I tell you that those who leave home or brothers or sisters or mother or father or children or fields for Me and for the Gospel will receive much more in this present age. They will receive a hundred times more houses, brothers, sisters, mothers, children, and fields—and persecutions as well; and in the age to come they will receive eternal life.

LUKE 9:59-62

He said to another man, "Follow Me." But that man said, "Sir, first let me go back and bury my father." Jesus answered, "Let the dead bury their own dead. You go and proclaim the Kingdom of God." Someone else said, "I will follow you, Sir; but first let me go and say goodbye to my family." Jesus said to him, "Anyone who starts to plow and then keeps looking back is of no use for the Kingdom of God."

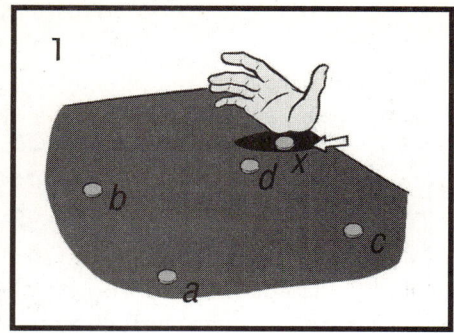

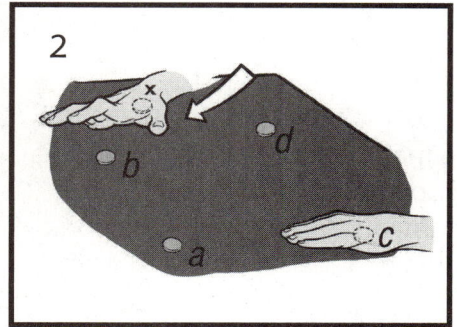

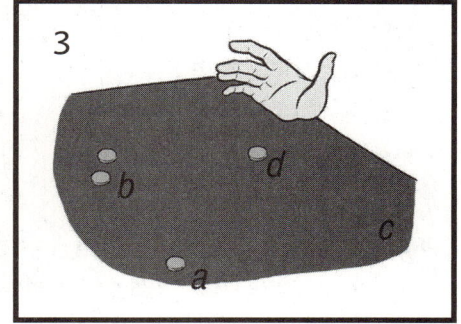

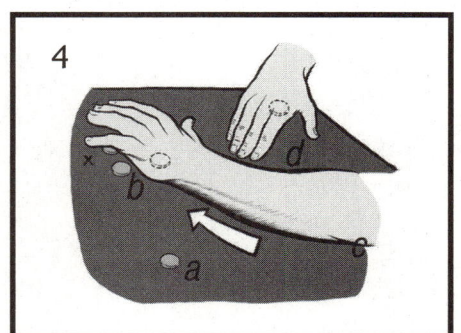

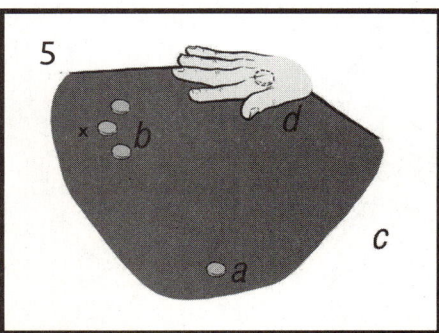

HOW YOU DO IT:

Show 4 of the coins on the table but hide the fifth coin (marked x in diagram 1) at the juncture of the base of your palm and wrist. Openly cover the object in position c, with your left hand. This is the coin that you will initially pretend to teleport. Wiggle the fingers of your right hand, making them seem to hover slightly above the table. Glide your right hand towards position b while dragging object x along. While your left hand is covering the coin in position c, apply pressure to it so that it sticks to the spot just below your palm. When you lift your hands, the coin at position c seemingly disappears while a second coin mysteriously appears in position b.

Now you should have one coin in position a, 2 coins in position in b, nothing in position c, one coin in position d and one coin hidden under your left wrist.

Cover the coin in position d with your right hand and glide your left hand toward position b while dragging the hidden coin. Push down on the coin in your right hand, making it stick to the base of your palm. Lift up your hands and your audience will think that the coin in position d has disappeared and reappeared in position b.

At this point you should have one coin in position a, 3 coins in position in b, nothing in position c, nothing in position d and one coin hidden under your right wrist.

Cover the coin in position a with your left hand while dragging the coin hidden under your right wrist to position b. Push down on the coin in your left hand, making it stick to the base of your palm. Release the coin under your right wrist onto the table and pull back both hands to your side of the table. Allow the one hidden under your left wrist to fall into your lap.

At this point 4 coins should be in position b.

> **HEBREWS 2:11**
> He purifies people from their sins, and both He and those who are made pure all have the same Father. That is why Jesus is not ashamed to call them His family.

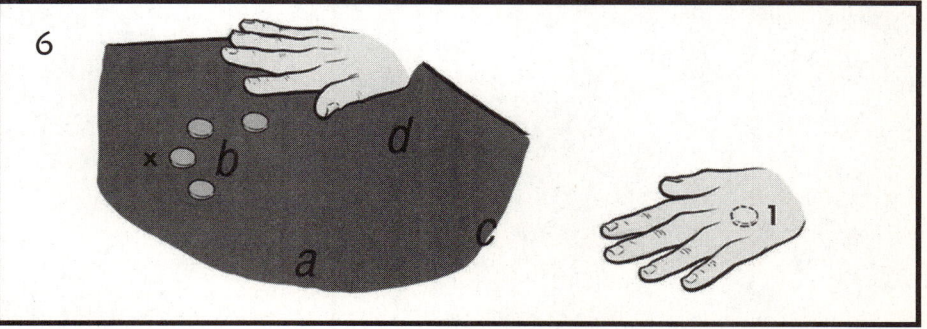

THE MORAL LAW (1950-1986)

By understanding good and evil, we come to make better choices in our lives.

WHAT YOU NEED:

2 decks of cards

WHAT THEY SEE:

Two piles of cards are shown to be identical in their order. A volunteer is given a choice of either pile and after altering the order of the cards substantially, the piles are examined to reveal that their orders haven't changed at all.

WHAT YOU SAY:

"How do we know God exists? There are many arguments that people have made throughout the millennia but a very interesting and simple one is this: because we all know what is 'good.' Who else could have put this inside of us even though no human person is perfectly good? Clearly Someone Who is perfectly good created in us the ability to know what is good. Who do you think that would be? That's right ... it's God."

"God put this idea of what is good inside us when He made us so that we can become better Children of God. All we need to do is follow what is in our hearts. The Church also gives us rules that use this 'natural goodness.' By following these rules, we can better understand God's will. Let's have an experiment. Let's see what it would be like if we created some rules that the 2 of us can follow. If we both follow them, what do you think will happen?"

(Perform the trick as described.)

"As you see, even though the order of the cards was altered, they automatically came back into the same order. If we understand what is good and right, we will always know what to do. If we accept the rules of what is right and good, we will be united to work together for a common good and for the greater glory of God."

ROMANS 12:6
So we are to use our different gifts in accordance with the grace that God has given us. If our gift is to speak God's message, we should do it according to the faith that we have.

2 CORINTHIANS 1:12
We are proud that our conscience assures us that our lives in this world, and especially our relations with you, have been ruled by God-given frankness and sincerity, by the power of God's grace and not by human wisdom.

2 CORINTHIANS 6:1
In our work together with God, then, we beg you who have received God's grace not to let it be wasted.

2 CORINTHIANS 8:9
You know the grace of our Lord Jesus Christ; rich as He was, He made himself poor for your sake, in order to make you rich by means of His poverty.

HOW YOU DO IT:

1. Take 2 piles of 13 cards and show that they are in random order but both are arranged in the same order as the other.

2. Turn both piles facedown.

3. Pick up either pile.

4. Deal 3 cards onto the table, one at a time.

5. Take the next 2 cards off the deck and put the top card under the other one while still holding them in your hand. (This will make it seem as if you are changing the order of the deck.)

6. Add the 2 cards to the pile on the table.

7. Deal 3 more cards, one at a time.

8. Take the next 2 cards off the deck and put the top card under the other one as you did before.

9. Add them to the pile.

10. Deal the last 3 cards one at a time.

11. Tell your audience that the order of the cards in the 2 piles is no longer the same.

12. Next, have a volunteer choose a pile.

13. Deal the remaining pile onto the table. (Have the volunteer direct you as to how many cards you should deal normally onto the pile, and how many you should "reverse" by using the method described in step 5. You can "reverse" as many cards as you want to by taking one card off the top of the deck and putting the next top card on top of it as you hold it in your hand.)

14. After all cards are dealt, turn the top card of each pile faceup to showing that they now match.

15. Continue turning the next top card of both piles simultaneously until all cards are faceup to show that the order of the 2 piles matches.

GRACE AND JUSTIFICATION (1987-2029)

God shines His magnificent grace upon us.

WHAT YOU NEED:

an 8-inch by 11-inch plastic sleeve for a ring binder
a small pitcher
a few sheets of a newspaper
glue or aquarium sealant
food coloring and water or milk

WHAT THEY SEE:

The catechist shows every page of a newspaper and then rolls it into a cone. He picks up a pitcher of milk and pours it into the cone. Despite this, the newspaper doesn't leak. The catechist opens the newspaper again to show that it is completely empty and the milk has disappeared. The newspaper is rolled up again and tipped over into a pitcher and, mysteriously, milk pours out.

WHAT YOU SAY:

"What is God's grace? It's the power that keeps the universe in existence. It is what blesses us and gives us faith. Does anyone have a special ability, like being really good at school or being a great athlete? Well ... that's God's grace. But even though we can't earn God's grace or control it, we are still required to be moral and ethical, to love one another, to receive the sacraments, which are means of receiving God's grace, to live out our baptismal promises, and to help bring about God's Kingdom on Earth. I guess that would make Christians pretty busy!"

"What does it mean to 'orient' ourselves to God? Imagine that this milk is God's grace. He loves to lavish it on us. It's ours for the taking. All we need do is orient our lives and behavior towards Christ. Grace is ever present. God bestows it on us and the rest of Creation. It permeates the entire universe."

(Pour the milk into the gimmick hidden in the rolled up newspaper.)

"God loves to pour out His grace into us."

(Open the newspaper and show that the milk has disappeared. The gimmick should remain hidden between sheets of newspaper.)

"But there's no way to control God's grace. We can't force Him nor can we control Him. What do you think would happen if we turned ourselves away from God? Would the grace come pouring out?"

(Close the newspaper. Turn it upside down raising the folded spine of the paper so that the liquid is trapped in the gimmick.)

"Well ... as you see ... we can't escape God's grace ... it's always with us ... but, the only way to thank God for His kindness and generosity is to obey His commands."

(Roll up the newspaper again and tip it the other way so that the liquid comes pouring out into the pitcher.)

"As you see, God's grace is still there. It's always with us. All we need to do is ask."

If I am not (in God's grace), may it please God to put me in it; if I am, may it please God to keep me there.
— St. Joan of Arc (when asked by her interrogators whether or not she felt she was in God's grace)

HOW YOU DO IT:

The gimmick to do this trick can be bought at a magic store but I will include the instructions here as it is a very easy piece of magic apparatus to make.

If you examine the accompanying diagram, you will note that if a fluid is poured into the newspaper, the liquid will get caught in the maze-like structure of the sleeve when the newspaper is slowly turned upside down. I prefer to not use milk as I don't like to waste food. Plain water wouldn't be the best choice as your class wouldn't be able to see it clearly. Try adding food coloring to the water for the best effect.

The gimmick is simply an 8 1/2 inch by 11-inch plastic sleeve used in a ring binder. Slit open all but one long side and, using a strong adhesive suitable for plastic, make a line of glue like the one described in the diagram. When the top plastic sheet is pressed against this you will have the elements of the gimmick. The opening at the top should be about 2 inches wide. When the glue is dry, you will be able to pour a liquid into this assemblage temporarily without it springing a leak. Glue this packet in between 2 sheets of a newspaper as described in the accompanying diagram.

2 CORINTHIANS 12:9
But His answer was: "My grace is all you need, for My power is greatest when you are weak." I am most happy, then, to be proud of my weaknesses, in order to feel the protection of Christ's power over me.

EPHESIANS 2:5
That while we were spiritually dead in our disobedience He brought us to life with Christ. It is by God's grace that you have been saved.

THE CHURCH: MOTHER AND TEACHER (2030-2051)

The Church is an expression of God's love.

WHAT YOU NEED:

a deck of cards

WHAT THEY SEE:

The catechist fans an imaginary deck of cards in his hands and asks the volunteer to "select" one. She announces the card she has chosen and, after a bit of comic by-play, the catechist directs her to the facedown card on the table. She finds that it matches her selected card exactly.

WHAT YOU SAY:

"When Jesus picked St. Peter as the rock upon which the Church would be built, this was the moment that the Catholic Church started. It wasn't Jesus's intention to have several competing churches; Christ's Body is one and the Church is the Protector and Guardian of Christ's Truth. The Church is, in a sense, our mother. Just as our own mothers protect us, so too, does the Church. The Church guides and teaches us just like our own mothers do.

"Let's have an experiment to show what I mean."

(Fan an imaginary deck of cards in front of a volunteer and ask her to mime taking one.)

"What card did you choose? What is your favorite card? What is your favorite card in the whole deck?"

(The volunteer announces her selection. Show her your prediction.)

"As you see, we're in sync. Our job as Catholic Christians, members of Christ's original Christian Faith, is to be in sync with our Church and pray for the eventual reunification of all Christians everywhere."

MATTHEW 16:18
And so I tell you, Peter: you are a rock, and on this rock foundation I will build My church, and not even death will ever be able to overcome it.

ACTS 20:28
So keep watch over yourselves and over all the flock which the Holy Spirit has placed in your care. Be shepherds of the Church of God, which He made His own through the blood of His Son.

1 CORINTHIANS 12:28
In the Church God has put all in place: in the first place apostles, in the second place prophets, and in the third place teachers; then those who perform miracles, followed by those who are given the power to heal or to help others or to direct them or to speak in strange tongues.

1 CORINTHIANS 14:12
Since you are eager to have the gifts of the Spirit, you must try above everything else to make greater use of those which help to build up the Church.

EPHESIANS 1:22
God put all things under Christ's feet and gave Him to the Church as supreme Lord over all things.

EPHESIANS 1:23
The Church is Christ's body, the completion of Him Who Himself completes all things everywhere.

EPHESIANS 5:29
None of us ever hate our own bodies. Instead, we feed them, and take care of them, just as Christ does the Church.

COLOSSIANS 1:18
He is the head of His body, the Church; He is the source of the body's life. He is the first-born Son, Who was raised from death, in order that He alone might have the first place in all things.

COLOSSIANS 1:24
And now I am happy about my sufferings for you, for by means of my physical sufferings I am helping to complete what still remains of Christ's sufferings on behalf of His body, the Church.

1 TIMOTHY 2:8
In every church service I want the men to pray, men who are dedicated to God and can lift up their hands in prayer without anger or argument.

1 TIMOTHY 3:1
This is a true saying: If a man is eager to be a Church leader, he desires an excellent work.

ACTS 14:23
In each church they appointed elders, and with prayers and fasting they commended them to the Lord, in Whom they had put their trust.

EPHESIANS 5:25
Husbands, love your wives just as Christ loved the Church and gave His life for it.

HOW YOU DO IT:

Have the queen of hearts face down on the table and slightly off to the side. Do not call undue attention to it. This trick works for women with about 90 percent certainty. It's 50-50 for men. It seems that most women, when asked what their favorite card is, will choose the queen of hearts. Young men will usually either pick the ace of spades (teenagers) or the jack of clubs (younger children).

It is imperative that you limit your volunteer's choices by specifically and clearly using the following formula, "What card did you choose? What is your favorite card? What is your favorite card in the whole deck?" Ask these 3 questions without pausing. This keeps the volunteer preoccupied and encourages her to pick the first card that occurs to her. More often than not, people will answer as I've explained above. In the case she doesn't select the card you had hoped, simply find her card in a deck of cards and force it on her using False Shuffle Force 3 on page 109.

> Is one religion as good as another? Is one horse in the Derby as good as another?
> —G.K. Chesterton

THE SECOND COMMANDMENT (2142-2167)

We show respect to God when we respect His name.

WHAT YOU NEED:

2 balloons
3 pennies

WHAT THEY SEE:

The catechist demonstrates 2 inflated balloons and 2 pennies. The volunteer is given one of each. Both the volunteer and the catechist rest their respective coins on their balloons and then cover them with their hands. Both shake their balloons but, suddenly, the catechist's coin enters the balloon without breaking it. It can be handed out for examination.

WHAT YOU SAY:

"Thou shalt not take the Lord's Name in vain. Do you know what that means? It means to not talk about Jesus in a silly or disrespectful manner. It means that we should be respectful of Him and those things that represent or symbolize Him, including His name."

"Imagine this balloon is God's presence and this penny is us. If we avoid using God's name in a silly or frivolous manner, that is, if we approach the Lord humbly as one of His children and treat Him as the Father, then we can join Him in His loving embrace."

(Hold your balloon with the penny inside it, hidden between 2 fingers. Hand another balloon and penny to your volunteer. Show that you also have a penny that is outside of the balloon. Direct the volunteer to cup her hands over her penny on the balloon and to shake it. Do the same with your balloon. Keep the penny on the outside of the balloon palmed and release your hold on the penny inside the balloon. Your balloon can be handed around while you secretly hide the palmed penny in your pocket.)

"Otherwise, we will always be outside of His Grace. Not because He is punishing us but because only the humble and the pure of heart can approach Him."

EXODUS 3:1-6
One day while Moses was taking care of the sheep and goats of his father-in-law Jethro, the priest of Midian, he led the flock across the desert and came to Sinai, the holy mountain. There the angel of the Lord appeared to him as a flame coming from the middle of a bush. Moses saw that the bush was on fire but that it was not burning up. "This is strange," he thought. "Why isn't the bush burning up? I will go closer and see." When the Lord saw that Moses was coming closer, he called to him from the middle of the bush and said, "Moses! Moses!" He answered, "Yes, here I am." God said, "Do not come any closer. Take off your sandals, because you are standing on holy ground. I am the God of your ancestors, the God of Abraham, Isaac, and Jacob." So Moses covered his face, because he was afraid to look at God.

PSALMS 51:10
Create a pure heart in me, O God, and put a new and loyal spirit in me.

1 TIMOTHY 1:5
The purpose of this order is to arouse the love that comes from a pure heart, a clear conscience, and a genuine faith.

2 TIMOTHY 2:22
Avoid the passions of youth, and strive for righteousness, faith, love, and peace, together with those who with a pure heart call out to the Lord for help.

HEBREWS 7:19
For the Law of Moses could not make anything perfect. And now a better hope has been provided through which we come near to God.

HEBREWS 10:22
So let us come near to God with a sincere heart and a sure faith, with hearts that have been purified from a guilty conscience and with bodies washed with clean water.

JAMES 4:8
Come near to God, and He will come near to you. Wash your hands, you sinners! Purify your hearts, you hypocrites!

2 CORINTHIANS 11:2
I am jealous for you, just as God is; you are like a pure virgin whom I have promised in marriage to one man only, Christ Himself.

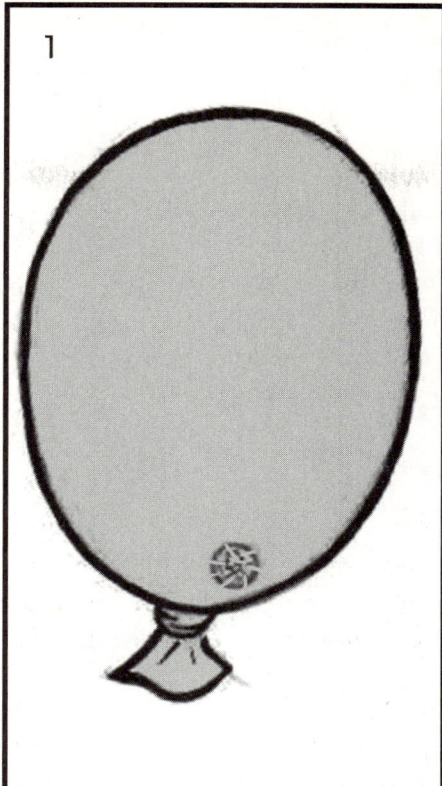

HOW YOU DO IT:

Place a penny inside your balloon before inflating it. Do not inflate it completely. This will allow extra latex so you can hide the coin between your fingers. This can be done by pinching the coin between 2 fingers as you hold the balloon in the palm of your hand or by holding the balloon at the knot and concealing it there. Openly show the other penny but palm it when you place it against the balloon. Hold the balloon lengthwise and, at the proper moment, shake the balloon and release your hold on the penny inside the balloon. It will look and sound as if it popped into the balloon. When you hand out your balloon to be examined, you can surreptitiously put the palmed penny in your pocket.

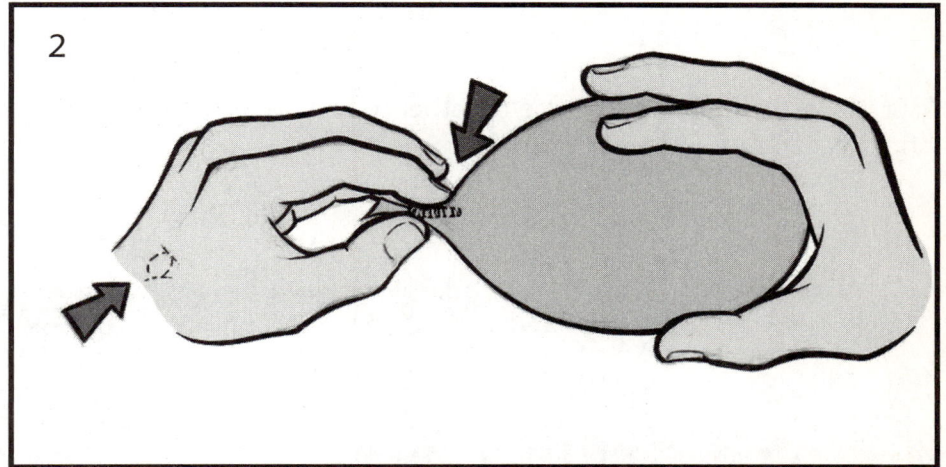

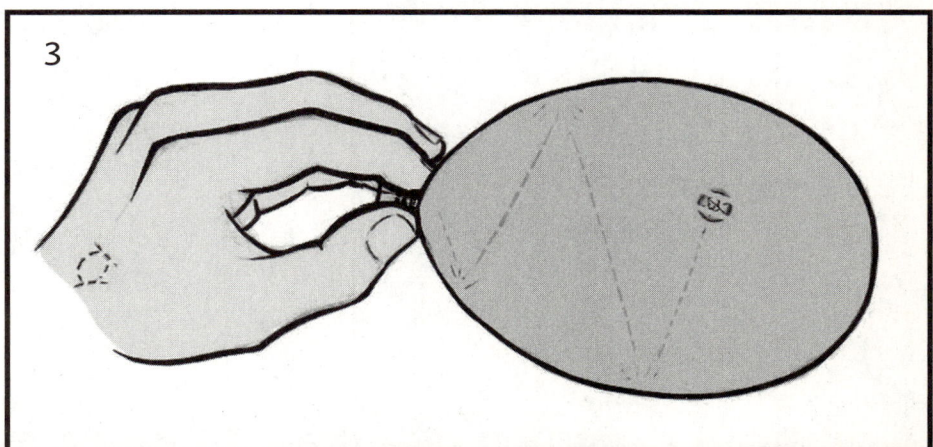

THE THIRD COMMANDMENT (2168-2195)

We demonstrate our love of God by keeping His day holy.

WHAT YOU NEED:

a rubber band

WHAT THEY SEE:

A rubber band is examined by a volunteer and returned to the catechist. He takes it with both hands. He stretches and ultimately breaks it. He rolls up the rubber band into a small ball and then tosses it to the table to show it has been restored.

WHAT YOU SAY:

"Why do we meet in church as a community every Sunday and on Holy Days of Obligation? Short answer: because God wants it. Long answer: because our pride and sinfulness distance us from God, and coming together as a community helps to heal that rift."

"Imagine this rubber band is us. Sin and pride pull at us as do the attentions and demands of the material and secular world. Sometimes we can distance ourselves so far from God and His Grace that we can seriously hurt ourselves spiritually, emotionally, and sometimes even physically."

("Break" the rubber band using the instructions described in the How You Do It section.)

"But, if we are humble and come together to pray as a community, we are accepting God's Grace in our lives ... and this gives us a chance to heal."

(Drop the "broken" rubber band onto the table. Show that it is intact.)

JOHN 4:47
When he heard that Jesus had come from Judea to Galilee, he went to Him and asked Him to go to Capernaum and heal his son, who was about to die.

JOHN 12:40
God has blinded their eyes and closed their minds, so that their eyes would not see, and their minds would not understand, and they would not turn to Me, says God, for Me to heal them.

ACTS 4:30
Reach out your hand to heal, and grant that wonders and miracles may be performed through the name of your holy Servant Jesus.

ACTS 28:27
Because this people's minds are dull, and they have stopped up their ears and closed their eyes. Otherwise, their eyes would see, their ears would hear, their minds would understand, and they would turn to Me, says God, and I would heal them.

HOW YOU DO IT:

This is a very easy trick to perform but will require a bit of practice to perfect. After receiving the rubber band back from the volunteer, flatten the rubber band into a line and conceal the 2 ends in your right hand (see diagram). Grab the rubber band with the left hand as well, and act as if you are stretching it with all your might. It is imperative that you strain your face as you would if you were really struggling to break a rubber band, otherwise the illusion will fail. Allow the "broken" rubber band to snap by releasing your right thumb and forefinger's grip of the extra 1/2 inch of rubber band. Roll it up into a small ball and drop it onto the table. The rubber band will automatically unravel to show that it has been restored.

CATECHETICAL TIP

When Christ's Apostles were sent out into the world to carry Christ's word, they too catechized. The Gospel Magician is simply following in their footsteps.

Catechesis is an essential ministry of the Church and is an important part of the ministries of evangelization and of the Word. We are all catechists even in our daily lives, in the same sense that we are all a priesthood of believers.

THE FOURTH COMMANDMENT (2196-2257)

By loving and respecting our parents, we come to know and love God.

WHAT YOU NEED:

a deck of cards

WHAT THEY SEE:

A volunteer is asked to cut a deck of cards and then to cut the 2 piles into 2 more piles for a total of 4. The magician adjusts the size of the piles and then produces queens on top of all 4 piles.

WHAT YOU SAY:

"How important is it to love and respect our parents? It's so important, one of the commandments God gave to Moses asks us specifically to do so. Don't you think it would be a little strange if God wanted us to be His children but didn't ask us to love our mothers and fathers?

"Imagine this deck is our society. If this deck is a society, how can we tell if any of these cards are in the same family? That's right ... they might look alike. How many people here look like their parents and brothers and sisters? Let's have an experiment."

> (Falsely shuffle the deck. Ask the volunteer to cut the deck in half. Have the volunteer cut 2 new piles again so that there are 4 in total. Keep an eye on which pile contains the 4 queens.)

"I don't think you cut the piles very evenly but don't worry, I work with non-professionals all the time. I'll straighten them out."

> (Maneuver 3 of the queens to the other piles.)

"What card did you choose? What is your favorite card? What is your favorite card in the whole deck?"

> (Turn over the top card of each of the piles.)

"All of these 4 cards belong to the same family. They even look alike! All of these cards stick together just as a family sticks together and supports its members. But a family can't remain strong if the children don't respect their parents. Christ asks us to love and respect our parents."

MATTHEW 19:19
Respect your father and your mother; and love your neighbor as you love yourself.

MARK 12:29-31; MATTHEW 22:39; GALATIANS 5:14
Jesus replied, "The most important one is this: 'Listen, Israel! The Lord our God is the only Lord. Love the Lord your God with all your heart, with all your soul, with all your mind, and with all your strength.' The second most important commandment is this: 'Love your neighbor as you love yourself.' There is no other commandment more important than these 2."

> He is truly great who
> hath a great charity
>
> — Thomas à Kempis,
> Imitation of Christ

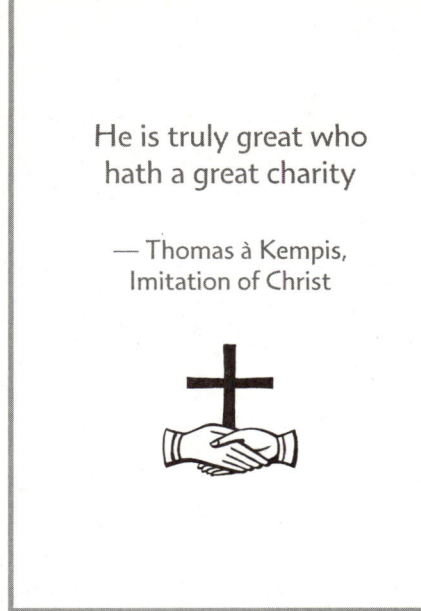

HOW YOU DO IT:

Before performing this trick, place the 4 queens on the top of a deck.

At the beginning of the performance, falsely shuffle the deck (use false shuffle 1 or 2 on page 109) and then invite a volunteer to cut the deck in half. Have the volunteer cut the 2 new piles again so that there are 4 of them.

Remember which pile contains the 4 queens. Tell your volunteer that she didn't cut the deck quite evenly so you will need to even them out. While doing so, casually maneuver the queens so that one rests on top of each pile. When you finish, ask the volunteer which card she likes the most. More frequently than not, she will prefer the queen. At this point, turn over the top card of each of the piles.

When performing this trick for young men, use the 4 aces. For younger boys, use the 4 jacks.

ROMANS 13:9; LUKE 10:27
The commandments, "Do not commit adultery; do not commit murder; do not steal; do not desire what belongs to someone else"—all these, and any others besides, are summed up in the one command, "Love your neighbor as you love yourself."

JAMES 2:8
You will be doing the right thing if you obey the law of the Kingdom, which is found in the scripture, "Love your neighbor as you love yourself."

THE FIFTH COMMANDMENT (2258-2330)

Jesus is Eternal Life.

WHAT YOU NEED:

a lemon
a black magic marker
heavy white paper
a pair of scissors
a ruler

WHAT THEY SEE:

Six blank cards are laid out on a tabletop and a volunteer selects one. The catechist turns over the others to find that they have the word "SIN" on them. The card selected by the volunteer is the only one that reads "JESUS."

WHAT YOU SAY:

"Do you know what "free will" is? We all have it. It's the ability to choose between good and evil. Even though we all know the difference between good and evil, we have to decide which one we will choose. That's why our free will is so important."

(Perform the trick as described in the How You Do It section.)

"As you see, your choices led you to Jesus. Jesus is life. He is Eternal Life. Just as the Bible teaches, 'I place before you life and death ... choose life.' "

DEUTERONOMY 30:19
I am now giving you the choice between life and death, between God's blessing and God's curse, and I call heaven and earth to witness the choice you make. Choose life.

ROMANS 5:12
Sin came into the world through one man, and his sin brought death with it. As a result, death has spread to the whole human race because everyone has sinned.

ROMANS 5:14
But from the time of Adam to the time of Moses, death ruled over all human beings, even over those who did not sin in the same way that Adam did when he disobeyed God's command. Adam was a figure of the One Who was to come.

ROMANS 5:17
It is true that through the sin of one man death began to rule because of that one man. But how much greater is the result of what was done by the one man, Jesus Christ! All who receive God's abundant grace and are freely put right with Him will rule in life through Christ.

ROMANS 5:21
So then, just as sin ruled by means of death, so also God's grace rules by means of righteousness, leading us to eternal life through Jesus Christ our Lord.

ROMANS 6:6
And we know that our old being has been put to death with Christ on His cross, in order that the power of the sinful self might be destroyed, so that we should no longer be the slaves of sin.

ROMANS 6:13
Nor must you surrender any part of yourselves to sin to be used for wicked purposes. Instead, give yourselves to God, as those who have been brought from death to life, and surrender your whole being to Him to be used for righteous purposes.

ROMANS 6:16
Surely you know that when you surrender yourselves as slaves to obey someone, you are in fact the slaves of the master you obey — either of sin, which results in death, or of obedience, which results in being put right with God.

HOW YOU DO IT:

The secret to this trick is a force known as "Magician's Choice." Procure some heavy paper and cut out 6 playing-card-sized pieces. Write the word "SIN" on 4 of the cards. On another, write the name, "JESUS." The last card should be blank on both sides. Stack the cards in the following order (from top to bottom) facedown on the table: SIN, JESUS, SIN, SIN, SIN, blank card.

When you are ready to perform this trick, place the stack of cards in your left hand in the order indicated. Expose the blank face of the bottom card to the audience. Turn the face of the bottom card to the table as you pretend to pull it out of the deck and place it facedown on the table. Instead remove the top card and place it facedown on the tabletop. This move is accomplished by holding the sides of the entire deck with the forefinger and thumb of the right hand, grabbing the whole deck momentarily with the left hand, and sliding it partially through the fingers of your right hand. Ultimately your left hand takes the top instead of the bottom card. Repeat this for all of the cards in your hands, making 2 rows of 3 facedown cards. When you come to the last card, show both sides to prove it is actually blank on both sides.

For this trick to work properly, you will need to force the JESUS card, this force is known as "Magician's Choice." Ask the volunteer to point to a row. If she points to the top row (which includes the JESUS card) move the bottom row a few inches away. If she points to the bottom row, move the bottom row a few inches away. (Now you understand why we call it "Magician's Choice." Either way, the magician gets what he wants.) Now that we've disposed of the row without the JESUS card, ask the volunteer to point to 2 cards. If she takes the JESUS card as one of her selections, move both cards towards her and ask her to choose one of them. The point it to get her to take the JESUS card. If when you ask her to take 2 cards and she chooses the non-JESUS cards, simply push them aside. This will leave the volunteer with the JESUS card.

At this point, turn over each of the SIN cards and form a fan in your hands. When you get to the double-blank card, simply place it behind the fan and immediately pull out one of the SIN cards and pretend it is one you just picked up. Close the fan of cards and bring your attention to the JESUS card. Turn it over and congratulate your volunteer for choosing Jesus. If you prefer, you can substitute Jesus's name with an iconic representation.

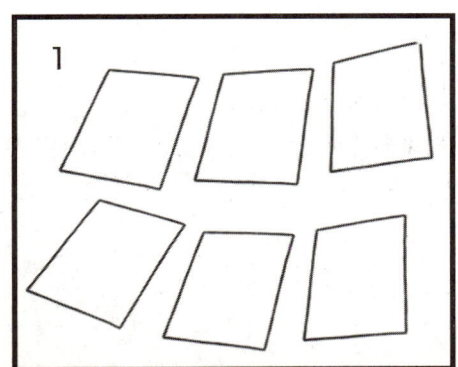

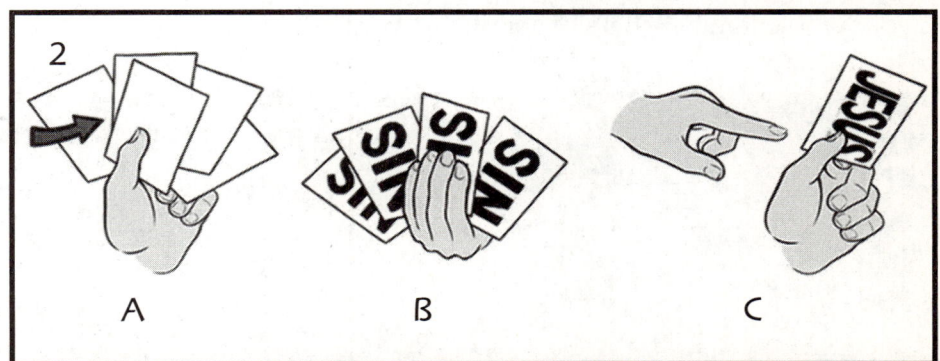

THE SIXTH COMMANDMENT (2331-2400)

We show respect by keeping our promises.

WHAT YOU NEED:

a deck of cards

WHAT THEY SEE:

The catechist displays 4 piles of cards. One is comprised of 4 aces, one of 4 kings, one of 4 queens, and one of 4 jacks. The catechist then assembles the cards into one pile. He invites a volunteer to cut this deck as often as she would like. After that, the cards are dealt into 4 piles. The catechist shows that each pile has one of each kind of card. He then gathers the piles one on top of the other again and asks the volunteer to cut them as often as she would like. When the cards are dealt into 4 piles each pile is shown to have reverted to its original configuration.

WHAT YOU SAY:

"Can anyone tell me what is adultery? Why is it bad? Has anyone here ever been happy if someone lied to you or cheated you? No one would ever say that they were pleased if someone did those things to them. It's the same thing with people who are married to each other. It would be wrong and very sad if a mother or father decided to love someone who wasn't their husband or wife. It's important for families, for society, for children, and for our own souls that if we decide to marry, we love only that one person."

"In these cards, we have 4 families: the Kings, the Queens, the Jacks and the Aces. They are most happy when they are together."

(Collect each pile, placing one on top of the other to form one large pile. Have your volunteer cut the pile as many times as she wishes. Once she is finished, deal cards into 4 separate piles. Show that each pile contains one of each type of cards.)

"But if they are separated and mixed up like this ... they will be unhappy. They are looking for each other for support but can't find each other. Let's see if we can help them preserve their families.

(Collect each pile, placing one on top of the other to form one large pile. Have your volunteer cut the pile as many times as she wishes. Once she is finished, deal cards into 4 separate piles. Show that each pile now contains 4 of the same cards.)

"So, the best thing to do is to stay with whom you promised to stay with. You, your spouse and your children ... your whole family will be happiest that way."

ROMANS 7:3
But now I tell you: if a man divorces his wife for any cause other than her unfaithfulness, then he is guilty of making her commit adultery if she marries again; and the man who marries her commits adultery also.

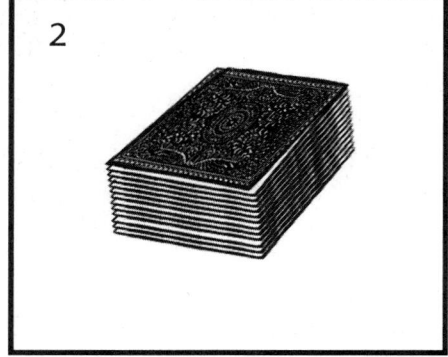

HOW YOU DO IT:

Display 4 piles of cards: 4 kings, 4 queens, 4 jacks and 4 aces. Collect them one on top of the other and ask your volunteer to cut them as many times as she would like. Deal the cards face down into 4 piles, and then turn them over to show that each pile now has one of every kind of card. Collect each pile and place them one on top of the other to form one large pile as you did before. Have your volunteer cut the large pile as many times as she wishes. Deal the cards out into 4 piles, and you will see that each of the piles are now made up of all the same kinds of cards (4 kings, 4 queens, etc., as before).

CATECHETICAL TIP

Start your performance with a group prayer; an Our Father and/or Hail Mary.

Wear a cross while you perform to remind your audience of your position as a teacher and not as merely a magician.

MATTHEW 15:19
For from your heart come the evil ideas which lead you to kill, commit adultery, and do other immoral things; to rob, lie, and slander others.

HEBREWS 13:4
Marriage is to be honored by all, and husbands and wives must be faithful to each other. God will judge those who are immoral and those who commit adultery.

MATTHEW 5:27-28
You have heard that it was said, "Do not commit adultery." But now I tell you: anyone who looks at a woman and wants to possess her is guilty of committing adultery with her in his heart.

175

THE SEVENTH COMMANDMENT (2401-2463)

What you do to the least of your brothers, that you do unto Me.

WHAT YOU NEED:

a 30-inch by 10-inch strip
  of plaid cloth
a hard-boiled egg
a needle and thread
  or sewing machine

WHAT THEY SEE:

An egg is openly shown and placed into a cloth bag. The bag is then turned upside down and inside out but the egg can't be found. The bag is righted and the volunteer is asked to reach into the bag. Instantly, she finds the egg and retrieves it.

WHAT YOU SAY:

"Though all of God's children are equal, the Church has a special dedication and preference for poor people. It's not because they are better, but because we can't be a community of Believers if we allow even one of our brothers or sisters to suffer because they lack food, clothing and shelter, education, medical care, and civil rights."

(Drop the egg into the bag. Turn the bag upside down to show that the egg has disappeared. Have a volunteer place her hand into the bag and check to see that it's gone. Make sure you hide the egg in your hand. Also, don't let her examine the bag too thoroughly.)

"It's just like this bag and this egg. It's always important to share what we have with those who are desperately in need. Some people think that giving something away, like an egg, means that it's disappeared completely. It's not true."

(Turn the bag over and let your volunteer retrieve the egg from the bag.)

"As God is with us always, He knows what we need before we ask Him. The more we give away ... the richer we are. He will never allow us to suffer because of our generosity."

MALACHI 1:10
The Lord Almighty says, "I wish one of you would close the Temple doors so as to prevent you from lighting useless fires on My altar. I am not pleased with you; I will not accept the offerings you bring Me."

MATTHEW 6:33
Instead, be concerned above everything else with the Kingdom of God and with what He requires of you, and He will provide you with all these other things.

MATTHEW 18:8-9
If your hand or your foot causes you to sin, cut it off and throw it away. It is better for you to enter into life maimed or crippled than with 2 hands or 2 feet to be thrown into eternal fire. And if your eye causes you to sin, tear it out and throw it away. It is better for you to enter into life with one eye than with 2 eyes to be thrown into fiery Gehenna.

HOW YOU DO IT:

Procure a 30-inch by 10-inch strip of plaid cloth. The more complex the pattern the better. The dotted lines depicted in the diagram are 10 inches apart. Fold the cloth strip at line B so that lines A and C meet. Do not sew this seam shut. Next fold Line D so that B and D meet. Sew the left and right sides of this assemblage.

Once done, you will note that the bag has 2 pockets, one right-side up and the other, upside down and hidden.

Openly drop a hard-boiled egg into the bag. Turn the bag upside down while simultaneously manipulating the egg so that it falls into the second, hidden pouch. The egg won't be able to fall out once it's hidden here.

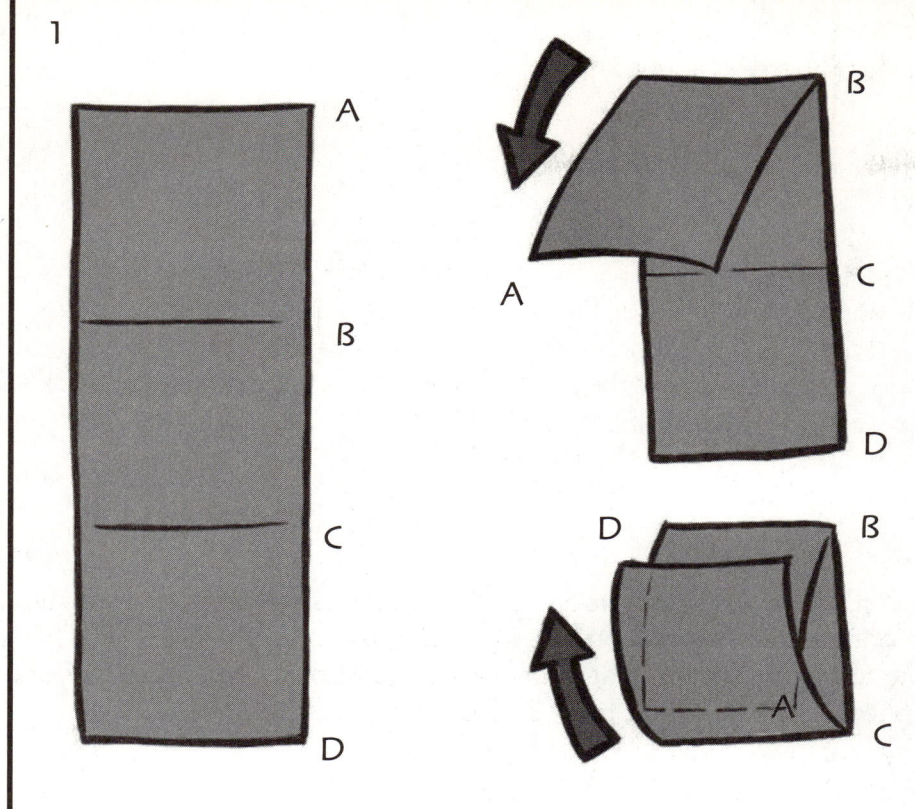

DEUTERONOMY 26:12
Every third year give the tithe—a tenth of your crops—to the Levites, the foreigners, the orphans, and the widows, so that in every community they will have all they need to eat. When you have done this?

JOHN 4:14
But those who drink the water that I will give them will never be thirsty again. The water that I will give them will become in them a spring which will provide them with life-giving water and give them eternal life.

1 CORINTHIANS 10:13
Every test that you have experienced is the kind that normally comes to people. But God keeps His promise, and He will not allow you to be tested beyond your power to remain firm; at the time you are put to the test, He will give you the strength to endure it, and so provide you with a way out.

THE EIGHTH COMMANDMENT (2464-2513)

By understanding the nature of truth, we come to experience God.

WHAT YOU NEED:

a pair of dice

WHAT THEY SEE:

The catechist offers a pair of dice for examination. The dice are rolled and the numbers that show up are used for the trick. The catechist picks up the dice, exposing the chosen faces towards his class. He turns his hand to show the reverse side of the dice and then the obverse once again. This is repeated. The last time he turns his hand, the dice show completely different numbers. The trick is repeated 2 more times.

WHAT YOU SAY:

"Do you know why we humans can speak? It's so that we can give answers to questions and to give information. It absolutely is not so that we can lie. No one ever asks a question presuming that the answer will be a lie. That would be ridiculous. We expect everyone to tell the truth ... that's why we ask questions. I don't think anyone here likes to be lied to. Why would anyone who doesn't want to be lied to want to lie to someone else?"

> (Ask your volunteer to roll a pair of dice.)

"Watch these 2 dice. Can you see the numbers that are showing? What are they?"

> (Show the numbers that were rolled between your fingers.)

"Now, what's on the other side?"

> (Show the actual backside of the exposed numbers.)

"Let's go back again ... here's the front."

> (Show the original numbers that were rolled.)

"What's on the other side?"

> (Show the actual backside of the exposed numbers.)

"Now ... tell me what the numbers are on the original side? Are you sure?"

> (Execute the Paddle Move.)

"It seems that's incorrect. Let's try it again ..."

> (Perform the trick 2 more times.)

"As you see, without the truth, we are only wasting our time and energy. It's a bit frustrating, isn't it? It's like when we lie to people and when people lie to us. We all want to be told the truth. That's why it's important to always be truthful."

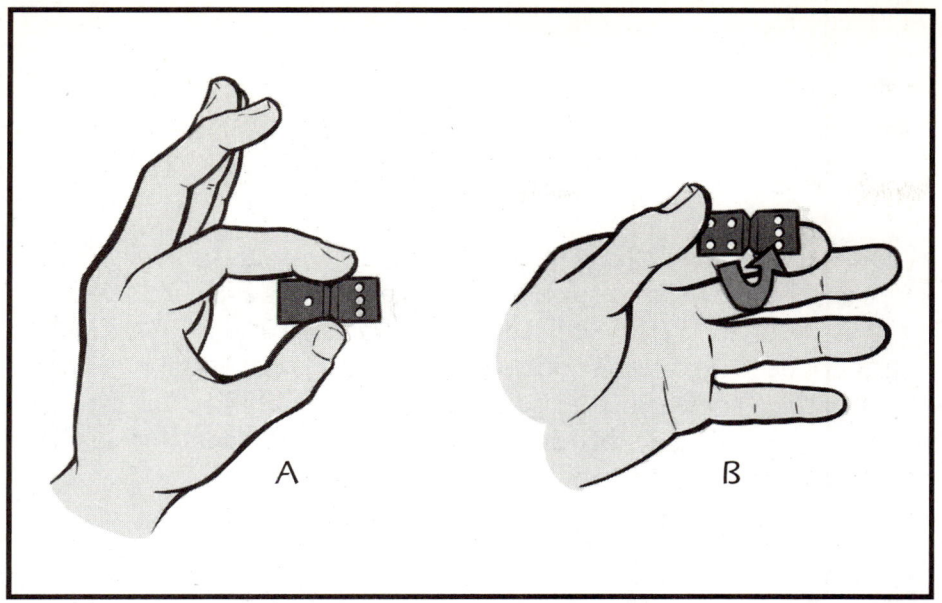

ROMANS 3:13
Their words are full of deadly deceit; wicked lies roll off their tongues, and dangerous threats, like snake's poison, from their lips.

EPHESIANS 4:29
Do not use harmful words, but only helpful words, the kind that build up and provide what is needed, so that what you say will do good to those who hear you.

2 CORINTHIANS 11:3
I am afraid that your minds will be corrupted and that you will abandon your full and pure devotion to Christ — in the same way that Eve was deceived by the snake's clever lies.

HEBREWS 4:13
There is nothing that can be hid from God; everything in all Creation is exposed and lies open before His eyes. And it is to Him that we must all give an account of ourselves.

1 PETER 3:10
As the scripture says, "If you want to enjoy life and wish to see good times, you must keep from speaking evil and stop telling lies."

REVELATIONS 14:5
They have never been known to tell lies; they are faultless.

HOW YOU DO IT:

This maneuver is called "The Paddle Move." It's an easy sleight-of-hand trick and the basis of many magic tricks. Refer to the diagram to understand how to hold the dice. The principle move is to rotate the thumb in relation to the forefinger. Hold 2 dice between the thumb and forefinger. Move the thumb towards yourself and the index finger away, rolling the dice between your fingers. This action exposes the sides of the dice that were towards the thumb initially. This would be very obvious and not terribly entertaining if you kept your hand still. Instead, keeping in mind the magicians' maxim that "the large movement hides the small movement," rotate your wrist as you roll the dice between your fingers. This will obscure any sneakiness on your part.

CATECHETICAL TIPS

Catechesis is not merely an intellectual pursuit. It is more appropriately a spiritual development whose end is a greater acceptance of Christ's salvation and submission to His will. Though an academic understanding is essential to this development, the main goal of catechesis is growth in faith.

Engage your parish priest and theology professors at local Catholic universities/seminaries to help you understand topics you will present in your performance/lesson.

TO BEAR WITNESS TO THE TRUTH (2471-2513)

As Christians, we are witnesses for Christ.

WHAT YOU NEED:

a lot of paper napkins

WHAT THEY SEE:

A volunteer is asked to come on stage and to sit facing the audience. The catechist shows her a small ball of paper napkins and asks her to concentrate on it. Even though she concentrates on it, the ball disappears in front of her. The catechist offers to use a larger ball. Several more napkins are added and again, the ball disappears in front of her. The catechist offers to use a still larger ball and adds more paper napkins. But, again, the ball disappears in front of her.

WHAT YOU SAY:

"I'll need a volunteer to help me with this trick."

> (Have your volunteer sit on a chair facing the audience. Perform the trick as described in the How You Do It section.)

"Sometimes we can get caught up in our own perceptions and judgments of things. We frequently trust ourselves more than we trust God. It's a sin related to pride. When we think that we can understand everything about a person or a situation we should remember that each of us has a different perspective. Sometimes we know where the napkins are disappearing to and sometimes we don't. This doesn't mean that we should refrain from being ethical or exhorting others to be ethical also. But we shouldn't condemn people. In fact, we should pray for them and for their conversion. Pray to God that their eyes are opened and that they no longer remain blind to the truth."

ROMANS 1:25
They exchange the truth about God for a lie; they worship and serve what God has created instead of the Creator Himself, Who is to be praised forever! Amen.

ROMANS 9:1
I am speaking the truth; I belong to Christ and I do not lie. My conscience, ruled by the Holy Spirit, also assures me that I am not lying.

COLOSSIANS 3:9
Do not lie to one another, for you have put off the old self with its habits.

HEBREWS 6:18
There are these 2 things, then, that cannot change and about which God cannot lie. So we who have found safety with Him are greatly encouraged to hold firmly to the hope placed before us.

1 PETER 2:22
He committed no sin, and no one ever heard a lie come from His lips.

MAGIC TIPS

Consider joining a magic club to help hone your skills as an artist.

Read over a trick several times very carefully before presenting it.

Make the trick your own. If you think you know of a way to improve a trick in this book, go for it!

CATECHETICAL TIPS

Magic is among the very few art forms that successfully incorporates a variety of different learning styles including the visual, audio and tactile. As such, Gospel Magic is an appropriate and highly flexible tool in that it can be adapted to a wide range of comprehension levels.

Magic tricks are meant to be supplementary and ancillary to the catechism that you are teaching. They should never supplant regular catechetical classes as it would be disrespectful to the subject at hand and confusing to your classes.

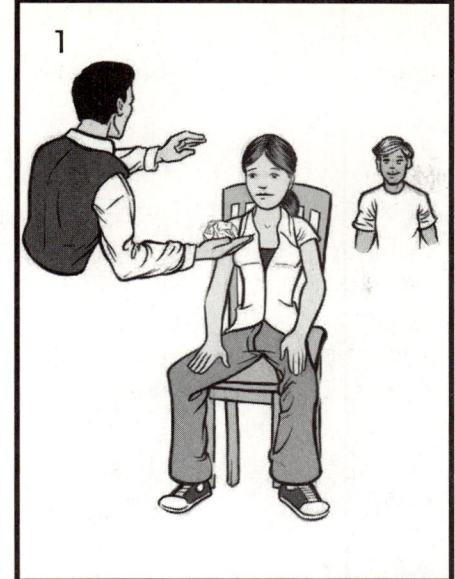

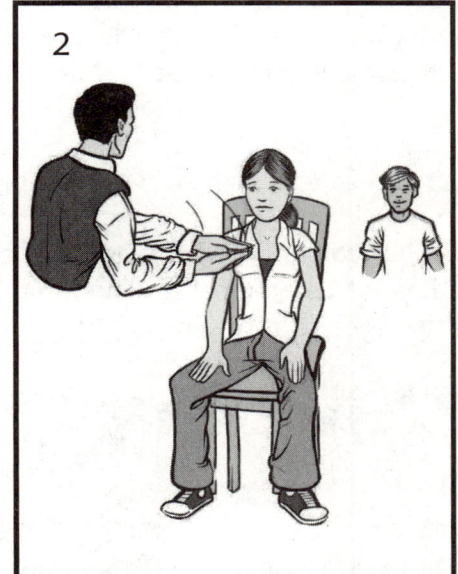

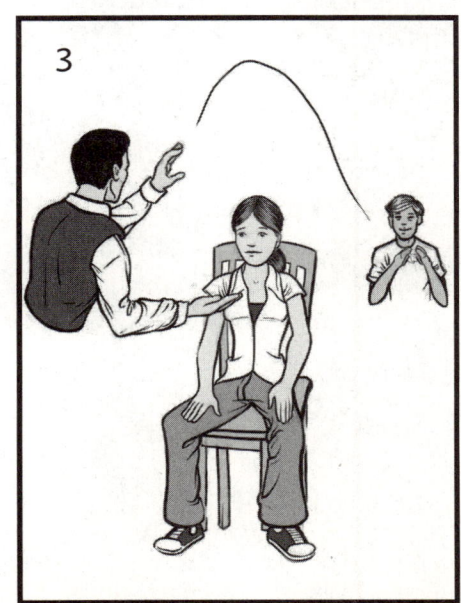

HOW YOU DO IT:

Unbeknownst to your volunteer, but very apparent to the rest of your audience, you are actually tossing the paper napkin ball to a confederate behind the seated volunteer. Obviously you will not be able to fool the audience but you will be able to fool the volunteer even if only for the duration of the trick.

The trick is very self-explanatory. The simple move is to hold the increasingly larger paper ball in the palm of your left hand as you lean over the volunteer. Clap your right hand over the left and cover it 3 times, counting aloud each time. At the second clap, grab the ball with your right hand and toss it over your volunteer's head. Slam your hand down quickly, and immediately open both of your hands to show that the ball has disappeared. Repeat this 2 more times with an increasingly larger ball of paper napkins.

Let nothing disturb thee;
Let nothing dismay thee;
All thing pass;
God never changes.
Patience attains all
that it strives for.
He who has God finds
he lacks nothing:
God alone suffices.

— St. Teresa of Avila

THE NINTH COMMANDMENT (2514-2533)

Through God's love and grace we come to know the difference between good and evil.

WHAT YOU NEED:

a deck of cards
a manila envelope
a pair of scissors
the prediction paper
   (cutout on page 243)

WHAT THEY SEE:

The catechist lays 2 cards faceup on a tabletop and places a prediction envelope in plain sight. The volunteer is given an absolutely free choice of either card. She chooses one and then the magician checks the prediction. The prediction is shown to be correct.

WHAT YOU SAY:

"Did you ever have a problem making the right decision? The truth is, you probably knew what you were supposed to do. Most people instinctively know what is good. Let's see what it means to make the correct decision. You have a choice now. Which card will you choose?"

(Ask the volunteer to choose either the king or queen of hearts. Cut the envelope based on the card she chooses. Remove the larger half of the prediction paper from the envelope and show it to your audience.)

"People don't have special magic powers but you knew what was in the envelope. When we trust ourselves, we usually come to the right decision. If you trust yourself, follow the rules of the Church, and are open to the will of God, you will always make the right decisions in your life."

MATTHEW 5:27-32
You have heard that it was said, "Do not commit adultery." But now I tell you: anyone who looks at a woman and wants to possess her is guilty of committing adultery with her in his heart. So if your right eye causes you to sin, take it out and throw it away! It is much better for you to lose a part of your body than to have your whole body thrown into hell. If your right hand causes you to sin, cut it off and throw it away! It is much better for you to lose one of your limbs than to have your whole body go off to hell. It was also said, "Anyone who divorces his wife must give her a written notice of divorce." But now I tell you: if a man divorces his wife for any cause other than her unfaithfulness, then he is guilty of making her commit adultery if she marries again; and the man who marries her commits adultery also.

MATTHEW 15:19
For from your heart come the evil ideas which lead you to kill, commit adultery, and do other immoral things; to rob, lie, and slander others.

MARK 10:11-12
He said to them, "A man who divorces his wife and marries another woman commits adultery against his wife. In the same way, a woman who divorces her husband and marries another man commits adultery."

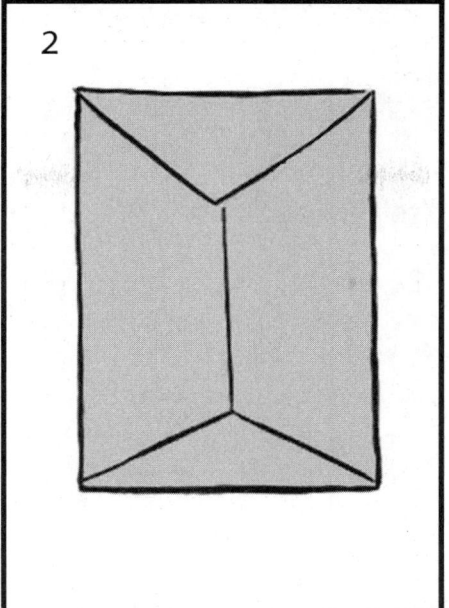
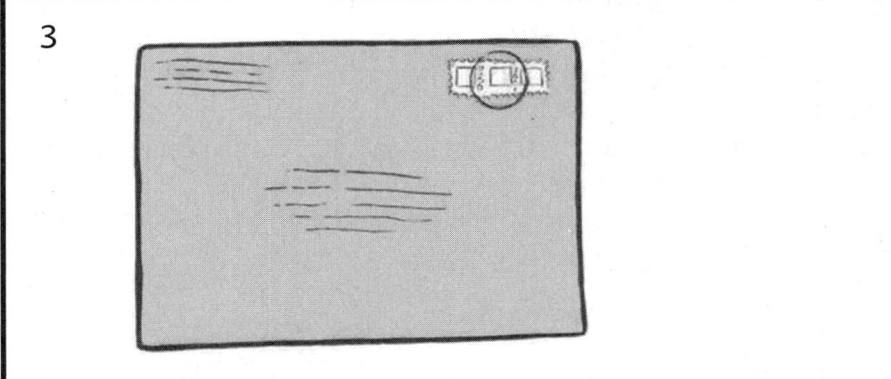
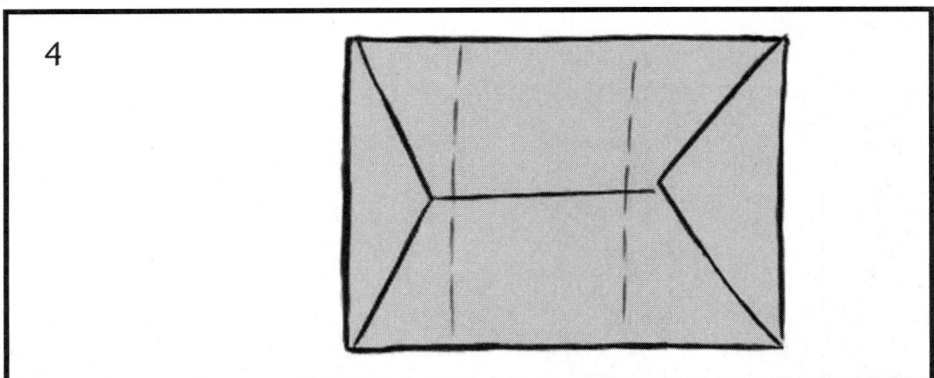

HOW YOU DO IT:

If you look at the prediction cutout on page 243 you'll note that the page can be cut on either line and still make a complete sentence. Cutting on the upper line makes the sentence: The chosen card will be the king of hearts. Cutting on the bottom line makes the sentence: The queen of hearts will be the chosen card. Photocopy the page, place the prediction in a manila envelope, and seal it. Mark the envelope with 2 lines that reflect the placement of the lines on the paper within. Make sure you mark the envelope exactly where the lines appear on the photocopied sheet so that you cut it correctly.

To add authenticity to the prediction, you can pretend to have mailed it many days, weeks or even months, before the performance. There's no need to actually mail it. Instead, ask the person at the post office to stamp the postage you've bought for it and simply hand it back to you.

Take the king of hearts and the queen of hearts out of the deck and ask your volunteer to choose one. If she chooses the king, cut the envelope on the upper line. If she chooses the queen, cut the envelope on the lower line. Take the larger half of the prediction card out of the envelope and show that it does indeed match her choice.

ROMANS 7:3
So then, if she lives with another man while her husband is alive, she will be called an adulteress; but if her husband dies, she is legally a free woman and does not commit adultery if she marries another man.

HEBREWS 13:4
Marriage is to be honored by all, and husbands and wives must be faithful to each other. God will judge those who are immoral and those who commit adultery.

THE TENTH COMMANDMENT (2534-2557)

Where your riches are, so too is your heart.

WHAT YOU NEED:

a Change Bag (see page 59)
a pair of scissors
2 identical ties
a confederate

WHAT THEY SEE:

The catechist asks for a male volunteer to step up and requests his tie for a small experiment. The tie is cut up into pieces and placed into a small bag. A small bit of it is seen at all times. Instantly, the tie is pulled out of the bag and is completely restored.

WHAT YOU SAY:

"What would pull us away from God? What can happen in our lives that would misdirect and confuse us? We can lose sight of God when we are too attached to physical goods and have lost our compassion for others. God doesn't abandon us, but sometimes we attempt to push God aside. Nothing good can come from being attached to material goods. Cast your bread upon the waters, and it will come back to you manifold. Do you remember the story of the young man who asked Christ what else he could do besides following the commandments? Jesus told him 'If you want to be perfect, go and sell all you have and give the money to the poor, and you will have riches in heaven; then come and follow Me.'"

(Ask for your confederate's tie and have a volunteer cut it up. Place the pieces into the Change Bag. After a bit of byplay, restore it.)

"As you see ... your goods are fine ... all you had to do was trust in the Lord. A truly spiritual person will not be overly concerned about the loss of physical possessions. As St. Paul reminds us, 'Do not be anxious.' This means we should give ourselves over to God's will if we hope to be happy in this lifetime."

MATTHEW 19:16-26

Once a man came to Jesus. "Teacher," he asked, "what good thing must I do to receive eternal life?" "Why do you ask Me concerning what is good?" answered Jesus. "There is only One Who is good. Keep the commandments if you want to enter life." "What commandments?" he asked. Jesus answered, "Do not commit murder; do not commit adultery; do not steal; do not accuse anyone falsely; respect your father and your mother; and love your neighbor as you love yourself." "I have obeyed all these commandments," the young man replied. "What else do I need to do?" Jesus said to him, "If you want to be perfect, go and sell all you have and give the money to the poor, and you will have riches in heaven; then come and follow Me." When the young man heard this, he went away sad, because he was very rich. Jesus then said to His disciples, "I assure you: it will be very hard for rich people to enter the Kingdom of heaven. I repeat: it is much harder for a rich person to enter the Kingdom of God than for a camel to go through the eye of a needle." When the disciples heard this, they were completely amazed. "Who, then, can be saved?" they asked. Jesus looked straight at them and answered, "This is impossible for human beings, but for God everything is possible."

GOSPEL MAGIC HISTORY

When he was a child, St. Don Bosco would gather the children of his village and repeat the homily he had heard that day.

St. Don Bosco learned his magic tricks from carnival magicians passing through his small town in Italy.

Catholic Magicians around the world celebrate St. Don Bosco's feastday by offering free performances for children in schools and hospitals.

Two of St. Nicholas Owen's brothers became priests and another printed illegal books for the outlawed Catholic community.

LUKE 12:33-34
Sell all your belongings and give the money to the poor. Provide for yourselves purses that don't wear out, and save your riches in heaven, where they will never decrease, because no thief can get to them, and no moth can destroy them. For your heart will always be where your riches are.

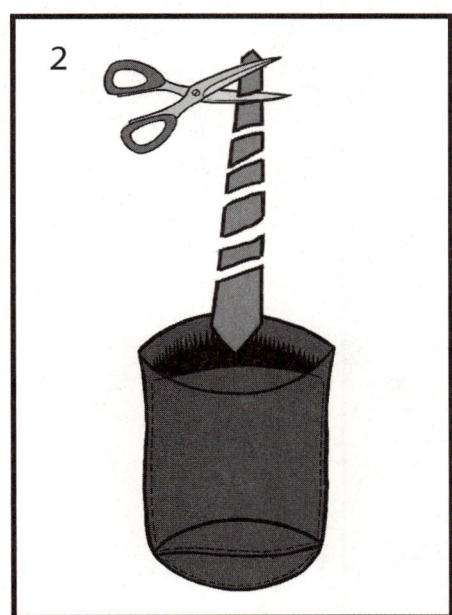

HOW YOU DO IT:

This magic trick is accomplished with the use of the Change Bag described on page 59. The male volunteer is a confederate. That is, he has agreed prior to the performance to help you and pretend as if he was not in on the scheme. Procure 2 identical inexpensive ties and give one of them to your confederate before the performance. Place its twin in one of the compartments of the Change Bag.

The rest of the trick is dependent upon good acting; both yours and that of your confederate. After he comes to the stage, ask to borrow his tie. He should do so reluctantly as no one gladly hands his tie over to a magician wielding a pair of scissors.

Ask for another volunteer to cut up the tie, allowing the pieces to fall into the unused compartment of the Change Bag. Your confederate should keep in mind how someone might react to seeing his tie cut into little pieces. His surprise and dismay will help waylay any of your audience's suspicions. After the tie is cut into pieces, look into the compartment with the intact tie and looked concerned as if the trick didn't quite go as well as you had hoped. Look into the second compartment and slowly pull out the now "restored" tie.

Part 4:
CHRISTIAN PRAYER

God's countenance is our reason because, just as we recognize someone by his face, so we recognize God through the mirror of reason. However, this reason has been deformed by human sin, since sin opposes us to God. The grace of Christ has put our reason right. Hence, the apostle Paul says to the Ephesians: "Be renewed in your minds" (Ephesians 4:23). The light in question in this psalm is thus the grace that restores God's image imprinted in our nature.

— St. Anthony of Padua (c.1195-1231),
Sermons for Sundays and Feasts of the Saints

IN THE OLD TESTAMENT (2558-2597)

The ancient forms of prayer show us the way to God.

WHAT YOU NEED:

2 handkerchiefs
a needle and thread
   or sewing machine
a Kennedy half-dollar coin

WHAT THEY SEE:

Both sides of a handkerchief are shown. All 4 corners are gathered together and a coin is placed inside the newly-formed pocket. Immediately, the catechist takes 2 corners of the handkerchief and shakes the cloth to show that the coin has disappeared. The corners of the handkerchief are gathered up again and, instantly, the coin is found once again.

WHAT YOU SAY:

"In the Old Testament, believers relied upon the temple to pray to God. Prayer usually included a sacrifice of an animal like a sheep or a goat. Prayer was inevitably asking God for something that the believer needed, like winning a battle or curing a disease that was affecting the entire community."

"Let's imagine this handkerchief is the temple at Jerusalem and this coin is God's love and presence. Solomon built the temple for God so that he could maintain God's presence in the midst of the Jewish people. But, of course, God is too important, too big, too wonderful to be contained inside a building created by humans."

(Shake the handkerchief and open it to show that the coin has disappeared.)

"As you see, although God's presence is among His people and in His tabernacle, He cannot be seen. But, even though you may not be able to see Him, if you seek Him, He will be found."

(Gather together the handkerchief's corners and reach in to retrieve the coin.)

GENESIS 1:1-5

In the beginning, when God created the universe, the earth was formless and desolate. The raging ocean that covered everything was engulfed in total darkness, and the Spirit of God was moving over the water. Then God commanded, "Let there be light" — and light appeared. God was pleased with what he saw. Then He separated the light from the darkness, and he named the light "Day" and the darkness "Night." Evening passed and morning came — that was the first day.

1 KINGS 19:8-12

Elijah got up, ate and drank, and the food gave him enough strength to walk forty days to Sinai, the holy mountain. There he went into a cave to spend the night. Suddenly the Lord spoke to him, "Elijah, what are you doing here?" He answered, "Lord God Almighty, I have always served you — you alone. But the people of Israel have broken their covenant with you, torn down your altars, and killed all your prophets. I am the only one left — and they are trying to kill me!" "Go out and stand before me on top of the mountain," the Lord said to him. Then the Lord passed by and sent a furious wind that split the hills and shattered the rocks — but the Lord was not in the wind. The wind stopped blowing, and then there was an earthquake — but the Lord was not in the earthquake. After the earthquake there was a fire — but the Lord was not in the fire. And after the fire there was the soft whisper of a voice.

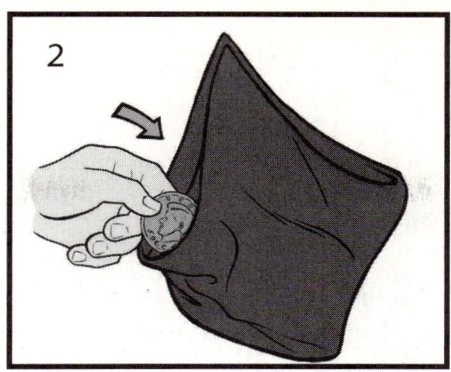
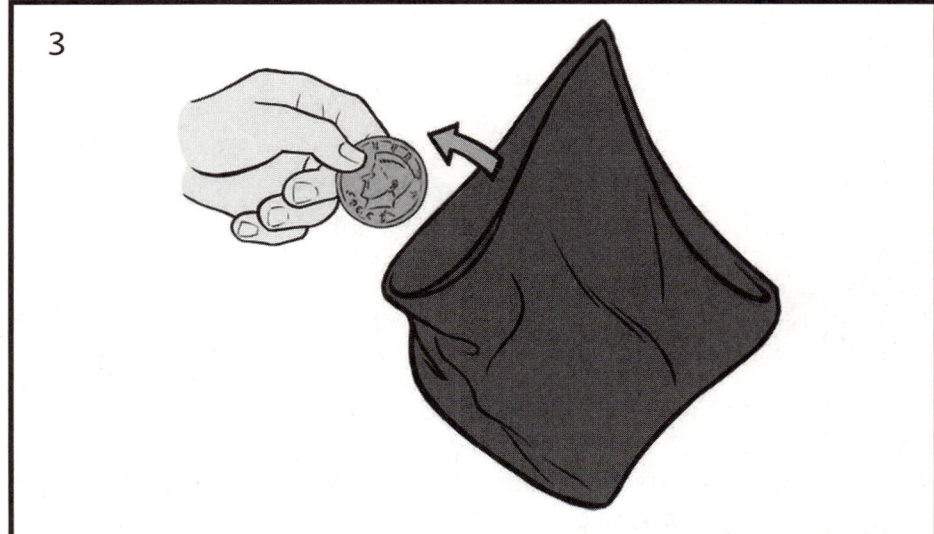

HOW YOU DO IT:

This is a specially constructed gimmick device known among Gospel Magicians as an "Angel's Handkerchief." It's actually 2 identical handkerchiefs sewn together in such a way as to form a hidden compartment between them. All seams except that of a 2-inch section on one side of the corner of the handkerchiefs are sewn together.

When you gather the corners of this handkerchief together, you will find that the secret pocket opens up immediately. Simply place the coin into the hole and it will slip to the bottom of the pocket. At this point, you can even ask a volunteer to touch the coin through the fabric to make sure that it really is there. Release the bottom 2 of the corners and show both sides of the handkerchief. To retrieve the coin, simply form the pouch again and reach into the secret pocket.

What we are looking for is What is looking. — St. Francis of Assisi

---

2 SAMUEL 24:25
Then he built an altar to the Lord and offered burnt offerings and fellowship offerings. The Lord answered his prayer, and the epidemic in Israel was stopped.

JOB 42:8
Now take 7 bulls and 7 rams to Job and offer them as a sacrifice for yourselves. Job will pray for you, and I will answer his prayer and not disgrace you the way you deserve. You did not speak the truth about me as he did.

1 KINGS 3:2
A temple had not yet been built for the Lord, and so the people were still offering sacrifices at many different altars.

1 KINGS 9:3
The Lord said to him, "I have heard your prayer. I consecrate this Temple which you have built as the place where I shall be worshiped forever. I will watch over it and protect it for all time."

IN THE FULLNESS OF TIME (2598-2622)

God has a plan for the world.

WHAT YOU NEED:

a deck of cards

WHAT THEY SEE:

The magician offers a volunteer a free choice of cards. The card is memorized and returned to the deck. Immediately, the magician locates the selected card.

WHAT YOU SAY:

"What is meant by the expression 'the fullness of time?' Generally, it refers to what ultimately happens according to God's plans for the world. Let me show you an example of what I mean. Choose any card and memorize it."

(Spy the bottom card of the deck in your hand while the volunteer is busy looking at her card.)

"Now ... let me remind you of everything we've done so far. We shuffled the deck. You chose a card completely randomly. There is no way for me to know what card you took. As I told you, the fullness of time means, waiting for something to happen ... like the way God asks us to wait and be patient for His plan to unfold. Should I make you wait any longer now? No? OK ... here's your card!"

(Reveal your spectator's card.)

"Sometimes, in the midst of our problems, when we wonder why God hasn't helped us immediately, we ask ourselves 'why?' This is a perfectly normal question. But, if we are patient and willing to accept God's timing, we will be rewarded with many gifts."

JEREMIAH 29:12-13
Then you will call to Me. You will come and pray to Me, and I will answer you. You will seek Me, and you will find Me because you will seek Me with all your heart.

ISAIAH 7:14
Well then, the Lord Himself will give you a sign: a virgin who is pregnant will have a son and will name Him 'Immanuel.'

LUKE 24:45-48
Then He opened their minds to understand the Scriptures, and said to them, "This is what is written: the Messiah must suffer and must rise from death 3 days later, and in His name the message about repentance and the forgiveness of sins must be preached to all nations, beginning in Jerusalem. You are witnesses of these things."

HOW YOU DO IT:

This trick is accomplished with the use of a key card. When the volunteer is examining her card, sneak a peek at the bottom card of the deck in your hand. When the volunteer returns the card to the top of the deck, cut the deck and complete the cut, placing the bottom half of the deck on top of the other half. This will make sure that the card you spied is on top of the volunteer's card. Once done, spread the deck in your hand and find the card you spied, the "key card." The card immediately underneath it is the volunteer's card.

MAGIC TIP
Use the best quality cards that you can afford, otherwise the cards will get shabby-looking and messy. Professional magicians will usually use Bee or Bicycle brands.

JOHN 11:27
"Yes, Lord!" she answered. "I do believe that You are the Messiah, the Son of God, Who was to come into the world."

JOHN 12:34
The crowd answered, "Our Law tells us that the Messiah will live forever. How, then, can you say that the Son of Man must be lifted up? Who is this Son of Man?"

ACTS 2:31
David saw what God was going to do in the future, and so he spoke about the resurrection of the Messiah when he said, "He was not abandoned in the world of the dead; His body did not rot in the grave."

ACTS 3:18
God announced long ago through all the prophets that His Messiah had to suffer; and He made it come true in this way.

IN THE AGE OF THE CHURCH (2623-2649)

Prayer is a lifeline to God.

WHAT YOU NEED:

a 3-foot length of rope
2 small matching magnets
a deck of cards
a single duplicate card
a top hat
a small box, or bag
white glue

WHAT THEY SEE:

The catechist gives a volunteer a choice of any card. The card is shuffled back into the deck and the deck is dropped into a cloth bag. A rope is introduced and lowered into the bag and, mysteriously, the selected card is lassoed by the rope.

WHAT YOU SAY:

"When you're sad, or happy, or mad, or lonely, what do you do? Do you ever call a friend? God is not only our Creator, but our Father, our Mother, our Brother and our Friend."

> (Force the card on your volunteer.)

"When we pray, it's like calling a good friend who will always take the time to understand us. Someone who will always love us."

> (Drop the shuffled deck into the top hat.)

"If we ever feel lost ... just like this card is lost, we can always trust that God will find us. Prayer is like a lifeline to God."

> (Drop the gimmicked rope into the top hat and retrieve the duplicate card.)

"God is always there to help us. He is waiting only for us to ask Him for His help. Prayer is the way we remain present to Him and He to us."

LUKE 15:11-32

Jesus went on to say, "There was once a man who had 2 sons. The younger one said to him, 'Father, give me my share of the property now.' So the man divided his property between his 2 sons. After a few days the younger son sold his part of the property and left home with the money. He went to a country far away, where he wasted his money in reckless living. He spent everything he had. Then a severe famine spread over that country, and he was left without a thing. So he went to work for one of the citizens of that country, who sent him out to his farm to take care of the pigs. He wished he could fill himself with the bean pods the pigs ate, but no one gave him anything to eat. At last he came to his senses and said, 'All my father's hired workers have more than they can eat, and here I am about to starve! I will get up and go to my father and say, "Father, I have sinned against God and against you. I am no longer fit to be called your son; treat me as one of your hired workers." ' So he got up and started back to his father. He was still a long way from home when his father saw him; his heart was filled with pity, and he ran, threw his arms around his son, and kissed him. 'Father,' the son said, 'I have sinned against God and against you. I am no longer fit to be called your son.' But the father called to his servants. 'Hurry!' he said.

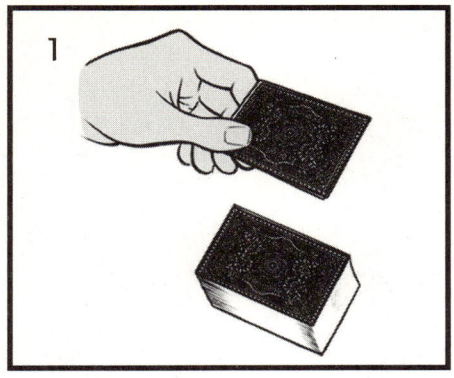

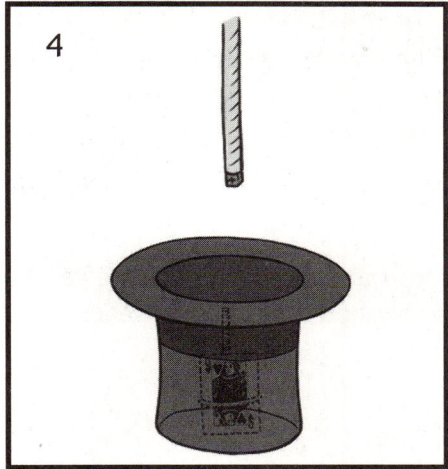
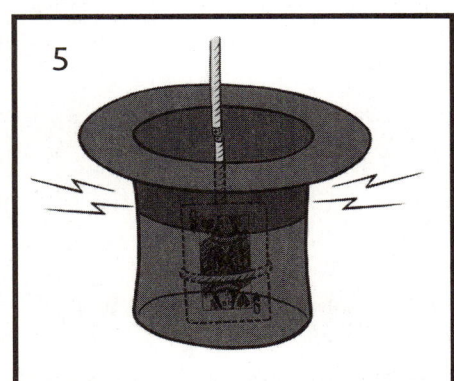
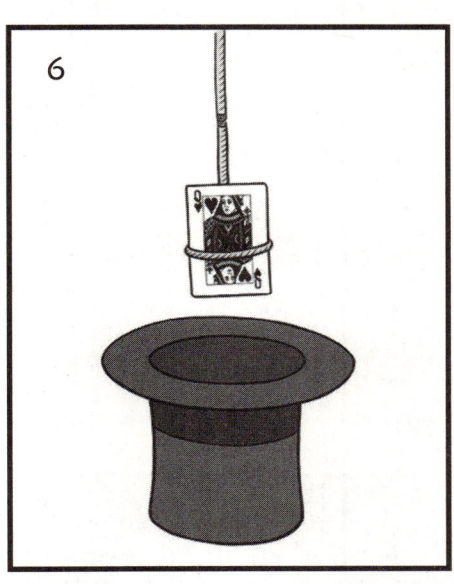

HOW YOU DO IT:

Cut off approximately 12 inches of rope and, using glue, embed a magnet into one end. Glue the other magnet into the end of the other length of rope. Make sure that they are oriented to attract each other and that they form what looks like an unbroken length of rope when they are in close proximity.

Tie the shorter piece of rope around the duplicate card. Knot the rope in back of the card, leaving the magnet end longer. Place the card with the shorter rope around it in a top hat (or bag or box).

Force the duplicate of the card that you have attached to the short end of the rope onto your volunteer. Use False Shuffle Force 3 on page 109. Have the volunteer return the card to the deck and allow the volunteer to give the deck a completely unnecessary but fair shuffle. Dump the cards into the top hat and lower the gimmicked rope into the hat. The magnet hidden in the rope that you lower into the top hat will engage the magnet hidden in the rope that is tied around the duplicate card and voila! The selected card will be lassoed and pulled out of the top hat.

(LUKE 15:11-32 continued)

'Bring the best robe and put it on him. Put a ring on his finger and shoes on his feet. Then go and get the prize calf and kill it, and let us celebrate with a feast! For this son of mine was dead, but now he is alive; he was lost, but now he has been found.' And so the feasting began. In the meantime the older son was out in the field. On his way back, when he came close to the house, he heard the music and dancing. So he called one of the servants and asked him, 'What's going on?' 'Your brother has come back home,' the servant answered, 'and your father has killed the prize calf, because he got him back safe and sound.' The older brother was so angry that he would not go into the house; so his father came out and begged him to come in. But he spoke back to his father, 'Look, all these years I have worked for you like a slave, and I have never disobeyed your orders. What have you given me? Not even a goat for me to have a feast with my friends! But this son of yours wasted all your property on prostitutes, and when he comes back home, you kill the prize calf for him!' 'My son,' the father answered, 'you are always here with me, and everything I have is yours. But we had to celebrate and be happy, because your brother was dead, but now he is alive; he was lost, but now he has been found.'"

AT THE WELLSPRINGS OF PRAYER (2652-2662)

The power of prayer leads us to God.

WHAT YOU NEED:

a large palming coin with deep rills

WHAT THEY SEE:

The catechist reaches behind a volunteer's ear and pulls out a coin.

WHAT YOU SAY:

"What can we expect from a lifelong commitment to prayer? We can hope for the grace to live in accordance with God's will. To love each other as He asked of us. Prayer teaches us to be humble and to accept His love in our hearts."

(Reach out to remove a coin from a volunteer's ear.)

"If we accept Christ in our hearts, He promises a life of love and incredible spiritual gifts. All we have to do is ask Him for them."

MAGIC TIP

Watch your angles. Magicians should always be aware of the placement of their audiences and volunteers. If necessary, don't be shy about asking your spectators to reposition themselves to your advantage. If they won't or can't move, go on to the next trick.

EXODUS 24:18
Moses went on up the mountain into the cloud. There he stayed for forty days and nights.

EXODUS 34:28
Moses stayed there with the Lord forty days and nights, eating and drinking nothing. He wrote on the tablets the words of the covenant—the Ten Commandments.

LUKE 10:38-42
As Jesus and his disciples went on their way, He came to a village where a woman named Martha welcomed Him in her home. She had a sister named Mary, who sat down at the feet of the Lord and listened to His teaching. Martha was upset over all the work she had to do, so she came and said, "Lord, don't You care that my sister has left me to do all the work by myself? Tell her to come and help me!" The Lord answered her, "Martha, Martha! You are worried and troubled over so many things, but just one is needed. Mary has chosen the right thing, and it will not be taken away from her."

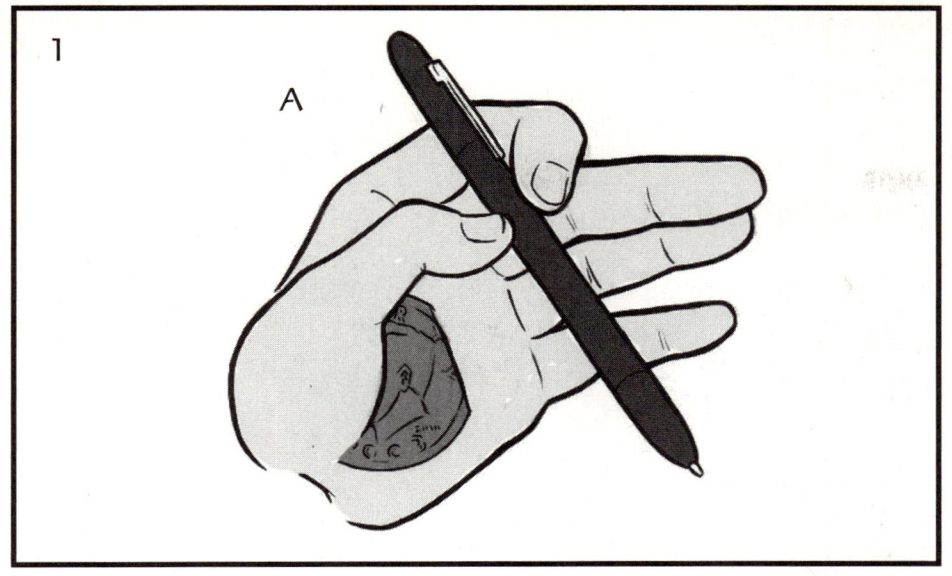

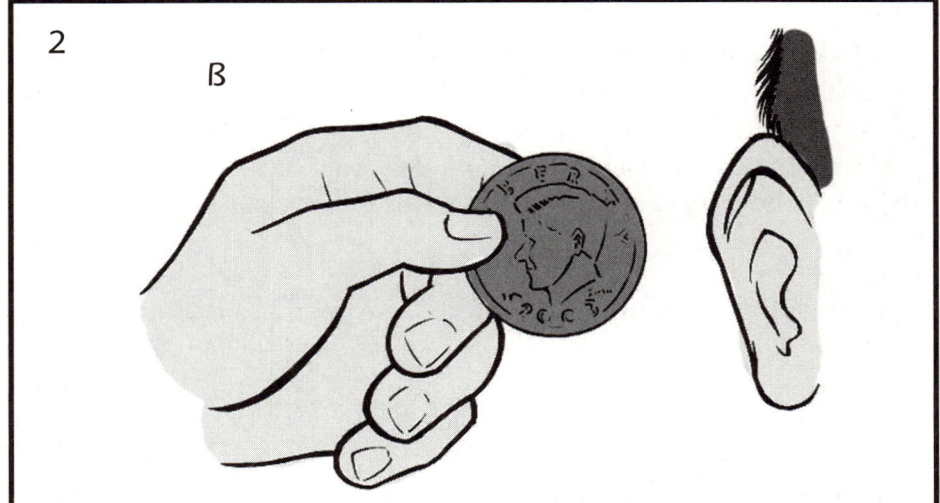

HOW YOU DO IT:

The Classic Palm is an easy sleight-of-hand maneuver to do, but difficult to master. It is the basis of nearly all coin magic. Procure a large, somewhat heavy coin. A Kennedy half-dollar is the smallest useable coin for a teenager or adult. Place the coin in the center of your dominant hand and allow it to settle into the natural contours of your palm. Next, curl your hand slightly and allow the skin of your palm to "grab" the coin. Once the coin is secure, allow your hand to rest naturally at your side. Hopefully the coin will not fall.

As you go about your day, keep the coin palmed in this manner. The more you practice, the easier it will be to palm coins. You will soon be able to write or pick up small objects without dislodging the coin. Once you are comfortable with hiding a coin in your hand, practice reaching behind people's ears and retrieving the coin. This is actually the easiest part of palming.

We must pray without tiring, for the salvation of mankind does not depend on material success; nor on sciences that cloud the intellect. Neither does it depend on arms and human industries, but on Jesus alone.
— St. Frances Cabrini

So she hung her love and her longing desire in this cloud of unknowing, and learned to love what she could not see clearly in this life by the light of understanding in her reason, nor truly feel in the sweetness of love in her affection; so much so that she paid little attention to whether she had been a sinner or not. Yes! And so often I think that she was so deeply affected in the love of the Godhead that she scarcely noticed the beauty of His precious and blessed body as He sat so handsomely speaking and teaching before her. It seems from the gospel that she was oblivious to anything else either bodily or spiritual.
— The Cloud of Unknowing

THE WAY OF PRAYER (2663-2682)

God uses prayer to develop a relationship with us.

WHAT YOU NEED:

a deck of cards

WHAT THEY SEE:

The magician chooses 2 cards from his deck and asks a volunteer to replace them anywhere she wishes. The magician retrieves the deck and tosses it in the air. Amidst the resulting shower of cards, he is able to immediately find the 2 previously lost cards.

WHAT YOU SAY:

"What is the need for prayer? Can we truly love God if we refuse to communicate with Him? Is it possible to have a relationship with anyone if we don't speak with that person? Communication is important for us. If we don't communicate with those around us, including God, how can we know their hearts and minds? When we communicate, we can get a lot accomplished. Imagine what our lives would be like if none of us could ask for the things we needed or tell others how much we love them or let them tell us how much they need us. It would be a very sad life."

"Right now, I want you to communicate mentally with me and tell me which were your 2 cards. Now that I know, let's see if I can find them for you."

(Toss the cards into the air, making sure you retain the top and bottom cards in your hand.)

"And here are your cards. When we communicate with God and those around us we can accomplish many things. Prayer allows us to commune with God. In that silence, we can listen to what He wants of us."

LUKE 1:13
But the angel said to him, "Don't be afraid, Zechariah! God has heard your prayer, and your wife Elizabeth will bear you a son. You are to name him John.

LUKE 4:1-2
Jesus returned from the Jordan full of the Holy Spirit and was led by the Spirit into the desert, where He was tempted by the Devil for forty days. In all that time He ate nothing, so that He was hungry when it was over.

LUKE 22:45
Rising from His prayer, He went back to the disciples and found them asleep, worn out by their grief.

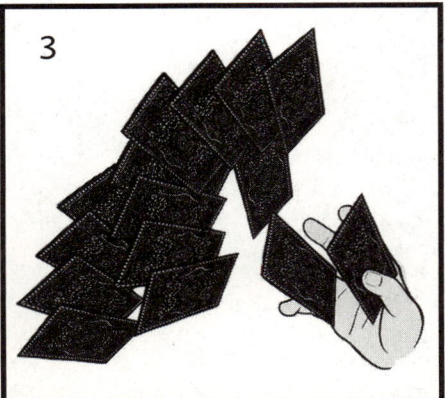

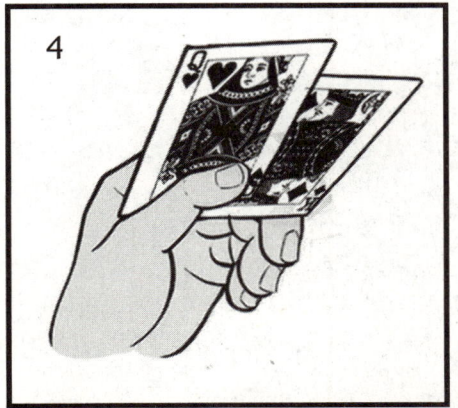

HOW YOU DO IT:

Secretly place the King of Diamonds on the top of the deck and the Queen of Hearts at the bottom of the deck. When you are ready to perform this trick, fan the deck towards yourself and openly remove the Queen of Diamonds and the King of Hearts. Show these cards to your volunteer and after she looks at them ask her to insert those 2 cards anywhere into the middle of the deck (the deck should still be fanned with the back towards volunteer).

Keep a fairly tight grip on the deck and concentrate on keeping hold of the top and bottom cards as you toss the deck into the air. As the cards tumble about you, pretend to "pull" the top and bottom cards from the shower of cards. Be nonchalant about it and smile widely. It is hoped that your audience will have forgotten the fact that these were not the exact cards shown in the beginning of the trick.

MAGIC TIP
Use the best quality cards that you can afford, otherwise the cards will get shabby-looking and messy. Professional magicians will usually use Bee or Bicycle brands.

> I have found and have known, by Your great mercy, that the love of a man's heart that is abandoned and broken and poor is most pleasing to You and attracts the gaze of Your Pity.
> — Thomas Merton, *Thoughts in Solitude*

197

GUIDES FOR PRAYER (2683-2696)

Those experienced in developing a relationship with God can teach us how to pray.

WHAT YOU NEED:

a deck of cards
a guillotine-style paper cutter
a pair of rounded manicure scissors

WHAT THEY SEE:

A volunteer is given a free and fair choice of any card. It's returned to the deck and the volunteer is asked to shuffle it. Instantly, the card is located.

WHAT YOU SAY:

"In prayer, we look for models to help us learn how to seek God. The Church's saints and mystics are all excellent guides from whom we can learn of the experience of approaching God in prayer."

(Motion to the deck of cards.)

"This deck is not like regular decks. It's for magicians who want to learn how to do magic tricks. It will help me figure out what card you take. It's my guide just like the saints and mystics in the Church are guides to prayer. Choose any card and make sure you show everyone what it is. Now please return it to the deck."

(Riffle the rest of the deck until you hear the short card. Cut the deck at that point and have the volunteer place her card on top of the short card. Then, false shuffle the deck.)

"Now ... my deck will help me identify your card. All of the Church's mystics and saints say that God whispers rather than shouts. Let's be quiet to listen to the deck as it tries to held me find your card."

(Listen for the distinctive sound of the short card as it slaps against the other cards. Ribbon spread the cards and identify the volunteer's card—the one on top of the short card.)

"We can't hear anything if we're shouting. The same goes for listening for God. He always speaks to us in the quiet of our hearts. Listening is the best kind of prayer."

EPHESIANS 6:18
Do all this in prayer, asking for God's help. Pray on every occasion, as the Spirit leads.
For this reason keep alert and never give up; pray always for all God's people.

JAMES 5:15
This prayer made in faith will heal the sick; the Lord will restore them to
health, and the sins they have committed will be forgiven.

PHILEMON 1:6
My prayer is that our fellowship with you as believers will bring about a deeper understanding of every blessing which we have in our life in union with Christ.

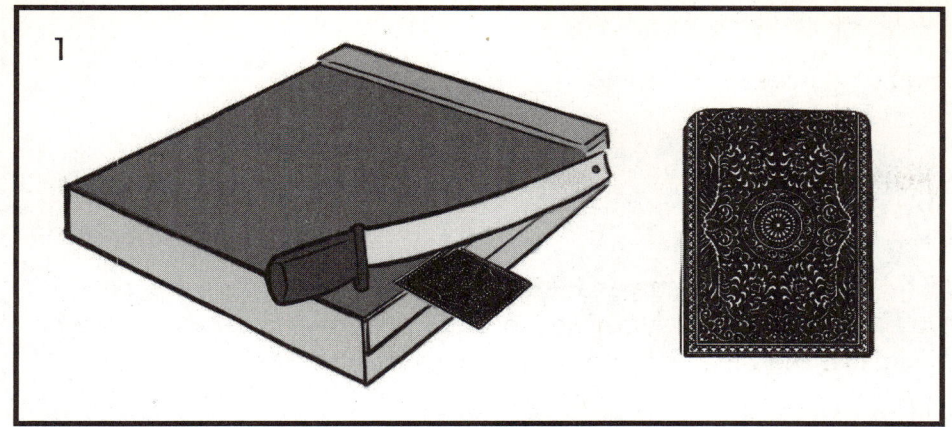

HOW YOU DO IT:

This is an old and fairly easy means of locating a selected card. The key is a gimmicked card known as a "short card." Using a guillotine-style paper cutter, trim any card by 1/32 inch. Make sure to round off the corners of the cut end with rounded manicure scissors.

short card

Place your prepared card someplace in the middle of the deck. Once the volunteer has made a fair choice, riffle the deck until you find the short card. With some practice, you will note that when you get to the short card, it will make a distinct sound. Once you find it, break the deck at that point and allow the volunteer to place her selected card on top of it. Falsely shuffle the deck (use false shuffle 1 or 2 on page 109).

When you are ready, riffle through the deck until you hear the distinct sound of the short card again. Cut the deck at that point and you will be able to locate the volunteer's card.

volunteer card

The purpose of prayer is the noughting of oneself and the all-ing of God.
— The Cloud of Unknowing

1 TIMOTHY 4:3-5
Such people teach that it is wrong to marry and to eat certain foods. But God created those foods to be eaten, after a prayer of thanks, by those who are believers and have come to know the truth. Everything that God has created is good; nothing is to be rejected, but everything is to be received with a prayer of thanks, because the word of God and the prayer make it acceptable to God.

THE LIFE OF PRAYER (2697-2865)

Prayer helps us grow as individuals and as part of God's family.

WHAT YOU NEED:

a 1-foot-square placard
a marker

WHAT THEY SEE:

The catechist demonstrates a simple placard that has an arrow printed on it. Despite the sign only having 2 obvious sides, it seems that the arrow is animated and can point, alternatively, in 4 different directions.

WHAT YOU SAY:

"We know that Christ came to us to point to the Father. His love for the Father is total and perfect."

>(Point upwards.)

"We can learn to look towards each other to help each other and to learn from each other."

>(Point right.)

"If we decide to not help each other and learn from each other, then where do we find ourselves?"

>(Point downwards.)

"What's the opposite of love? That's right ... it's sin. And no matter what, we can't make ourselves good just by ourselves no matter how hard we try."

>(Point left.)

"Do you know Who can help us? I think you already know. Who would do anything for us? Who wants us to be with Him? That's right ... it's God."

>(Point upwards.)

"Prayer allows us to speak to God. More accurately, it allows us to quiet ourselves so we can listen to God when He speaks to us. Those who lead a prayerful life see themselves becoming more humble and less sinful. They find see themselves putting their own needs aside as they become more conscious of their family and community. Prayer is truly one of God's most beautiful gifts."

ACTS 4:24
When the believers heard it, they all joined together in prayer to God: "Master and Creator of heaven, earth, and sea, and all that is in them!"

JAMES 5:16
So then, confess your sins to one another and pray for one another, so that you will be healed. The prayer of a good person has a powerful effect.

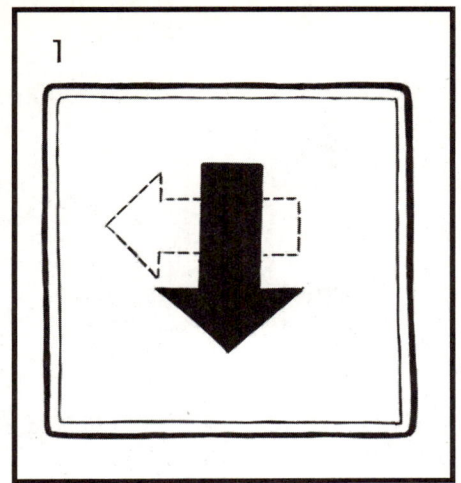

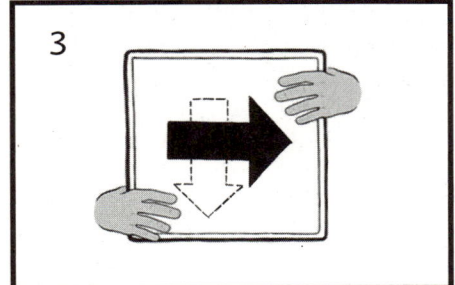

HOW YOU DO IT:

This trick was originally created by Melbourne Christopher. Create a one-foot-square, 2-sided placard like the accompanying diagram. On one side draw an arrow pointing to the right. Turn the page facedown so that the original arrow is pointing to the left. Now make an arrow that points down on the second side of the placard.

Practice this trick by standing in front of a mirror. Hold the sign as in Figure 2. You will note that the arrow points to the audience's right. Keep your right hand on the top right corner and your left hand on the bottom left corner and spin the card so that the reverse side faces the audience. The arrow will remain pointing to the audience's right. Next, move your hands to the placard's opposite corners as described in Figure 3. Now when you flip the sign over, the arrow will face the audience's left. While in this position, move your hands to the middle of the placard as described in Figure 4. If you turn over the placard, the arrow will point downwards. If you move your hands to the positions described in Figure 5 and turn the placard over, the arrow will point upwards.

It is imperative that you memorize the moves for this trick. This illusion is spoiled if you have to keep looking at the front of the placard to check your progress.

Make 4 signs: GOD, SIN, FAMILY & COMMUNITY and SELF. Place these 4 signs on the wall behind where you plan to stand to perform this trick. Place the GOD sign above your head. Place the SIN sign to your left. Place the COMMUNITY & FAMILY sign to your right and the SELF sign at your feet, preferably propped up on a small easel or stack of books.

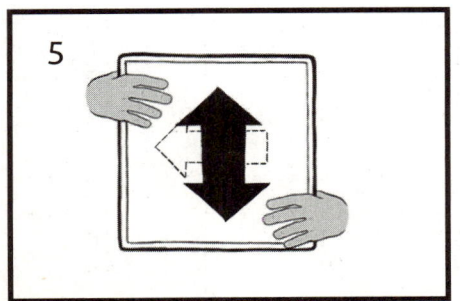

PERSEVERING IN LOVE (2742-2745)

Prayer changes us.

WHAT YOU NEED:

a faceted, plastic drinking glass,
a glass cutter
2 mirrors (they should be the same height as the plastic glass and as wide as the widest part of the glass)
caulking material
an 8-inch by 10-inch sheet of cardboard
a white handkerchief
a black handkerchief
a foulard
a pair of scissors

WHAT THEY SEE:

The catechist shows a black handkerchief and stuffs it into a glass resting on the table before him. A foulard is produced and placed over the glass. A moment later, he retrieves a white handkerchief from the glass.

WHAT YOU SAY:

"Did you ever want to meet God? Do you think that God wants to speak to you? What do you think it would be like to talk to Him? Do you know that we can speak to Him when we pray? It's true. And do you know what happens when we pray a lot and become closer and closer to Jesus? He can change us. He can make us perfect like Him."

(Show a black handkerchief and place it into glass. Cover the glass with a foulard.)

"Let's imagine the black handkerchief represents our sins. God can forgive us of our sins."

(Pick up the glass under the foulard and move it closer to the audience. In doing so, turn the glass around. Remove the foulard and take out the white handkerchief.)

"Our sinful selves can become good. Our stone hearts can be remade, full of compassion."

MATTHEW 4:2; MARK 1:13; LUKE 4:2
Where He stayed forty days, being tempted by Satan. Wild animals were there also, but angels came and helped Him.

COLOSSIANS 4:2
Be persistent in prayer, and keep alert as you pray, giving thanks to God.

1 TIMOTHY 2:8
In every church service I want the men to pray, men who are dedicated to God and can lift up their hands in prayer without anger or argument.

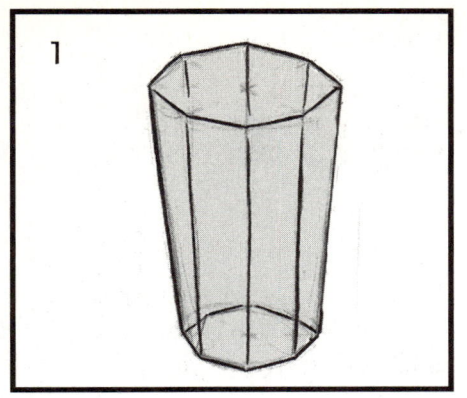
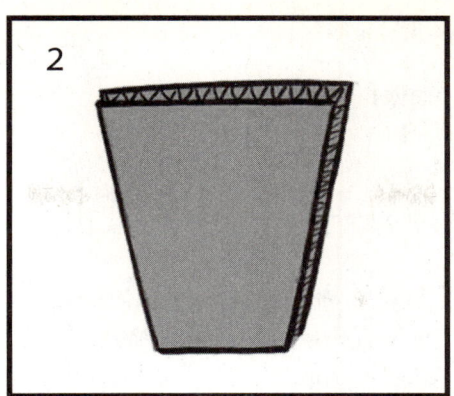

HOW YOU DO IT:

A Mirror Glass is very simple to construct. First, procure a faceted plastic drinking glass that is neither perfectly transparent nor perfectly opaque. One should be able to detect a brightly colored object resting inside the glass but not necessarily be able to see the outlines of the object clearly.

Cut a piece of cardboard to fit vertically across the center of the plastic drinking glass. You will need to make small adjustments to the cardboard with a pair of scissors. Once you are certain of the exact dimensions, cut 2 pieces of mirror using the cardboard as a template. Glue the 2 pieces back to back and use caulking material to affix the mirrors into the center of the plastic glass. Before performing the trick, stuff a white handkerchief into one of the compartments created by the mirror.

1 TIMOTHY 4:4-5
Everything that God has created is good; nothing is to be rejected, but everything is to be received with a prayer of thanks, because the word of God and the prayer make it acceptable to God.

JAMES 5:15
This prayer made in faith will heal the sick; the Lord will restore them to health, and the sins they have committed will be forgiven.

JAMES 5:16
So then, confess your sins to one another and pray for one another, so that you will be healed. The prayer of a good person has a powerful effect.

THE PRAYER OF THE HOUR OF JESUS (2746-2758)

Jesus is the aim and support of our prayer.

WHAT YOU NEED:

a dry, red magic marker
a fresh red magic marker
a photocopied page of
  a catechism book
an envelope
a blank sheet of paper

WHAT THEY SEE:

The catechist gives a marker and a photocopied page of the catechism to his volunteer. A sealed envelope is placed on the tabletop between them. The volunteer is told to hold the page facedown so that she cannot see it. She is then asked to draw a large X on the underside of the photocopy without looking at it. The photocopy is inspected and a single word appears at the juncture of the 2 lines. The envelope is consulted and is found to contain the same word.

WHAT YOU SAY:

"At Jesus's last hours on Earth, before His Passion and Crucifixion, he offered a final prayer that we call His 'Priestly Prayer.' In it, He asks His Father to 'let this cup pass but Your will be done and not Mine.' The purpose of all prayer is to bring oneself into sync with God. This requires a lot of time dedicated to prayer and changing your life so that you avoid sin. It means not opposing God. It means allowing God into your life. What would it be like if we opened ourselves up completely to God? I'd like to have an experiment."

(Hand the volunteer the dry magic marker and a photocopy of a page of the catechism.)

"Draw an X on the underside of the paper without looking."

(Retrieve the page and ask her to read out the word over which her lines crossed.)

"As you see, you made your X exactly over Jesus's Name. Let's see what the prediction had to say about what you would choose."

(Reveal the paper in the envelope with the word Jesus written on it.)

"This is what I meant by centering yourself in God. It means always choosing Jesus as your Brother, your Friend, your Savior. In all ways, in every way ... Jesus must be in your life."

ISAIAH 56:7
I will bring you to Zion, My sacred hill, give you joy in My house of prayer, and accept the sacrifices you offer on My altar. My Temple will be called a house of prayer for the people of all nations.

2 CHRONICLES 7:12; 1 KINGS 9:3
The Lord appeared to him at night. He said to him, "I have heard your prayer, and I accept this Temple as the place where sacrifices are to be offered to Me."

HOSEA 14:2
Return to the Lord, and let this prayer be your offering to Him: "Forgive all our sins and accept our prayer, and we will praise you as we have promised."

HOW YOU DO IT:

Write the name, Jesus on the blank sheet of paper and seal it inside an envelope. Photocopy a page of the catechism or a theology book where the name Jesus appears somewhere near the center of the page. Using your shakiest writing and the fresh magic marker, draw a large X that covers most of the page and centers over His name.

Holding the page upside down in front of your volunteer, have her uncap the dried out magic marker. Ask her to make an X on the underside of the paper without looking. Not knowing the marker is dried, she will think that she created the mark.

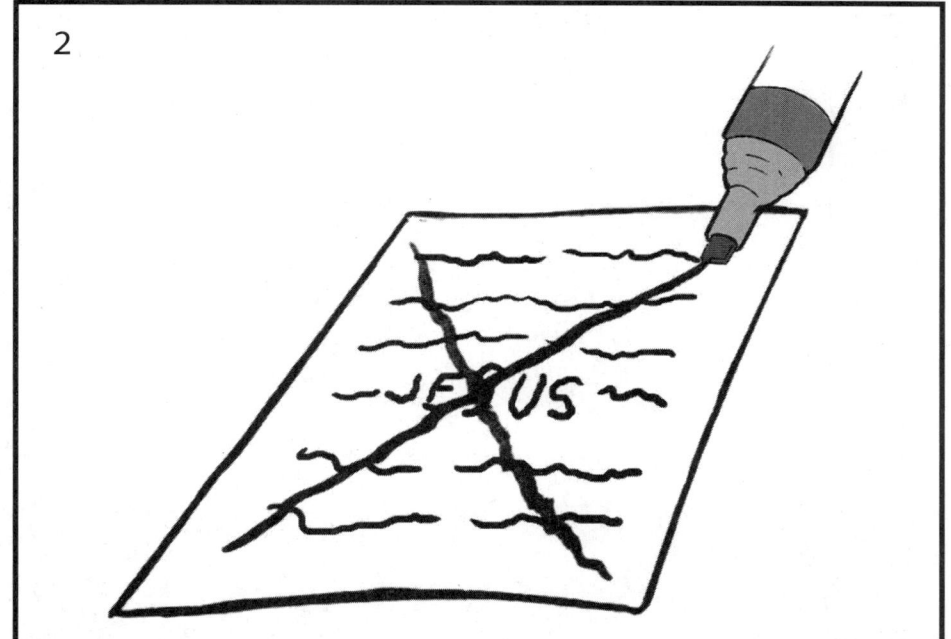

> I would rather live in a world where my life is surrounded by mystery, than one so small that my mind could comprehend it.
>
> — Harry Emerson Fosdick

MATTHEW 21:22
If you believe, you will receive whatever you ask for in prayer.

MATTHEW 26:26
While they were eating, Jesus took a piece of bread, gave a prayer of thanks, broke it, and gave it to His disciples. "Take and eat it," He said; "this is My body."

MARK 14:36
"Father," He prayed, "My Father! All things are possible for You. Take this cup of suffering away from Me. Yet not what I want, but what You want."

THE LORD'S PRAYER (2765-2766)

The Bible teaches and inspires us to lead prayerful lives.

WHAT YOU NEED:

a large handkerchief
a short length of monofilament or fishing line
confetti

WHAT THEY SEE:

The catechist shows his hands to be completely empty. He tosses some confetti into the air, quickly moves his hands apart, and a large handkerchief instantly appears between them.

WHAT YOU SAY:

"Living a life of prayerful attentiveness to the Spirit includes reading Scripture. The Lord speaks to us through the Bible and helps bring about change in our hearts. Our prayers allow the Spirit to put aside our sinfulness and for us to take on His holiness. It happens suddenly!"

(Toss the confetti and engage your thumbs into the monofilament's loops. Produce the handkerchief.)

"The change in our lives can be both beautiful and powerful!"

Abba Lot went to see Abba Joseph and he said to him, "Abba, as far as I can, I say my little office, I fast a little, I pray and meditate, I live in peace and as far as I can I purify my thoughts. What else can I do?" Then the old man stood up and stretched his hands toward heaven; his fingers became like ten lamps of fire and he said to him, "If you will, you can become all flame."
— St. Joseph of Panephysis

---

1 KINGS 19:11-12

"Go out and stand before me on top of the mountain," the Lord said to him. Then the Lord passed by and sent a furious wind that split the hills and shattered the rocks — but the Lord was not in the wind. The wind stopped blowing, and then there was an earthquake — but the Lord was not in the earthquake. After the earthquake there was a fire — but the Lord was not in the fire. And after the fire there was the soft whisper of a voice.

MATTHEW 6:7-13

When you pray, do not use a lot of meaningless words, as the pagans do, who think that their gods will hear them because their prayers are long. Do not be like them. Your Father already knows what you need before you ask him. This, then, is how you should pray: "Our Father in heaven: May your Holy Name be honored; may your Kingdom come; may Your will be done on earth as it is in heaven. Give us today the food we need. Forgive us the wrongs we have done, as we forgive the wrongs that others have done to us. Do not bring us to hard testing, but keep us safe from the Evil One"

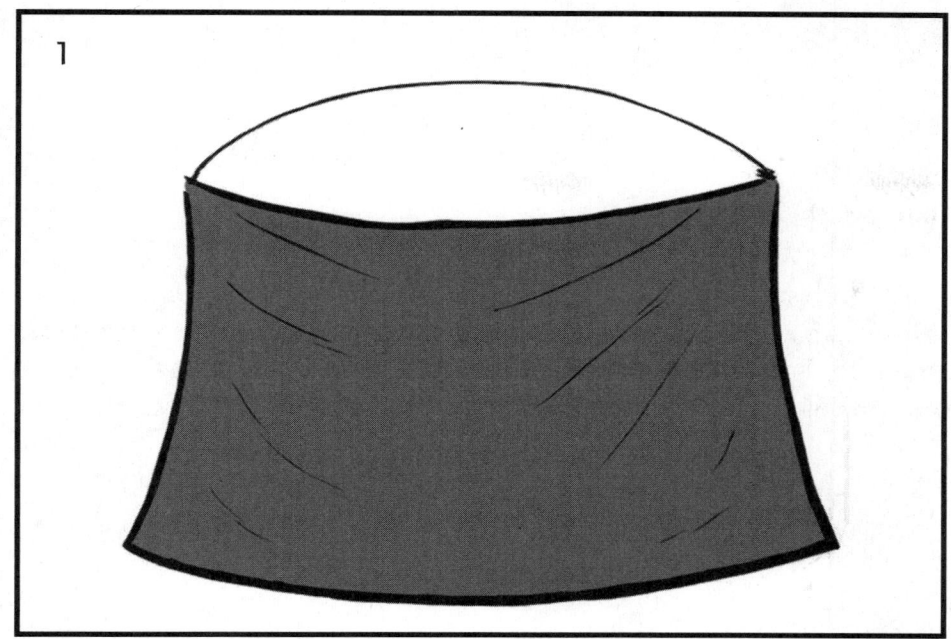

HOW YOU DO IT:

This is a very visual bit of magic. Cut about a yard of monofilament and tie its ends to 2 corners of a large handkerchief. Fold the handkerchief into a small packet and slip it into your jacket or shirt in the

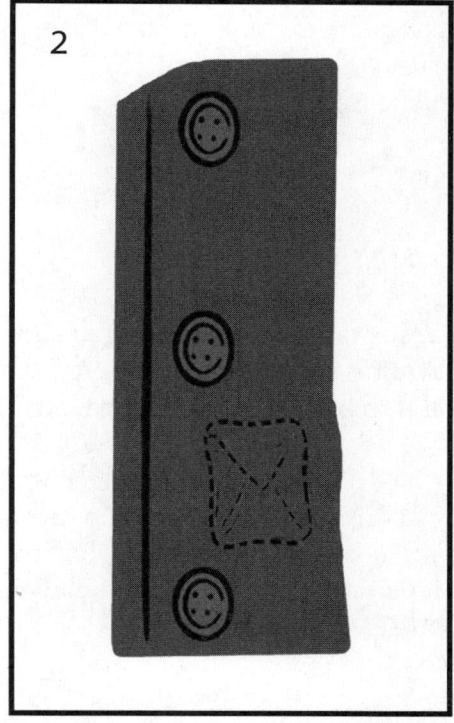

opening between 2 buttons. Push most of the monofilament line into the hidden space with the handkerchief but allow a small loop to rest on your shirt or jacket so that you have easy access to it.

When you are ready to perform this trick, throw some confetti into the air in the space immediately in front of you and hook your thumbs into the monofilament loop. Quickly pull your hands apart and the handkerchief will unfold in between your outstretched hands. The confetti is mostly for misdirection and to obscure the movement of your hands as you produce the handkerchief. You might also wish to consider adding some confetti to the folds of the handkerchief before you place it inside your jacket or shirt.

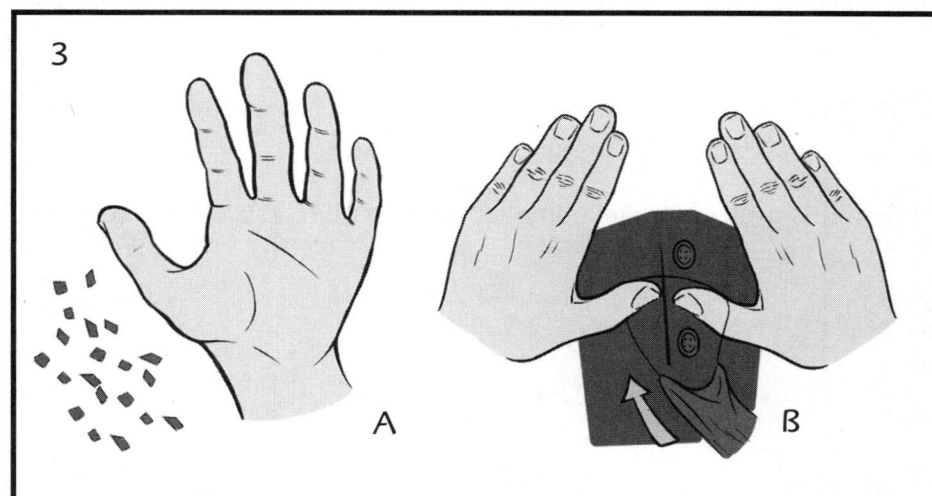

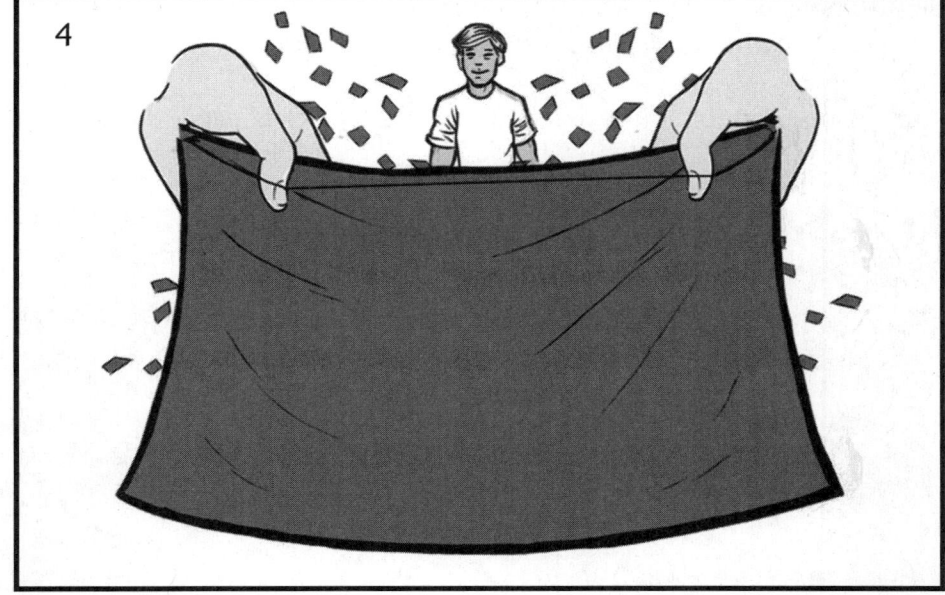

OUR FATHER WHO ART IN HEAVEN (2777-2802)

Prayer restores us.

WHAT YOU NEED:

a Change Bag (see page 59)
several sheets of photocopy paper
glue
rubber cement

WHAT THEY SEE:

The catechist invites a volunteer to stand beside him as they both rip up sheets of paper. When finished, the catechist and the volunteer open their hands to show that the catechist's paper has been restored but the volunteer's is still shredded. The catechist offers the volunteer another chance and produces a small, black, cloth bag. He places the pieces of her failed attempt into the bag and, a few seconds later, pulls out a restored sheet of paper.

WHAT YOU SAY:

"Jesus taught us how to pray and reminded us that God already knows what we need before we ask for it. What is the purpose of prayer? It's meant to bring us closer to God; to ask God to be a part of all of our lives and to bless all of our endeavors."

(Hand your volunteer a piece of paper and take the gimmicked one for yourself. Rip up the gimmicked paper as she rips up hers.)

"If God isn't involved with building the house, it's useless to try building it on your own. We all have to orient ourselves to God."

(Restore your paper. Your volunteer won't be able to do so.)

"Don't worry ... let's try something else."

(Place her ripped pieces into the Change Bag.)

"Now, you've tried once to restore what was broken and what happened? It didn't work. But if you try again, if you place yourself in God's hands, everything is possible. That which was wounded is healed. That which was lost is found. That which was torn up can become whole, just like this piece of paper."

(Let your volunteer reach into the Change Bag to retrieve and open the intact piece of paper that was hidden in the other compartment.)

MATTHEW 7:24-27

So then, anyone who hears these words of Mine and obeys them is like a wise man who built his house on rock. The rain poured down, the rivers flooded over, and the wind blew hard against that house. But it did not fall, because it was built on rock. But anyone who hears these words of Mine and does not obey them is like a foolish man who built his house on sand. The rain poured down, the rivers flooded over, the wind blew hard against that house, and it fell. And what a terrible fall that was!

MATTHEW 5:48

You must be perfect—just as your Father in heaven is perfect.

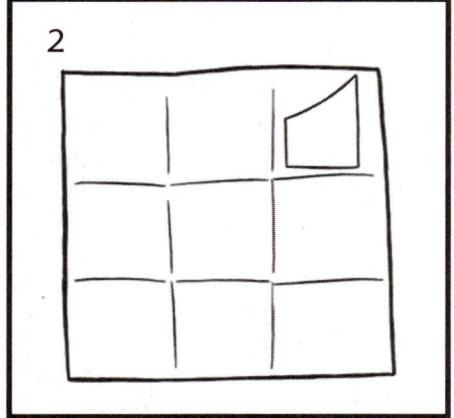

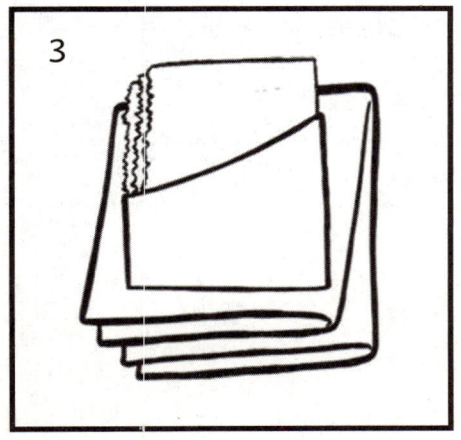

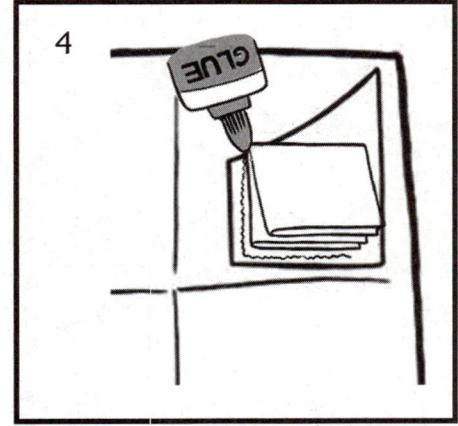

HOW YOU DO IT:

To perform this trick, you will need a Change Bag as described on page 59. Fold up one sheet of paper (we'll call this paper A) and place it in one of the pockets of the Change Bag. Create a small angled pocket on the upper right corner of another sheet (paper B). You should glue the left and bottom sides of the pocket but leave the top and right sides open. Fold another sheet (paper C) so that the creases divide the paper into 9 equal squares. Glue the back of paper C to the pocket on the back of paper B. The folded paper (C) should not show when you hold up the front of paper B to your audience. Invite a volunteer to come on stage to rip up a piece of paper as you do the same. Don't let your volunteer see the extra folded sheet.

Rip up paper B, keeping the pocket and paper C intact and hidden in the upper right corner of the backside. If you keep ahold of the section with the pocket, this will be easier. When the pieces of paper are small enough (the smallest should be about the size of a ninth of the whole paper) you can slide them into the prepared pocket. Turn the back of the assemblage toward the audience and open the other side to show a seemingly restored paper.

Of course the volunteer will not have the same luck with her ripped up paper.

Ask her to try again. Direct her to place the ripped-up pieces into the empty pocket of the Change Bag. Take this opportunity to review what has happened so far. Magicians refer to this as "time misdirection." Have the volunteer reach into the Change Bag to retrieve the intact paper that was hidden in the other compartment.

> **PSALM 127:1**
> If the Lord does not build the house, the work of the builders is useless; if the Lord does not protect the city, it does no good for the sentries to stand guard.
>
> **MATTHEW 5:16**
> In the same way your light must shine before people, so that they will see the good things you do and praise your Father in heaven.
>
> **MATTHEW 6:14**
> If you forgive others the wrongs they have done to you, your Father in heaven will also forgive you.
>
> **MATTHEW 6:26**
> Look at the birds: they do not plant seeds, gather a harvest and put it in barns; yet your Father in heaven takes care of them! Aren't you worth much more than birds?
>
> **MATTHEW 11:25**
> At that time Jesus said, "Father, Lord of heaven and earth! I thank You because you have shown to the unlearned what You have hidden from the wise and learned."

BUT DELIVER US FROM EVIL (2850-2854)

We rest in God and He keeps us safe.

WHAT YOU NEED:

a roll of Lifesavers
a 3-foot length of string thin
   enough to accommodate a
   Lifesavers candy
   (a shoe lace works well)
a foulard

WHAT THEY SEE:

The catechist asks a volunteer to open a roll of Lifesavers. He strings them on a length of string and covers them with a foulard. He reaches under the foulard and instantly releases the candy without damaging the string.

WHAT YOU SAY:

"In the 'Our Father' prayer, we ask God to protect us from evil. Even though we should always avoid doing bad things, we need His grace to protect us from other influences. Spiritual danger is much more damaging than is physical danger. Let's have a demonstration. I'm going to place these Lifesavers on this string."

(String the candies on as explained. Cover the candies and string with a foulard.)

"How does God keep us from evil? These candies seem to be trapped on this string."

(Break the first candy and allow the others to slip off into your hand. Show them to your audience.)

"Whenever we feel trapped either in sin or in trouble, we can ask God for help. All things are possible with the Lord. He can even save us from ourselves."

MATTHEW 4:1-11

Then the Spirit led Jesus into the desert to be tempted by the Devil. After spending forty days and nights without food, Jesus was hungry. Then the Devil came to Him and said, "If you are God's Son, order these stones to turn into bread." But Jesus answered, "The scripture says, 'Human beings cannot live on bread alone, but need every word that God speaks.'" Then the Devil took Jesus to Jerusalem, the Holy City, set Him on the highest point of the Temple, and said to Him, "If you are God's Son, throw yourself down, for the scripture says, 'God will give orders to His angels about You; they will hold You up with their hands, so that not even Your feet will be hurt on the stones.'" Jesus answered, "But the scripture also says, 'Do not put the Lord your God to the test.'" Then the Devil took Jesus to a very high mountain and showed Him all the kingdoms of the world in all their greatness. "All this I will give you," the Devil said, "if You kneel down and worship me." Then Jesus answered, "Go away, Satan! The scripture says, 'Worship the Lord your God and serve only Him!'" Then the Devil left Jesus; and angels came and helped Him.

MATTHEW 6:7-13

When you pray, do not use a lot of meaningless words, as the pagans do, who think that their gods will hear them because their prayers are long. Do not be like them. Your Father already knows what you need before you ask Him. This, then, is how you should pray: "Our Father in heaven: May Your holy name be honored; may Your Kingdom come; may Your will be done on earth as it is in heaven. Give us today the food we need. Forgive us the wrongs we have done, as we forgive the wrongs that others have done to us. Do not bring us to hard testing, but keep us safe from the Evil One.'"

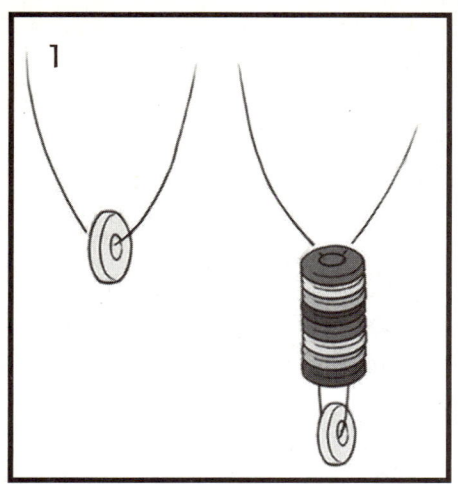
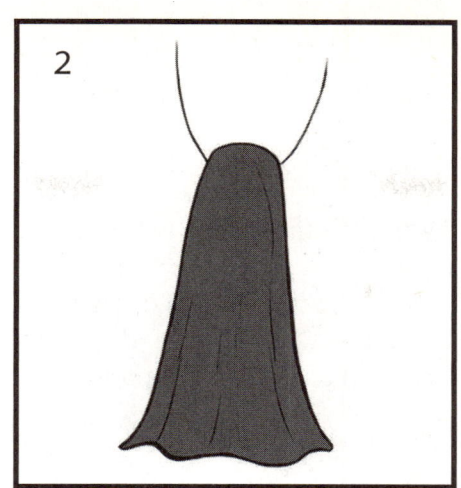
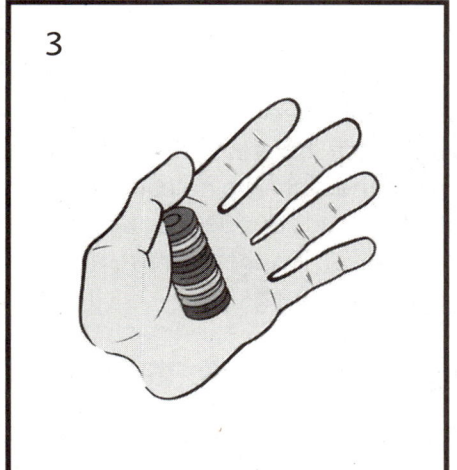
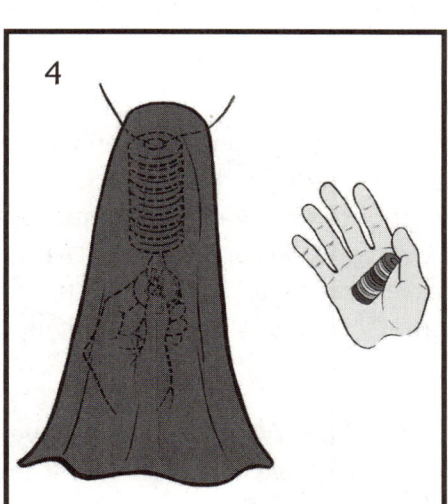

HOW YOU DO IT:

Thread one end of a string through a Lifesavers candy. We'll say this first candy is red. Next add 7 more candies, putting both ends of the string through the hole, so that the additional candies are stacked horizontally on the first one, which is still oriented vertically. Palm another red Lifesavers in your right hand. Have a volunteer hold both ends of the string. Drape your foulard over this assemblage. Under cover of the foulard, break the first Lifesavers with your fingers and conceal the 2 pieces in your hand by covering them with the duplicate Lifesavers. Hand out the candies to your audience members and quickly dispose of the broken pieces either by popping them into your mouth or your pocket.

LUKE 7:50
But Jesus said to the woman, "Your faith has saved you; go in peace."

JOHN 10:9
I am the gate. Those who come in by Me will be saved; they will come in and go out and find pasture.

ACTS 2:21
And then, whoever calls out to the Lord for help will be saved.

ACTS 13:47
For this is the commandment that the Lord has given us: "I have made you a light for the Gentiles, so that all the world may be saved."

ROMANS 5:10
We were God's enemies, but He made us His friends through the death of His Son. Now that we are God's friends, how much more will we be saved by Christ's life!

ROMANS 9:27
And Isaiah exclaims about Israel: "Even if the people of Israel are as many as the grains of sand by the sea, yet only a few of them will be saved."

FINAL DOXOLOGY (2855-2865)

We show our thankfulness to God in prayer.

WHAT YOU NEED:

2 quarters
access to a table vise
a rubber mallet
rags or towels

WHAT THEY SEE:

The catechist asks for a quarter and hands it out for examination. He places it in a spectator's hand and, after concentrating on the quarter, she opens her hand to find that the coin is noticeably bent.

WHAT YOU SAY:

"A 'doxology' is a short hymn of praise offered to God. Some people wonder why it is that we praise God at all. If He is the Creator of the universe, then He really doesn't need our thanks. He doesn't really need anything. The truth is God is so wonderful that He doesn't need anything but that doesn't mean that we shouldn't offer Him praise. Could we go even a single day at home without being grateful to our parents and friends for helping us? Would any of us want to live in a world where everyone was ungrateful? It's not that God needs our devotion and love but what kind of children would we be if we decided not to thank Him for His mercy and kindness? It's natural to thank whoever gives us the things we need, especially if we specifically ask for those things."

"Imagine being given something extraordinary and not reacting to it at all? That would be very strange. Look around you ... we have so much to be thankful for. We are alive. We have our health, our families, and our many successes. We have this beautiful world in which we live. How many small, delightful surprises offer us the opportunity for gratitude every day? How many of these opportunities do we miss? Probably a lot of them."

(Borrow a quarter from a volunteer and use a Shuttle Pass to switch it for a bent one. Invite a volunteer to assist you. Rest the bent coin on her outstretched palm and have her lightly cup her other hand to conceal the bent coin. Ask her to concentrate on the coin. Ask her if she feels the coin moving. Ask her to examine the coin in her hand.)

"As you see, we have wonderful things happening constantly around us. Now all you need to do is be thankful for them."

REVELATIONS 21:1-3

Then I saw a new heaven and a new earth. The first heaven and the first earth disappeared, and the sea vanished. And I saw the Holy City, the new Jerusalem, coming down out of heaven from God, prepared and ready, like a bride dressed to meet her husband. I heard a loud voice speaking from the throne: "Now God's home is with people! He will live with them, and they shall be His people. God Himself will be with them, and He will be their God."

HOW YOU DO IT:

Prepare a quarter by wrapping it in rags or towels and placing it in the grips of table vise. Make sure that at least half of the quarter is exposed. Cover the exposed part of the quarter with another rag. Take a rubber mallet and beat the quarter until it bends. Alternatively, you can ask the proprietor of a hardware store to bend a quarter for you. After you ask one of your audience members for a quarter, perform a Shuttle Pass to exchange the flat coin with the bent one (see instructions below on how to do the Shuttle Pass). Pocket the borrowed coin.

Ask your volunteer to keep her left hand completely flat. Place the bent quarter in her outstretched hand keeping it hidden from view with your hand. Before releasing it, have her cup her right hand and place it lightly over the quarter without actually touching it. Step a few feet away from her and ask her to close her eyes and breathe deeply. Most people cannot stand perfectly still; they will inevitably rock almost imperceptibly. If you've placed the coin so that it wobbles slightly as it rests on its bent edge, the volunteer will report that she can feel the coin actually move. After a bit of byplay, ask her to uncover her hand and examine the quarter.

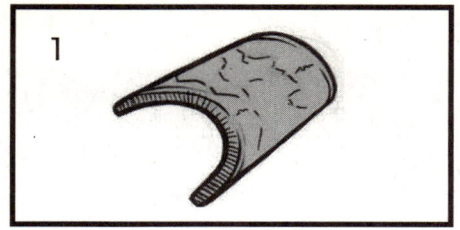

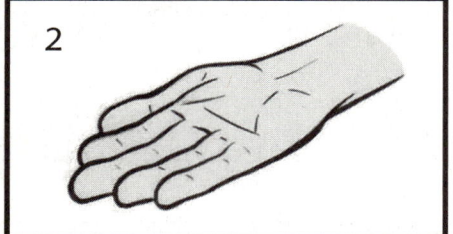

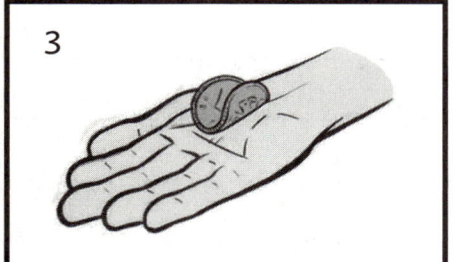

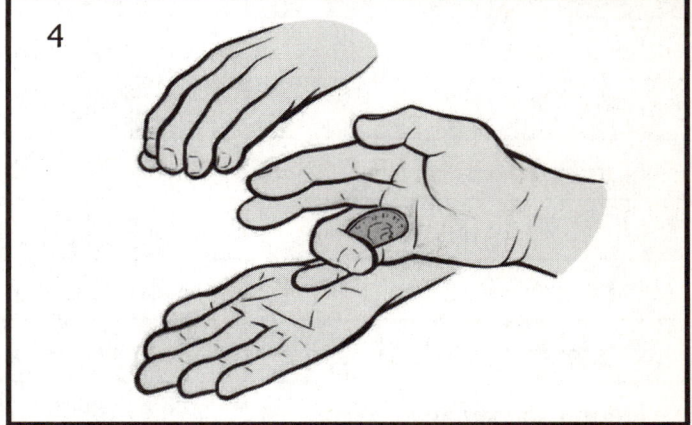

SHUTTLE PASS

This maneuver is designed to surreptitiously switch one coin for another coin.

Put a coin/disk into the center of your left palm. We'll call this coin A. Practice keeping coin A hidden while moving your hand as if it were empty. Magicians refer to this as "palming." Openly show the other coin/disk (ß) on the palm of your right hand. At this point, your left hand will be facedown and your right hand will be faceup. Simultaneously, flip both hands, making it seem as if you are tossing coin ß from your right hand into your left. You should actually palm coin ß in your right hand. Your left hand, now faceup, will be holding coin A and your right hand will be facedown. Keep coin ß palmed in your right hand and use the right hand facedown to pick up the exposed coin in your left hand.

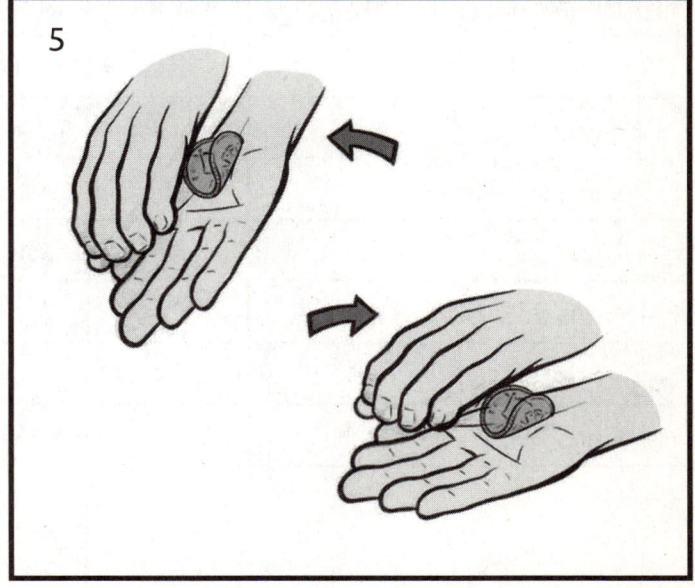

213

BIBLE PASSAGES AND TRICKS THAT APPLY

BIBLICAL PASSAGE	MAGIC TRICK/SECTION FROM CATECHISM
Genesis 1:1-30	Man: The Image of God, 140; In the Old Testament, 188
Genesis 3:1-24	Where Sin Abounded, Grace Abounded All the More, 68; Man's Freedom, 144
Genesis 17:5-15	The Power of the Keys, 102; Liturgical Diversity and the Unity of the Mystery, 118
Genesis 32:28	The Power of the Keys, 102
Genesis 40:13	He Ascended into Heaven and Is Seated at the Right Hand of the Father, 84
Exodus 3:1-6	The Revelation of God, 46; The Second Commandment, 166
Exodus 17:9-13	Jesus Christ Was Buried, 78
Exodus 18:21	Moral Conscience, 150
Exodus 20:2-17	The Ninth Commandment, 182
Exodus 24:18	At the Wellsprings of Prayer, 194
Exodus 34:28	At the Wellsprings of Prayer, 194
Leviticus 16:17	Participation in Social Life, 158
Leviticus 19:2	Participation in Social Life, 158
Numbers 16:5	The Second Commandment, 166
Numbers 27:17	Participation in Social Life, 158
Deuteronomy 5:18	The Ninth Commandment, 182
Deuteronomy 9:9-25	The Joint Mission of the Son and the Spirit, 88
Deuteronomy 30:1-19	Man's Freedom, 144; The Morality of Human Acts, 146; Moral Conscience, 150; The Fifth Commandment, 172
Joshua 1:11	He Ascended into Heaven and Is Seated at the Right Hand of the Father, 84
1 Samuel 9:24	The Morality of Human Acts, 146
2 Samuel 12:13-25	The Power of the Keys, 102; The Final Purification, or Purgatory, 106
2 Samuel 24:25	In the Old Testament, 188
1 Kings 3:2	In the Old Testament, 188
1 Kings 8:13-60	Jesus Christ Suffered Under Pontius Pilate, Was Crucified, Died and Was Buried, 76; Liturgical Diversity and the Unity of the Mystery, 118; In the Old Testament, 188
1 Kings 9:3	In the Old Testament, 188; The Prayer of the Hour of Jesus, 204
1 Kings 17:12	The Liturgy – Work of the Holy Trinity, 112

1 Kings 19:8-12	In the Old Testament, 188
1 Kings 19:11-12	The Lord's Prayer, 206
2 Kings 20:5	He Ascended into Heaven and Is Seated at the Right Hand of the Father, 84
1 Chronicles 16:31	Liturgical Diversity and the Unity of the Mystery, 118
2 Chronicles 1:11	The Morality of Human Acts, 146; Moral Conscience, 150
2 Chronicles 2:5-6	In the Old Testament, 188
2 Chronicles 7:12	The Prayer of the Hour of Jesus, 204
2 Chronicles 20:9	In the Old Testament, 188
2 Chronicles 29:15-16	In the Old Testament, 188
2 Chronicles 31:2	In the Old Testament, 188
Esther 4:16	He Ascended into Heaven and Is Seated at the Right Hand of the Father, 84
II Maccabees 12:43-45	The Final Purification, or Purgatory, 106
Job 42:8	In the Old Testament, 188
Psalms 5:4	The Final Purification, or Purgatory, 106
Psalms 11:4	In the Old Testament, 188
Psalms 15:1-5	The Final Purification, or Purgatory, 106
Psalms 23:1-6	Christian Funerals, 136
Psalms 24:3-6	The Final Purification, or Purgatory, 106
Psalms 47:8	Liturgical Diversity and the Unity of the Mystery, 118
Psalms 51:10-11	The Second Commandment, 166; The Joint Mission of the Son and the Spirit, 88
Psalms 82:8	Liturgical Diversity and the Unity of the Mystery, 118
Psalms 91:9-16	Christian Funerals, 136
Psalms 102:19-22	Liturgical Diversity and the Unity of the Mystery, 118
Psalms 119:7	The Second Commandment, 166
Psalms 127:1	Our Father Who Art in Heaven, 208
Proverbs 6:26-32	The Ninth Commandment, 182
Ecclesiastes 12:11	The Hierarchical Constitution of the Church, 96

BIBLE PASSAGES AND TRICKS THAT APPLY (continued)

Wisdom 3:1-7	The Final Purification, or Purgatory, 106
Sirach 33:2	The Hierarchical Constitution of the Church, 96
Isaiah 2:4	Liturgical Diversity and the Unity of the Mystery, 118
Isaiah 6:1-8	The Final Purification, or Purgatory, 106
Isaiah 7:14	The Son of God Became Man, 70; Born of the Virgin Mary, 74; In the Fullness of Time, 190
Isaiah 52:15	Liturgical Diversity and the Unity of the Mystery, 118
Isaiah 56:7	Liturgical Diversity and the Unity of the Mystery, 118; The Prayer of the Hour of Jesus, 204
Jeremiah 2:21	The Morality of the Passions, 148
Jeremiah 21:8	The Morality of the Passions, 148; Moral Conscience, 150
Jeremiah 29:12-13	In the Fullness of Time, 190
Ezekiel 16:32	The Ninth Commandment, 182
Daniel 9: 17-25	The Sacrament of Penance and Reconciliation, 126; Final Doxology, 212
Daniel 12:2-10	The Final Purification, or Purgatory, 106
Hosea 14:2	The Prayer of the Hour of Jesus, 204
Zechariah 3:7	The Angels, 66
Zechariah 13:9	The Final Purification, or Purgatory, 106
Malachi 3:1-3	Born of the Virgin Mary, 74; Jesus Christ Suffered Under Pontius Pilate, Was Crucified, Died and Was Buried, 76; The Final Purification, or Purgatory, 106
Micah 6:8	The Desire for God, 44
Haggai 2:9	Jesus Christ Suffered Under Pontius Pilate, Was Crucified, Died and Was Buried, 76; The Final Purification, or Purgatory, 106
Matthew 1:20	The Joint Mission of the Son and the Holy Spirit, 88
Matthew 2:13	The Angels, 66
Matthew 3:11-17	The Joint Mission of the Son and the Holy Spirit, 88; The Sacrament of Baptism, 120
Matthew 4:1-18	Participation in Social Life, 158; But Deliver Us From Evil, 210
Matthew 5:1-48	I Believe, 52 in One God, 56; The Final Purification, or Purgatory, 106; The Beatitudes, 142; The Ninth Commandment, 182; Our Father Who Art in Heaven, 208
Matthew 6:1-33	The Father, 58; The Life of Prayer, 200; I Believe, 52 in One God, 56; The Sacrament of Penance and Reconciliation, 126; Our Father Who Art in Heaven, 208
Matthew 7:1-27	From Thence Will He Come Again to Judge the Living and the Dead, 86; The Father, 58; Our Father Who Art in Heaven, 208
Matthew 8:5-13	I Believe, 52

Matthew 9:6-28	The Power of the Keys, 102; The Anointing of the Sick, 128
Matthew 10:1-32	The Father, 58; The Anointing of the Sick, 128
Matthew 11:1-25	The Apostolic Tradition, 48; Our Father Who Art in Heaven, 208
Matthew 12:10-50	He Ascended into Heaven and Is Seated at the Right Hand of the Father, 84; From Thence Will He Come Again to Judge the Living and the Dead, 86; The Anointing of the Sick, 128; Participation in Social Life, 158
Matthew 13:15	The Anointing of the Sick, 128
Matthew 14:33	The Revelation of God, 46
Matthew 15:19	The Sixth Commandment, 174
Matthew 16:15-19	The Power of the Keys, 102
Matthew 18:8–35	The Almighty, 60; On the Third Day He Rose from the Dead, 82; The Sacrament of Penance and Reconciliation, 126
Matthew 19:9-16	The Ninth Commandment, 182; The Tenth Commandment, 184
Matthew 21:22	The Prayer of the Hour of Jesus, 204
Matthew 22:25-39	The Fourth Commandment, 170
Matthew 25:31-46	The Last Judgment, 108
Matthew 27:2-60	The Revelation of God, 46; Jesus Christ Was Buried, 78, He Ascended into Heaven and Is Seated at the Right Hand of the Father, 84; The Paschal Mystery in the Church's Sacraments, 114; The Sacrament of the Eucharist, 124; Christian Funerals, 136
Matthew 28:1-20	The Angels, 66; The Paschal Mystery in the Church's Sacraments, 114
Mark 1:1-13	The Sacrament of Penance and Reconciliation, 126; Persevering in Love, 202
Mark 2-1:12	The Power of the Keys, 102
Mark 3:25	Participation in Social Life, 158
Mark 4:12-24	From Thence Will He Come Again to Judge the Living and the Dead, 86; The Power of the Keys, 102
Mark 6:2-34	The Apostolic Tradition, 48
Mark 8:29	I Believe, 52
Mark 9:29	Sacramentals, 134
Mark 10:6-30	The Paschal Mystery in the Church's Sacraments, 114; Participation in Social Life, 158; The Ninth Commandment, 182
Mark 11:25	The Sacrament of Penance and Reconciliation, 126
Mark 12:31-37	I Believe, 52; The Fourth Commandment, 170
Mark 13:11	The Joint Mission of the Son and the Spirit, 88

BIBLE PASSAGES AND TRICKS THAT APPLY (continued)

Mark 14:1-61	I Believe, 52; The Church is the Temple of the Holy Spirit, 92; The Sacrament of the Eucharist, 124; The Prayer of the Hour of Jesus, 204
Mark 16:6	On the Third Day He Rose from the Dead, 82
Luke 1:13-79	The Angels, 66; The Son of God Became Man, 70; Mary – Mother of Christ, Mother of the Church, 100; The Way of Prayer, 196
Luke 2:1-20	The Angels, 66; The Son of God Became Man, 70
Luke 3:21-22	The Sacrament of Confirmation, 122
Luke 4:1-2	The Way of Prayer, 196
Luke 5:24	The Power of the Keys, 102
Luke 6:37	From Thence Will He Come Again to Judge the Living and the Dead, 86; The Power of the Keys, 102; The Sacrament of Penance and Reconciliation, 126
Luke 7:50	But Deliver Us From Evil, 210
Luke 8:20-21	Participation in Social Life, 158
Luke 9:2-62	I Believe, 52; I Believe in the Resurrection of the Body, 104; The Liturgy – Work of the Holy Trinity, 112; Participation in Social Life, 158
Luke 10:9-42	The Joint Mission of the Son and the Spirit, 88; The Liturgy – Work of the Holy Trinity, 112; The Sacrament of Confirmation, 122; The Fourth Commandment, 170; At the Wellsprings of Prayer, 194; Our Father Who Art in Heaven, 208
Luke 11:4-17	The Sacrament of Confirmation, 122; The Creator, 63; The Sacrament of Penance and Reconciliation, 126; Participation in Social Life, 158
Luke 12:12-59	The Final Purification, or Purgatory, 106; The Sacrament of Confirmation, 122; The Tenth Commandment, 184
Luke 14:26	Participation in Social Life, 158
Luke 15:11-89	On the Third Day He Rose from the Dead, 82; In the Age of the Church, 192
Luke 16:18-31	The Final Purification, or Purgatory, 106; The Ninth Commandment, 182
Luke 18:7-9	The Last Judgment, 108
Luke 22:1-46	Celebrating the Church's Liturgy, 116; The Sacrament of the Eucharist, 124; Christian Funerals, 136; The Way of Prayer, 196
Luke 23:33-49	Jesus Christ Was Buried, 78; The Sacrament of Penance and Reconciliation, 126; Christian Funerals, 136
Luke 24:45-48	In the Fullness of Time, 190
John 1:10-41	The Desire for God, 44; I Believe, 52; Where Sin Abounded, Grace Abounded All the More, 68; The Sacrament of Confirmation, 122
John 2:18-22	Jesus Christ Suffered Under Pontius Pilate, Was Crucified, Died and Was Buried, 76
John 4:14-47	Only One Faith, 54; The Incarnation, 72; The Third Commandment, 168
John 5:22-30	The Last Judgment, 108
John 6:32-54	Our Father Who Art in Heaven, 208; The Creator, 63; The Final Purification, or Purgatory, 106; The Liturgy – Work of the Holy Trinity, 112; Christian Funerals, 136

John 7:16	The Creator, 63
John 8:12	The Revelation of God, 46
John 9:39	The Last Judgment, 108
John 10:9	But Deliver Us From Evil, 210
John 11:27	Only One Faith, 54
John 12:34-40	The Third Commandment, 168; In the Fullness of Time, 190
John 14:2-26	The Incarnation, 72; The Joint Mission of the Son and the Spirit, 88; Liturgical Diversity and the Unity of the Mystery, 118
John 15:1-8	The Desire for God, 44; The Church is the Temple of the Holy Spirit, 92
Luke 17:3	The Sacrament of Penance and Reconciliation, 126
John 19:14-42	Jesus Christ Suffered Under Pontius Pilate; Was Crucified, Died and Was Buried, 76; Jesus Christ Was Buried, 78
John 20:10-23	He Descended into Hell. On the Third Day He Rose Again, 80; The Paschal Mystery in the Church's Sacraments, 114
Acts 1:2-14	The Hierarchical Constitution of the Church, 96; Participation in Social Life, 158
Acts 2:1-38	Jesus Christ Was Buried, 78; The Joint Mission of the Son and the Spirit, 88; I Believe in the Resurrection of the Body, 104; Liturgical Diversity and the Unity of the Mystery, 118; In the Fullness of Time, 190; But Deliver Us From Evil, 210
Acts 3:18	In the Fullness of Time, 190
Acts 4:24-30	The Third Commandment, 168; The Life of Prayer, 200
Acts 5:19-29	The Incarnation, 72; The Angels, 66
Acts 6:4	The Life of Prayer, 200
Acts 8:27-31	Sacred Scripture, 50
Acts 9:22	Only One Faith, 54
Acts 10:4	The Angels, 66
Acts 12:7	The Angels, 66
Acts 13:47	But Deliver Us From Evil, 210
Acts 14:23	The Church: Mother and Teacher, 164
Acts 17:29-31	The Last Judgment, 108
Acts 18:28	Only One Faith, 54
Acts 20:7-28	The Church: Mother and Teacher, 164; Celebrating the Church's Liturgy, 116

BIBLE PASSAGES AND TRICKS THAT APPLY (continued)

Acts 28:27	The Third Commandment, 168
1 Corinthians 1:10-23	Jesus Christ Was Buried, 78; The Church is the Temple of the Holy Spirit, 92; But Deliver Us From Evil, 210
1 Corinthians 3:11-15	The Final Purification, or Purgatory, 106
1 Corinthians 6:15-19	The Joint Mission of the Son and the Spirit, 88; The Church is the Temple of the Holy Spirit, 92
1 Corinthians 7:19	The Incarnation, 72
1 Corinthians 10:13-16	The Church is the Temple of the Holy Spirit, 92
1 Corinthians 11:2-26	I Believe in the Resurrection of the Body, 104; The Liturgy – Work of the Holy Trinity, 112
1 Corinthians 12:1-14	The Gifts and Fruits of the Holy Spirit, 152
1 Corinthians 13:1-12	The Sacrament of Matrimony, 132; Man: The Image of God, 140
1 Corinthians 14:1-26	The Sacrament of Holy Orders, 130
1 Corinthians 15:2-56	He Ascended into Heaven and Is Seated at the Right Hand of the Father, 84; I Believe in the Resurrection of the Body, 104; Man: The Image of God, 140; The Fifth Commandment, 172; But Deliver Us From Evil, 210
2 Corinthians 1:12	The Moral Law, 160
2 Corinthians 2:7	The Power of the Keys, 102
2 Corinthians 3:18	Man: The Image of God, 140
2 Corinthians 4:4	Man: The Image of God, 140
2 Corinthians 6:1	The Moral Law, 160
2 Corinthians 8:1-9	The Moral Law, 160
2 Corinthians 11:2-3	The Second Commandment, 166; The Eighth Commandment, 178
2 Corinthians 12:9-20	Grace & Justification, 162
Ephesians 1:7-23	Grace & Justification, 162; The Church: Mother and Teacher, 164
Ephesians 2:5-19	Grace & Justification, 162; Participation in Social Life, 158
Ephesians 4:24-32	The Power of the Keys, 102; Man: The Image of God, 140; The Eighth Commandment, 178
Ephesians 5:25-28	The Sacrament of Matrimony, 132; The Church: Mother and Teacher, 164
Ephesians 6:18	Guides for Prayer, 198
Philemon 1:6	Guides for Prayer, 198
Hebrews 1:3	Man: The Image of God, 140
Hebrews 2:4-28	The Final Purification, or Purgatory, 106; Participation in Social Life, 158

Hebrews 4:13	The Eighth Commandment, 178
Hebrews 5:12	Sacred Scripture, 50
Hebrews 6:18	To Bear Witness to the Truth, 180
Hebrews 7:19	The Second Commandment, 166
Hebrews 8:12	The Power of the Keys, 102
Hebrews 9:27-28	The Final Purification, or Purgatory, 106
Hebrews 10:19-22	The Second Commandment, 166; I Believe in the Resurrection of the Body, 104
Hebrews 11:27	The Mystery of the Church; In the Old Testament, 188
Hebrews 12:14-23	The Final Purification, or Purgatory, 106
Hebrews 13:4-20	The Ninth Commandment, 182
1 Peter 1:3-12	The Joint Mission of the Son and the Spirit, 88; I Believe in the Resurrection of the Body, 104
1 Peter 2:22	To Bear Witness to the Truth, 180
1 Peter 3:10-22	The Final Purification, or Purgatory, 106; But Deliver Us From Evil, 210; The Eighth Commandment, 178
1 Peter 4:5-10	The Last Judgment, 108
2 Peter 1:10-15	Moral Conscience, 150
2 Peter 3:10	Born of the Virgin Mary, 74
1 John 2:3-20	The Incarnation, 72; The Joint Mission of the Son and the Spirit, 88
1 John 4:16	Christian Funerals, 136
1 John 5:1-17	Only One Faith, 54; The Incarnation, 72; The Fifth Commandment, 172
Revelations 1:18	I Believe in the Resurrection of the Body, 104
Revelations 7:17	The Hierarchical Constitution of the Church, 96
Revelations 12:7-17	But Deliver Us From Evil, 210
Revelations 14:5	The Eighth Commandment, 178
Revelations 20:1-15	The Final Purification, or Purgatory, 106
Revelations 21:1-3	Final Doxology, 212
Revelations 21:25-27	The Final Purification, or Purgatory, 106
Revelations 22:6	The Angels, 66

TRICKS ACROSS RELIGIONS

To assist Protestant and Orthodox Gospel Magicians as they navigate this book, I've prepared a chart with the help of theologians from several Christian traditions, that describes the applicability of these tricks to Protestant and Orthodox, as well as Catholic theologies.

MAGIC TRICK SECTION FROM CATECHISM	Catholic	Protestant	Orthodox
PART 1: THE PROFESSION OF FAITH			
THEOLOGY	CHURCHES		
The Desire for God	†	†	†
The Revelation of God	†	†	†
The Apostolic Tradition	†	†	
Sacred Scripture	†	†	†
I Believe	†	†	†
Only One Faith	†	†	†
I Believe in One God	†	†	†
The Father	†	†	†
The Almighty	†	†	†
The Creator	†	†	†
The Angels	†	†	†
Where Sin Abounded, Grace Abounded All the More	†	†	†
The Son of God Became Man	†	†	†
The Incarnation	†	†	†
Born of the Virgin Mary	†	†	†
Jesus Christ Suffered Under Pontius Pilate, Was Crucified, Died and Was Buried	†	†	†
Jesus Christ Was Buried	†	†	†
He Descended into Hell. On the Third Day He Rose Again	†	†	†
On the Third Day He Rose from the Dead	†	†	†
He Ascended into Heaven and Is Seated at the Right Hand of the Father	†	†	†

MAGIC TRICK SECTION FROM CATECHISM	Catholic	Protestant	Orthodox
From Thence Will He Come Again to Judge the Living and the Dead	†	†	†
The Joint Mission of the Son & the Spirit	†	†	†
The Mystery of the Church	†	†	†
The Church is the Temple of the Holy Spirit	†	†	†
The Church is One	†	†	†
The Hierarchical Constitution of the Church	†		†
Communion in Spiritual Goods	†	†	†
Mary – Mother of Christ, Mother of the Church	†		†
The Power of the Keys	†		†
I Believe in the Resurrection of the Body	†	†	†
The Final Purification, or Purgatory	†		
The Last Judgment	†	†	†
PART 2: THE CELEBRATION OF THE CHRISTIAN MYSTERY			
THEOLOGY	CHURCHES		
The Liturgy – Work of the Holy Trinity	†	†	†
The Paschal Mystery in the Church's Sacraments	†	†	†
Celebrating the Church's Liturgy	†	†	†
Liturgical Diversity and the Unity of the Mystery	†	†	†
The Sacrament of Baptism	†	†	†

MAGIC TRICK SECTION FROM CATECHISM	Catholic	Protestant	Orthodox
The Sacrament of Confirmation	†		†
The Sacrament of the Eucharist	†		†
The Sacrament of Penance and Reconciliation	†	†	†
The Anointing of the Sick	†	†	†
The Sacrament of Holy Orders	†	†	†
The Sacrament of Matrimony	†	†	†
Sacramentals	†	†	†
Christian Funerals	†	†	†
PART 3: **LIFE IN CHRIST**			
THEOLOGY	CHURCHES		
Man: The Image of God	†	†	†
The Beatitudes	†	†	†
Man's Freedom	†	†	†
The Morality of Human Acts	†	†	†
The Morality of the Passions	†	†	†
Moral Conscience	†	†	†
The Gifts and Fruits of the Holy Spirit	†	†	†
Sin	†	†	†
The Person & Society	†	†	†
Participation in Social Life	†	†	†
The Moral Law	†	†	†
Grace & Justification	†	†	†
The Church: Mother and Teacher	†	†	†
The Second Commandment	†	†	†

MAGIC TRICK SECTION FROM CATECHISM	Catholic	Protestant	Orthodox
The Third Commandment	†	†	†
The Fourth Commandment	†	†	†
The Fifth Commandment	†	†	†
The Sixth Commandment	†	†	†
The Seventh Commandment	†	†	†
The Eighth Commandment	†	†	†
To Bear Witness to the Truth	†	†	†
The Ninth Commandment	†	†	†
The Tenth Commandment	†	†	†
PART 4: **CHRISTIAN PRAYER**			
THEOLOGY	CHURCHES		
In the Old Testament, 188	†	†	†
In the Fullness of Time	†	†	†
In the Age of the Church	†	†	†
At the Wellsprings of Prayer	†	†	†
The Way of Prayer	†	†	†
Guides for Prayer	†	†	†
The Life of Prayer	†	†	†
Perservering in Love	†	†	†
The Prayer of the Hour of Jesus	†	†	†
The Lord's Prayer	†	†	†
Our Father Who Art in Heaven	†	†	†
But Deliver Us From Evil	†	†	†
Final Doxology	†	†	†

MAGICIAN'S GLOSSARY

Abracadabra – a "magic" word used by modern stage magicians as a means by which to build suspense or to "cause" a magic effect. In reality, it is derived from ancient pagan and Gnostic prayers. The word was originally believed to cure disease.

Acetabularii (Latin: "vinegar cup") – ancient Roman magicians who specialized in performing the cups and balls trick.

Act – the collected tricks and routines performed by a magician at a single performance.

Ambitious Card – a trick where a selected card continually rises to the top of the deck.

Angel's Handkerchief – a set of 2 handkerchiefs sewn together in such a way as to create a secret, hidden pocket.

Apparatus – the magic equipment used by a magician.

Appearance – the act or instance of an object seemingly coming into sight.

Aquitment – a sleight-of-hand maneuver whereby a small object, usually a coin or a ball, is secretly passed from one hand to another in such a way as to give the idea that both hands are empty.

Backpalm – a sleight-of-hand maneuver whereby a magician hides a card or coin on the back of his hand.

Billet – a small piece of folded paper upon which a message has been written.

Black Art – the principle of using black cloth and special lighting in order to conceal black objects.

Break – a slight physical separation between sections of a deck of cards for the purpose of locating and controlling the movement of a selected card.

Catholic Magicians Guild – an international fraternity of Catholic Gospel Magicians.

Change Bag – a bag with a secret compartment used to change one item for another.

Clairvoyance – the supposed ability to sense objects or situations at a distance.

Clean – a magic trick is considered "clean" if the hands, props, and immediate area can be examined after performance of the trick without fear that the secret will be revealed.

Closer – the last trick or routine performed in a magician's act.

Close-up Magic – magic that is performed within 3 feet of an audience. Usually done while seated at a table. Card and coin magic is usually considered close-up magic.

Comedy Magic – a magic trick, routine, or act that is performed lightly for comical effect.

Confederate – an assistant who secretly assists a magician in accomplishing a trick.

Control – any of dozens of means by which a card is maneuvered to a specific part of a deck.

Court Card – a jack, queen, or king.

Crimp – to bend a corner of a card so as to identify it or to otherwise use it to locate another card.

Disappearance – the act or instance of an object seemingly disappearing from sight.

Ditch – to get rid of a gimmick without allowing a spectator to see what you are doing.

Double Lift – a sleight-of-hand maneuver used to lift 2 cards as one.

Effect – 1) a magic trick, 2) what a magic effect appears like to an audience, as opposed to its "method."

Escape Artist – a magician who performs escapes.

ESP (Extra-sensory Perception) – the supposed ability to sense objects and situations at a distance.

Exposure – the unethical revealing of a magic secret.

Face – the side of a playing card that shows its value and suit.

False Count – any of several means of counting cards while simultaneously concealing one or more cards.

False Deals – any of several means of simulating a fair deal.

False Shuffle – any of several means of seemingly shuffling a deck of cards that actually doesn't disturb the order of the cards.

Fellowship of Christian Magicians – an international organization of Christian Gospel Magicians.

Finale – the last magic trick of a performance.

Finger Palm – a way to palm a small object, usually a coin, so that it is concealed in the crook of one's fingers.

Flash – to inadvertently expose a trick's gimmick during the performance.

Flourish – a display of skill usually with cards or coins.

Force – to secretly make a volunteer perform a desired action without her knowledge. Usually to choose a specific card.

Foulard – a large handkerchief.

Gimmick – a specially designed device unknown to the audience that allows the magician to perform a magic trick.

Glide – to slide a card back in order to access the card beneath it. Used to either to identify or deal it.

Glimpse – a quick and secret glance at a card in order to identify it.

Gospel Magic – magic used to instruct a theological or catechetical lesson.

Hocus Pocus – nonsense phrase equivalent to "abracadabra." Some scholars believe the word is a corruption of the phrase "hoc ist corpus" used in the Latin Mass and is therefore meant as an anti–Catholic pejorative.

Hypnosis (also known as "Mesmerism") – tricks in which the performer seemingly induces a state that resembles sleep and in which the subject responds to suggestions.

Illusion – a magic trick.

Illusionist – a magician.

Impromptu Magic – a trick or tricks that can be done without any extensive preparation.

Index – the value of a card (i.e., ace through king.)

Iron Man – a marked and stacked deck of cards. The Destiny Deck is an example of an iron man.

Jog – to allow a card or group of cards to protrude from the deck almost imperceptibly in order to locate a specific card.

Key Card – a card that has either been surreptitiously glimpsed or specifically planted so as to give the magician an idea of a selected card's location.

Lapping – the action of tossing or otherwise discarding a small object onto one's lap while seated as one performs close-up magic.

Lay person – in Catholic parlance, a non-cleric and/or a non-religious. Amongst magicians, a "lay person" refers to a non-magician.

Legerdemain – (french–"light of hand") magic, sleight-of-hand.

Levitation – the apparent violation of the law of gravity.

Locate – the act of finding a selected card from an otherwise shuffled deck.

Magician's Choice – any of several means by which a volunteer can appear to have a free choice but is actually guided to choose what the magician wishes.

Magicienne – a female magician.

Marked Deck – a deck of cards that is secretly marked in such a way to allow a magician to identify or otherwise control each card.

Mentalism – magic of the mind. There are 4 subdivision of mentalism: 1) ESP, 2) Telepathy, 3) Precognition and 4) Telekinesis.

Method – the actual secret behind a magic trick, as opposed to its "effect."

Mirror Box – a production box that utilizes a mirror to create the illusion that it is empty. In reality, the mirror creates a hidden compartment accessed through a second door.

Mirrored Glass – a drinking glass that is outfitted with a small mirror placed in such a way as to create a hidden compartment.

Misdirection – the act of distracting one's audience so that a magician might accomplish yet another action surreptitiously. Magicians might use physical, psychological, verbal, or time-based distractions.

Move – an example of sleight-of-hand.

Opener – the first trick or routine performed in a magician's act.

Overhand Shuffle – the standard means of shuffling a deck of cards.

Packet Effect – a trick that can be performed without special or extensive preparation straight from the package.

Palming – any of several means by which a small object is concealed in one's hand.

Palming Coin – a coin suitable for palming. The larger the coin, the better suited it is for palming.

Parlor Magic – magic that is performed at least 6 feet away from an audience and usually done impromptu.

Pass – a sleight-of-hand maneuver used to secretly move a card to a new position in the deck.

Patter – the words or story that a magician says as part of his performance, principally used as a form of misdirection and entertainment.

Peek – a surreptitious means by which the magician can glimpse at a card's identify.

Pip Card – any non-court card in a deck.

Poker-size Cards – normal-sized cards, larger than bridge-sized cards.

Precognition – the supposed psionic ability to know the future.

Prediction – a piece of paper upon which a magician writes a statement about a future event or action such as the name of a card a spectator will select before she selects it.

Prestidigitation – (coined by French magician Jules DeRovere in 1815;) it literally means "fast fingers."

Presto – an Italian word meaning "quickly" used humorously by magicians at the moment of revelation.

Production – the manifestation or revelation of an object or objects.

Prop – a theatrical object used during a magician's performance.

Repertoire – all the tricks that a magician is capable of performing.

Restoration – the physical destruction and reconstitution of an object.

Revelation – the act of revealing the final stage of a magic trick. Most commonly used with card and mentalism tricks.

Rhine Deck – a deck of 25 cards comprised of 5 symbols repeated 5 times each and used in mentalism tricks. The Phenomena Deck is based on the original Rhine Deck.

Riffle – to move through a deck of cards by depressing the corner and then releasing each card in rapid succession.

Riffle Shuffle – springing 2 halves of a deck so they randomly dovetail into each other.

Servante – a pouch or shelf positioned on the magician's side of a performance table which allows him to secretly deposit or retrieve small objects.

Short Card – a card that has been purposefully shorten by approximately 1/32 of an inch and used as a locator card to help find an otherwise freely selected card.

Shtick (also schtick) – a performer's routine or gimmick.

Shuffle – to randomly mix a deck of cards.

Shuttle Pass – a coin sleight-of-hand maneuver which gives the impression that a coin has been passed to another hand when, in reality, it actually has been switched for another coin.

Silk – a handkerchief usually made of thin, highly compressible silk or nylon.

Sleeving – the act of secretly slipping a small object into your jacket's sleeve.

Sleight-of-hand – a trick performed surreptitiously with the hands.

Spectator Success/Failure – a comical magic trick wherein the performer always succeeds but the audience member loses.

Stacked Deck – a pre-arranged deck of cards.

Stage Illusion – a large-scale magic trick that involves humans or animals such as "Lady to Tiger."

Steal – taking an object without the audience's knowledge.

Street Magic – the act of busking or performing magic on city streets and parks.

Stripper Deck – a deck of cards trimmed to be wedge-shaped. Cards that are reversed are easily found, even though "lost" in the deck. Also known as a "Tapered Deck" or "Wizard Deck."

Suit – one of the 4 sets of playing cards in a deck, (i.e., clubs, hearts, spades and diamonds).

Switch – to secretly exchange a small object (e.g., a card or coin) for another.

SYM (Society of Young Magicians) – the kids' organization attached to the Society of American Magicians.

Sympathetic Reaction – a magic trick in which a pair of objects are somehow "linked," in that whatever happens to one will seem to happen to the other.

Telekinesis – the supposed psionic ability to move objects with one's mind.

Telepathy – the supposed psionic ability to communicate between minds.

Teleportation – a switch, exchange, or relocation of an item.

Theme act – an act based around a central premise or prop. All Gospel Magic is necessarily a themed act.

Thumb Tip – a fake plastic thumb used by magicians to conceal small, compressible objects.

Time Misdirection – using one's patter to stall for time in the hope of confusing one's audience.

Topit – a large, secret pocket in the lining of a jacket for hiding objects. The topit was originally developed by thieves in the Middle Ages.

Torn & Restored – a trick involving an object which is torn up and then immediately repaired.

Transformation – one of the basic tricks in magic, in which an object changes into an entirely different item.

Transposition – one of the basic tricks in magic in which 2 or more objects or people exchange places.

Turn/No-Turn – a coin sleight-of-hand maneuver which, when executed properly, gives the impression that both sides of a coin have been shown. In reality, one side has been shown twice.

Value – a card's index or number as opposed to its suit.

Vanish – a sleight-of-hand maneuver that causes something to disappear.

Voila – a French term for "here it is" used by magicians at the moment of revelation.

Woofle Dust – a non-existent powder used as an excuse for a magician to put his hand into his pocket to deposit or retrieve a secretly palmed object.

CUTOUT SECTION

The following pages are meant to be carefully removed from this book and used for the tricks indicated.

To be used with "Jesus Christ Suffered Under Pontius Pilate, Was Crucified, Died and Was Buried," page 76

To be used with "The Joint Mission of the Son and the Holy Spirit," page 88

To be used with "The Church is the Temple of the Holy Spirit," page 92

233

To be used with "Mary – Mother of Christ, Mother of the Church," page 100

To be used with "Mary – Mother of Christ, Mother of the Church," page 100
Enlarge as needed to fit your jacket.

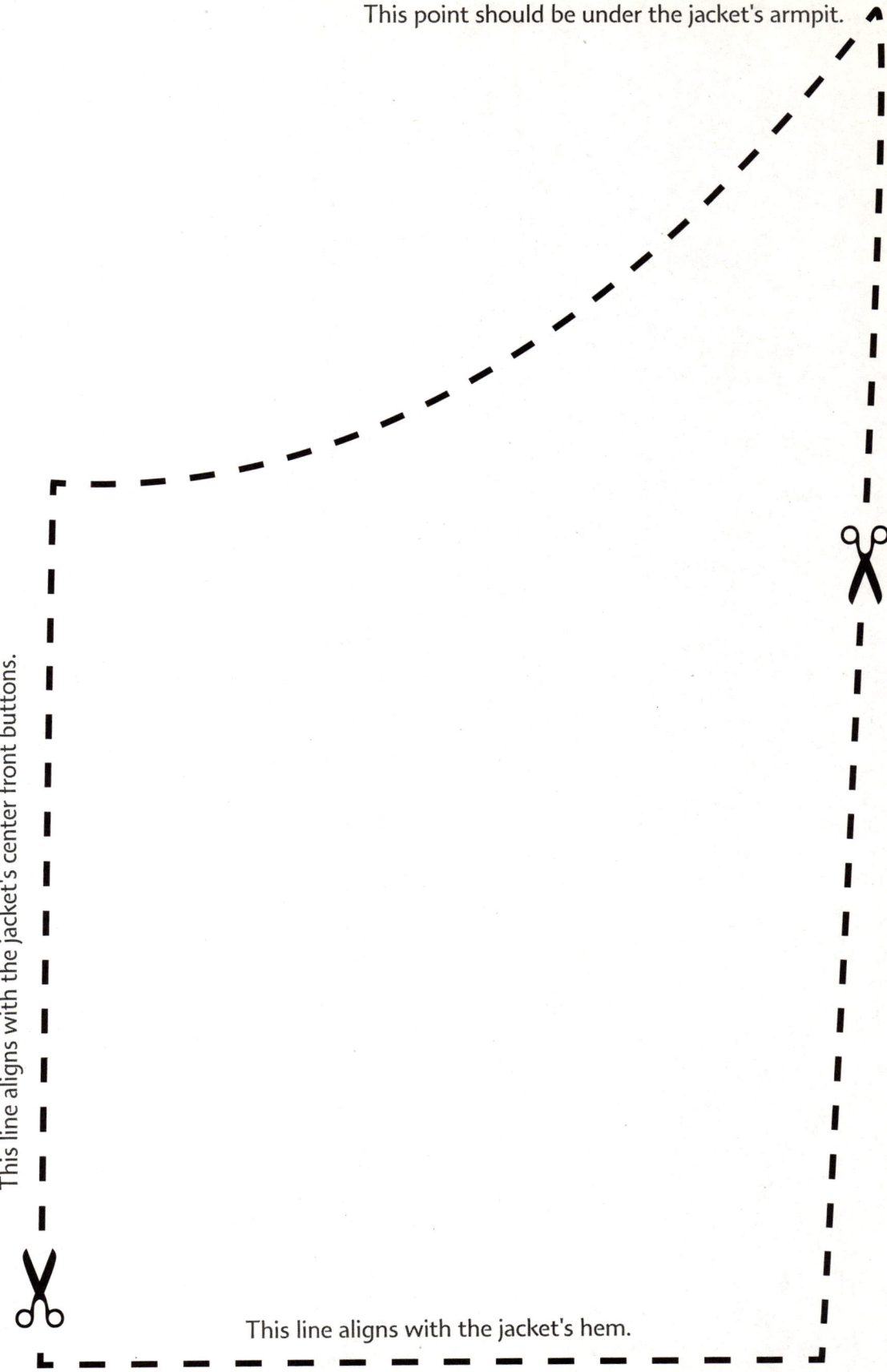

To be used with "The Sacrament of Holy Orders," page 130

To be used with "The Person & Society," page 156

To be used with "The Ninth Commandment," page 182

THE QUEEN OF HEARTS WILL BE

THE CHOSEN CARD

WILL BE THE KING OF HEARTS

About the Author

ANGELO STAGNARO has been a mentalist and magician since the age of thirteen and has performed as the magician "Erasmus" on stage, television, and street corners in over a dozen countries, including Asia, Africa, and Europe. Stagnaro publishes the successful and informative Smoke & Mirrors electronic magazine (e-zine). Information on this is available on his website www.KismetMagic.com.

His previous magic book, Conspiracy: A Guide to Mentalist Codes, (published by H&R Magic Books in Texas in 2004) is a compilation of coded mentalist team effects and was well received by the magic community. His other works, Something from Nothing, The Other Side, Shibboleth, Spur of the Moment and MasterMind were published by Manipulix Publishing in Lalling, Germany.

Stagnaro's articles about magic have appeared in "Genie" and "The Joey." His articles about Catholicism have appeared in Catholic News Service, National Catholic Register, America, US Catholic, National Catholic Reporter, and The Catholic Herald (UK.)

Angelo has taught the Rite of Christian Initiation of Adults (RCIA) in Indiana and New York. He currently performs mentalism and Gospel Magic in the Greater New York City area and in Europe.

About the Graphic Artist, Editor, and Designer

SEAN PRYOR, graphic artist, was born in Freehold, New Jersey in 1983. He earned his Associate's Degree in Fine Arts at Mercer County Community College in 2004 and his Bachelor of Fine Arts at New York City's School of Visual Arts in 2008. He is currently focused primarily on comics illustration.

Pryor's comics range from symbolic science fiction and horror to low-brow, satirical comedy. He also creates flyers for independent bands.

SYLKE JACKSON, technical writer/project editor, was born in Rockland County, New York and is a freelance writer and editor. Recent projects include Legends of Pop, Chemistry 101, Weather 101, Lighthouses Coast to Coast, and award-winning film The Baby. She holds a BA cum laude in Literature from Yale University.

EVE VATERLAUS, designer, was born in Nassau, Bahamas and educated at Rhode Island School of Design in Providence, RI, (BFA in Painting), École des Beaux Arts in Geneva, Switzerland, and School of Visual Arts in New York City. Her work spans many media, including painting, sculpture, fabric painting, graphic and web design.

About the Iconographer

ADE BETHUNE, (Baroness Adélaide de Bethune, January 12, 1914 – May 1, 2002) was born into a noble Belgian family that emigrated to the United States after World War I. She was a Catholic liturgical artist who is most closely associated with The Catholic Worker and with the modern liturgical movement.

The story of Ade Bethune is an important chapter in the cultural history of the 20th century. Bethune made unique contributions to the fields of sacred art, architecture, and social justice as an artist, writer, and liturgical consultant. Her life encompassed over half a century of significant work, which flowed from her early association with Dorothy Day and the publication of her pictures in The Catholic Worker.

In addition to her art, Bethune was also interested in Catholic social activism, spirituality, and ecumenism. She was particularly devoted to providing hospitality to the poor and elderly. In 1969, she founded the Church Community Housing Corporation in Newport County, RI in order to design and build housing for the poor. In 1991 she founded "Star of the Sea" in order to renovate a Carmelite convent into housing for the elderly.

Collection

St. Catherine University in St. Paul Minnesota owns Ade Bethune's papers and artwork. Materials in the Ade Bethune collection represent Ade Bethune's entire career from art school at the National Academy of Design and Cooper Union in New York in the 1930s to her final projects in the early years of the 21st century.

The iconography in this book is a selection from the more than 2000 drawings in the Ade Bethune collection. The collection includes 200 graphics encompassing the seasons of the liturgical calendar, various saints, and original brush and ink drawings created for The Catholic Worker newspaper and other publications. The collection also contains many of Bethune's writings, including a selection of pamphlets and articles and correspondence with Dorothy Day, Graham Carey, and others.

Inquiries about the Collection

If you would like more information about Ade Bethune or the collection at St. Catherine University, the website is: www.stkate.edu/library/spcoll/bethune.html.

Please direct your questions to:
Curator, Ade Bethune Collection, St. Catherine University, 2004 Randolph, St. Paul, MN, 55105.
The phone number is (651) 690-6599.
E-mail comments may be sent to: dkloiber@stkate.edu.

Special Thanks

Special thanks to Ms. Deborah Kloiber, Curator of the Ade Bethune collection for her kind generosity and assistance with this project.

About the Consultants

Fr. Jerry Jecewiz, "Priesto," Brooklyn Diocesan priest

Fr. Silvio Mantelli, SDB, "Mago Sales," Salesian priest, Gospel Magician, Director of Fondazione Mago Sales

Fr. Boudewijn Spittaels, SDB, "Bodo," Salesian priest, Gospel Magician

Glenn Hister, Gospel Magician

Chris Knabenshue, Gospel Magician, Co-Chairman of the Catholic Magicians' Guild

Fr. Daniel Rolland, OP, Dominican priest, Gospel Magician

Bishop Paul A. Zipfel, Bishop of the Diocese of Bismarck, North Dakota

Fr. James Blantz, CSC, Holy Cross priest, Gospel Magician

Br. John Hamman, SM, Marianist Brother, (deceased)

Fr. Steve Gibson, CSC, "The Sermonator," Holy Cross priest, Gospel Magician

Fr. Mark Thesing, CSC, Holy Cross priest, Notre Dame University, Business Manager for Student Affairs

Sr. Carol Ann Nawracaj, OSF, Bernardine Franciscan Sister, Gospel Magician, Supervisor of Society of Young Magicians, Executive Director of Villa Maria Education Center

Fr. Nicholas Argentieri, Diocesan priest, Gospel Magician

Fr. James Mueller, SM, Marianist Priest, Gospel Magician, Campus Minister, Chaminade High School

Michael Loyet, President of St. John Vianney High School, St. Louis

Fr. Jim Miller, Diocesan Priest, Fort Worth Diocese, Gospel Magician

David Calavitta, Gospel Magician, Catholic Youth Minister, St. Thomas More Church, Irvine, California

Fr. Michael Court, SDB, Salesian priest, Gospel Magician

Fr. Larry Lorenzoni, SDB, Salesian priest, Gospel Magician

Br. Martin de Porres Schmidt, OFM Cap., Capuchin friar, Gospel Magician

Fr. Mark Davis, Diocese of Toledo, Ohio, Diocesan priest, Gospel Magician

Br. Jim Zettel SDB, Salesian Brother, Gospel Magician

Fr. John R Blaker, Diocese of Oakland, California, Diocesan priest, Gospel Magician

Joel Howlett, Gospel Magician

Fr. Vincent Pazhukkakulam, O.Carm., "Magicachan," Carmelite priest, Gospel Magician

Fr. Cyprian Murray, OFM, Cap., MI, President of the Society of American Magicians (1989-90)

Thanks to Fr. John Serio SDB for providing the photo of Saint Don Bosco on the Dedication page

ADE BETHUNE
List of Illustrations

Page	Code
Page i –	ABC3420o
Page 1 –	ABC4565
Page 10 –	ABC3414
Page 12 –	ABC3460o
Page 14 –	ABC3432
Page 15 –	ABC5706
Page 16 –	ABC4808
Page 21 –	ABC5706
Page 22 –	ABC3627
Page 23 –	ABC6547-2
Page 27 –	ABC5705
Page 31 –	ABC3636
Page 37 –	ABC3414
Page 39 –	ABC3404
Page 40 –	ABC6312
Page 43 –	3448-D
Page 62 –	ABC6111
Page 63 –	ABC6065
Page 79 –	ABC3442ßo
Page 80 –	ABC4518
Page 93 –	ABC5706-2
Page 95 –	ABC3636
Page 111 –	ABC5643
Page 117 –	ABC4518
	ABC3404
Page 129 –	ABC3627
Page 139 –	ABC4904
Page 149 –	ABC4564
Page 161 –	ABC3434o
	ABC3432ßo
Page 165 –	ABC3636
Page 181 –	ABC4809
Page 185 –	ABC3627
Page 187 –	ABC4027
Page 227 –	ABC3432Do
Page 228 –	ABC5737
Page 234 –	ABC5794
Page 235 –	ABC5632
Page 249 –	ABC3438ßo
Page 250 –	ABC5706-1
Page 252 –	ABC5916

RESOURCES FOR MINISTRY

Gregory A. Popcak, Ph.D. and Lisa Popcak
A MARRIAGE MADE FOR HEAVEN
The Secrets of Heavenly Couplehood

This parish-based marriage enrichment program written by leading experts on Catholic marriage and family life is designed to lead couples to an immediate and personal experience of the spiritual significance of their marital relationship. Couples will be equipped with practical tools needed to create a marriage that will "make the angels smile ... and the neighbors sick with jealousy." A special feature of the program is the authors' trademark ability to explain wholly orthodox Catholic thought (including the Theology of the Body) in intuitive and appealing ways, with gentle humor and references to the best research in marriage and family psychology. The program is a series of 12 monthly "date nights" for married couples to gather for ongoing education and support. From the opening commitment ceremony to the concluding recommitment ceremony 12 months later, each session includes opening and closing prayers with responses, a video presentation, questions for review, a group discussion exercise (where couples reflect on actual cases), the Heavenly Home Improvement Plan (daily action steps for each couple), Heavenly Witness (couple sharing of experiences), the Marital Imperative Exercise (marital mission statement), and Heavenly Hullabaloo (group social). Throughout the book are questionnaires, quizzes, assessment tools, checklists, and activities lists for couples to use weekly and daily.
978-0-8245-2532-3 Leader Guide with DVD
978-0-8245-2534-7 Couple Workbook

RESOURCES FOR MINISTRY

Edward P. Hahnenberg
MINISTRIES
A Relational Approach

"Directs a fresh, well-focused light on the theological and pastoral issues relating to ministry in today's church. This clear, creative, and authoritative work deserves serious and wide attention."

—**Donald Cozzens,** author of **The Changing Face of the Priesthood**

978-0-8245-2103-5, paperback

Christoph Cardinal Schönborn
WITH JESUS EVERY DAY
How Believing Transforms Living

Tracing the life of Jesus and how the faith was passed on through the ages to our present time, this book offers a clear and accessible presentation of the tradition of faith and the responses it gives for the basic questions of life.

978-0-8245-2420-3, cloth

Christoph Cardinal Schönborn
THE SOURCE OF LIFE
Exploring the Mystery of the Eucharist

Focusing on the beauty and power of the Holy Eucharist, the cardinal explores the Jewish roots of the Christian story as well as the deep division that the understanding of the Eucharist has created within Christian communities.

978-0-8245-2477-7, cloth

Joseph Cardinal Ratzinger
(Pope Benedict XVI)
THE YES OF JESUS CHRIST
Spiritual Exercises in Faith, Hope, and Love

An invitation to rediscover the Christian basis for hope. By exercising our spirituality through continual practice in Christian life, we hear again the distinctly Christian message that our ability to say Yes to ourselves and one another can only come from God's Yes in Christ.

978-0-8245-2374-9, paperback

MAY THE BLESSING
OF ALMIGHTY GOD
FATHER, SON & HOLY SPIRIT
DESCEND UPON YOU AND
REMAIN WITH YOU FOREVER

Check your local bookstore for availability.
To order directly from the publisher, visit our website at
www.cpcbooks.com

THE CROSSROAD PUBLISHING COMPANY